The *Poetics* of Aristotle

The *Poetics* of Aristotle

translation and commentary

Stephen Halliwell

The University of North Carolina Press
Chapel Hill

First published in Great Britain 1987 by
Gerald Duckworth & Co. Ltd.
The Old Piano Factory
43 Gloucester Crescent, London NW1

First published in the United States 1987
by The University of North Carolina Press

10 09 08 07 06   11 10 9 8 7

Library of Congress Cataloging-in-Publication Data

Aristotle
    The Poetics of Aristotle.

    Bibliography: p.
    Includes index.
    1. Poetry—Early works to 1800.   2. Aesthetics—
Early works to 1800.   I. Halliwell, Stephen.   II. Title.
PN1040.A513   1987b   808.2   87-16255
ISBN 0-8078-1763-5
ISBN-13: 978-0-8078-4203-4 (pbk.: alk. paper)
ISBN-10: 0-8078-4203-6 (pbk.: alk. paper)

THIS BOOK WAS DIGITALLY PRINTED.

Photoset in North Wales by
Derek Doyle & Associates, Mold, Clwyd.
Printed and bound in Great Britain by
Robert Hartnoll (1985) Ltd., Bodmin, Cornwall.

Contents

Preface

This book is intended to provide a type of guidance and interpretative stimulus to the study of the *Poetics* which is not at present easily available to the Greekless reader. Translations of the work are usually accompanied by separate notes on particular points, but what many students and other readers may find more valuable, I believe, is a continuous exposition which follows with critical attention the structure and implications of Aristotle's argument. Comparison with the one already available work of this kind, by Golden and Hardison (see Further Reading), will show why there has not seemed to me much risk of duplicating their views.

To base such a commentary on someone else's version of the work would have entailed making too many defensive qualifications of a distracting kind. As it is, I have at any rate been able to achieve consistency between the translated text and the commentary, and this has been my main justification for adding to the already large number of English renderings of the treatise. Without launching on a disquisition concerning translation, I would wish to say that my version stays close to the best Greek text we have of the *Poetics*, while striving to be as clear and intelligible as it can honestly be made. The *Poetics* is not as garbled or unreadable as is sometimes alleged. On the other hand, I cannot claim to have given any real impression of Aristotle's idiosyncratic style: anyone who wants *that* will have to learn Greek.

In writing my commentary, I had in mind chiefly such readers as serious students of Greek literature in translation, of Drama, and of European literature in general – as well as interested readers of a less easily classifiable kind. Most points of factual detail have been dealt with in the Glossary, so that I was free in the commentary to concentrate on ideas and argument. I

presume that anyone who has a real interest in the work does not
wish to be served up only *idées reçues* (from which the *Poetics*
continues to suffer, particularly in general textbooks on poetry
and criticism), and I have not shirked strong judgements of a
kind which may provoke the questioning reader into thinking
independently about Aristotle's intentions and achievement.

Where appropriate, I have indicated ways in which Aristotle's
views might be brought to the test of surviving tragedy. We are
fortunate in possessing the two plays which he cites most often,
Sophocles' *Oedipus Tyrannus* and Euripides' *Iphigeneia in
Tauris*: all readers of the *Poetics* should also read these texts in
conjunction with the treatise (together with as many other Greek
tragedies as possible), and should be prepared to think carefully
about them in relation to the theory of tragedy. My own views on
ways in which I believe Aristotle misrepresents, or offers heavily
one-sided approaches to, these plays, will emerge clearly enough,
but the reader will want to test my views too against the works
themselves.

Although some of the arguments presented here are inevitably
close to those which I have put forward at greater length in my
study, *Aristotle's Poetics* (London & Chapel Hill, NC 1986), this
smaller work was separately conceived and is not intended as a
potted version of the earlier one. I have managed to include in
both the Introduction and the Commentary many points and
suggestions which did not find a place in the larger book.

S.H.

Guide for the reader

Where works of secondary literature are cited without full details, these will be found in the guide to Further Reading.

The Greek text used for the translation is that edited by R. Kassel, *Aristotelis de Arte Poetica Liber* (Oxford 1965). Significant departures from this text are mentioned in the Textual Notes (see below, pp. 66-8).

A small number of specific references to surviving works of Greek poetry have been identified in footnotes to the translation; but for details such as names, titles, and technical terms, the reader should consult the Glossary.

The following notations are used in the translation:

*   indicates a textual problem; refer to Textual Notes.

...   marks a lacuna in the Greek text

[...]   indicates an omission, usually of technicalities, from the translation. Such omissions have been kept to a minimum, and will be found mostly in chs. 22 and 25, where Ar. gives a number of quotations whose relevant points cannot be successfully rendered into English.

( )   ordinary parentheses are used purely for the clearer presentation of the argument, including small exegetical supplements such as occasional cross-references, and the use of letters, (a) etc., in passages where Ar. lists a series of points.

Introduction

What we now call Aristotle's *Poetics* is part of a work which was compiled some time between the 360s and the 320s B.C. (Aristotle's dates are 384-322), for use, either as lecture notes or in some other way, in the education of young philosophers. It was never intended to be available to a wide public, and it was in any case not designed to be read as an elegantly polished composition. Its author was a prolific, profound and wide-ranging thinker whose major interests were in the natural world, in logic, in ethics and in metaphysics. Aristotle, like all educated Greeks, knew a great deal of poetry intimately, but it does not seem to have been among his deepest concerns, and he turned his philosophical attention to it perhaps chiefly because he saw ways of justifying this traditional element of Greek culture against his own teacher, Plato (427-347), who had condemned poetry as false, immoral and psychologically damaging.[1]

The *Poetics* was preserved together with Aristotle's other teaching materials after his death, but at some point it lost its second book, in which comedy and perhaps iambic satire were discussed. It was never at all well known in antiquity (though a few of its ideas were disseminated by other, now lost, Aristotelian works), and it was only with the fresh interest of Italian humanists in the sixteenth century that it assumed a central place in current literary theory and criticism, which it then retained, not only in Italy but also in France, England and elsewhere, until the burgeoning Romanticism of the eighteenth century distanced itself from the work as part of a reaction against the neo-classicism with which the *Poetics* had become so

---

[1] For fresh consideration of Plato's attitudes to poetry see Else, *Plato and Aristotle on Poetry*, part I, and the Introduction to my forthcoming edition of *Republic* Book 10.

closely associated.[2]

Why, today, should anyone other than a student of Aristotle trouble to read this incomplete treatise, produced in a remote philosophical school and written in a less than prepossessing style? Even if we can accept the usual description of the work as literary criticism or theory, it is undeniable that these subjects as now commonly pursued share few presuppositions with the method of the *Poetics*. Aristotelian authority in these matters waned long ago, and while revivals have occasionally been advocated, they are not likely to win many converts. It requires no special reflection to recognise that we cannot hope to turn to the work for immediate or practical help with the understanding of literature in general, since so much of the literature we know was written in cultural contexts very different from anything envisaged by Aristotle. So what justification can be given for continuing to read the *Poetics*?

Three major reasons can be picked out to form an answer to this question. First, the *Poetics* has a unique status for us in relation to the poetry of Attic culture, since it is the only substantial document surviving from classical Athens (though Aristotle himself was not Athenian) which is devoted to a positive consideration of tragic drama. The modern reader of Greek tragedy can hardly afford to ignore the ideas on the genre held by a highly intelligent Greek who was able to see the plays of the Athenian dramatic tradition produced in the theatre within half a century of the death of Sophocles and Euripides, and who had access, both written and oral, to earlier views on tragedy which went back to the lifetimes of these playwrights. We shall see that it would be a mistake to treat what Aristotle has to say about tragedy as necessarily authoritative, but the critical concepts which he uses, and the judgements which he bases on them, do give us a valuable way of testing and refining our own appreciation of extant Greek tragedy.

The *Poetics* also deserves to be read for a rather different sort of reason, namely on account of its historical influence. I shall later offer some observations on the course which this influence has taken, concentrating particularly on English literary criticism. Such an enquiry is worthwhile not just for its own historical sake, but because at least some of the ideas and

[2] See pp.17ff. below.

principles which we continue to employ and encounter in modern criticism were gradually formed in a tradition on which the interpretation of Aristotle's treatise repeatedly impinged.

But while the *Poetics* has been influential in the development of thinking about literature, it has also in the course of time come to seem as a whole very remote; and this fact, paradoxically, provides a final and more general reason for continuing to study it. The major concern of the work, as my commentary will try to demonstrate, is theoretical: that is to say, it bears systematically and prescriptively on the intrinsic nature of poetry, and on the values and conceptions involved both in its composition and in the experience of it. This theoretical point of view is inevitably conditioned by various factors, not only concerning Greek poetry and culture in general, but also arising from Aristotle's individual outlook and philosophical mentality. But, while we cannot expect simply to perpetuate or share Aristotle's ideas on poetry, we can benefit from the effort of confronting the premises and standards on which they rest. This argument does not, of course, apply uniquely to the *Poetics*; but Aristotle's work, by the very features which now lend it a certain intellectual remoteness, can still offer a particular challenge and stimulus to anyone who is prepared to examine its arguments seriously and carefully, and in the process also to reflect on his own basic assumptions about poetry.

The running commentary supplied on each chapter of the *Poetics* in this book is intended precisely to aid this effort of understanding and reflection. In the remainder of the Introduction I would like to expand on the first two of the three reasons I have given for reading Aristotle's treatise on poetry: its special relation to Greek tragedy, and its historical influence on later literary criticism.

*

Tragedy was more than a century and a half old when Aristotle first came to Athens to study in Plato's Academy in 367 B.C. By this date the Athenians were not only producing new plays each year for their dramatic festivals, but were also encouraging the revival of older works. This practice, which seems so familiar to us, was in fact a recent development, only some two decades old, in the Athenian theatre. In part, it reflected a dawning sense that tragedy had enjoyed in the previous century a level of poetic and dramatic achievement which could perhaps no longer be matched by living playwrights. The Athenians were starting to look back to the careers of Aeschylus (c. 525-456), Sophocles (c. 496-406) and Euripides (c.485-406) as something of a 'great age' of tragedy.[3] But tragedy was, nonetheless, still flourishing in Attic culture, and the *Poetics*, which mentions a number of works first performed during Aristotle's own lifetime, would hardly have taken the form that it does if its author had not felt that at least some of the ideals of tragic drama were continuing possibilities in the poetry of his own day.

The place of tragedy in Athenian culture had evidently produced ideas about the genre and its standards long before Aristotle's arrival in the city. The very fact of official competition between performing playwrights implied the existence of principles of preference and discrimination in Athenian audiences. By the later part of the fifth century the comic poet Aristophanes could build whole plays, such as *Thesmophoriazusae* and *Frogs*, around themes drawn from contemporary tragedy; and he clearly expected his audience – which was also the audience of tragedy – to enjoy the details of the debate on dramatic principles and values which he stages between Aeschylus and Euripides in *Frogs*. Aristophanes allows us to glimpse a range of factors which might have played a part in ordinary Athenian attitudes to tragic drama: factors ranging from major questions of morality, through aspects of theatrical technique (dramatic silences in Aeschylus, ragged heroes in Euripides), to delicate points of poetic style and tone.

Despite these tantalising hints of the Athenian experience of tragedy during the very lifetime of Sophocles and Euripides, Aristophanes' comic function makes it difficult for us reliably to infer connected arguments or general approaches which might have been met with at this time. Plato, by contrast, does offer a coherent and serious view of tragedy, but it is one whose philosophical hostility to poetry and its traditional values could clearly not have been widely shared. Aristotle's understanding of

---

[3] It has often been observed that the first explicit evidence for a sense of the exceptional status of Aeschylus, Sophocles and Euripides is to be found in Aristophanes' *Frogs* (esp. the implication of 785-94). What is not often noted is that the trio of tragedians were treated exceptionally in their own lifetimes by virtue of the frequency with which they were 'granted a chorus' for performance. For a further indication of fourth-century recognition of the standards set by the previous century, see p.6 below on *Poetics* 18.

tragedy is also that of a philosopher, and certainly cannot be used as direct evidence for normal Athenian attitudes. But Aristotle's positive aim of trying to do justice to the nature of dramatic tragedy, and his willingness, as in other areas of his thought, to take account of existing views on the subject, make the *Poetics* a much more promising document for anyone who wishes to form some idea of how Greek tragedy may have been interpreted in its original culture.

In addition to its own arguments, the *Poetics* gives us occasional references to earlier or contemporary convictions about tragedy, on the part either of individuals or of audiences, and these help to confirm that by the middle of the fourth century a climate of critical views and standards concerning the genre was firmly established in Athens. From the end of ch. 4, for example, we gather the existence of a detailed, though perhaps purely oral, tradition about the stages of tragedy's theatrical development. This not only connects with the work which Aristotle himself towards the end of his life carried out on the records of tragic performances, but also significantly indicates that Athenian culture could now look back on, and try to find order in, the entire history of a major poetic genre. This must be borne in mind when reading *Poetics* 4, where Aristotle offers his own sketch of tragedy's evolution (within that of poetry as a whole). While I shall argue in my commentary that the chapter presents an abstract scheme resting on Aristotle's own philosophical conceptions, it is clear enough that this was at least worked out against the background of an already existing interest in tragedy's history.[4]

Elsewhere in the *Poetics* we can catch a handful of allusions to views on tragic style and related matters.[5] Ch. 8's rejection of a 'central character' as the basis for dramatic unity (contrary to what 'some believe') may well have some relevance to particular types of tragedy, though it must be admitted that Aristotle illustrates his point from epic. Ch. 13 is more direct: here we are twice referred to a preference, shared it seems by some critics

[4] Cf. Aristophanes *Frogs* 939ff. for hints of a sense of tragedy's historical development.

[5] In addition to the explicit citation of existing attitudes, Ar. may sometimes be arguing against current ideas without saying so. This is possible, if unprovable, in the case of his emphatic remarks on the relation between action and character in ch. 6.

and by audiences, for a 'double' plot in which an equilibrium of poetic justice is attained at the end. Aristotle's testimony that audiences *wanted* such ethically satisfying endings is of great importance, and it should be remembered in all generalisations about the Athenian experience of tragedy. At the same time it would be a mistake to suppose that Aristotle is referring to the behaviour of *all* audiences all of the time. He cannot be, for in this same chapter he also tells us that, when properly staged, Euripides' unhappy endings 'make the most tragic impression', and the reference is again clearly to existing Athenian audiences.

It is easily overlooked that what these observations have in common is the confident implication that general tendencies of preference or taste could be discerned in contemporary audiences of the Athenian theatre. That is itself a valuable glimpse of the lively reception of tragedy in the fourth century, and there are others. In ch. 17 Aristotle cites an actual instance of an audience's displeasure at a playwright's dramaturgical incompetence (it seems from other evidence that an audience could sometimes go so far as to whistle a performance off the stage);[6] this passage supplies an interesting illustration of Aristotle's willingness (rare among Greek philosophers) to use, when appropriate, ordinary people's experience as confirmation of a general principle or tenet.

In ch. 18, by contrast, we are told that people wrongly expect the individual poet to excel simultaneously in all the various types of tragedy. This passage tells us two things of significance: first, that the categories set out in this section (including, it should be noted, the distinctive notion of the 'complex' tragedy) were related in Aristotle's mind to judgements on the genre that were being fairly widely made in Athenian culture; second, that at least some Athenians were disposed to apply more stringent standards of criticism in certain areas than Aristotle thought reasonable. There may also be here a further suggestion, in the reference to earlier poets good at each type, of a tendency by Aristotle's day to judge contemporary tragedians by the finest achievements of the previous century (cf. p.4 above). At any rate, a context of strongly held feelings about standards in the

---

[6] See A. Pickard-Cambridge, *Dramatic Festivals of Athens* 2nd edn. (Oxford 1968) pp. 272-3, adding the evidence of Plato *Laws* 876b on the noise of theatre audiences.

genre is clearly attested; and this is finally confirmed by a passing reference in ch. 24 to the way in which lack of variety 'causes the rejection' of tragic plays in performance.

These various passages evidently do not fit together to produce a full or coherent picture of fourth-century attitudes to tragedy, but they are useful as pointers to the fact that, notwithstanding its distinctively philosophical setting, the *Poetics* was compiled consciously against a wider cultural background of estimates of tragedy at Athens in Aristotle's own day. This fact can also serve to dispel a misconception which may interfere with our understanding of the treatise. The *Poetics'* various references to audiences and current judgements of tragedy show collectively that Aristotle was not a closeted theorist who stood completely detached from the popular culture to which tragic drama belonged. Further evidence on the point could be adduced from elsewhere (such as the appreciative remark on the difference between Theodorus' and other actors' voices at *Rhetoric* 3.2.4). Insofar as Aristotle diverged from ordinary views of tragedy, or even from the ordinary practice of playwrights, he did so from conscious intellectual convictions and reasoning, not because of a cloistered remoteness from the realities of the subject.

If we now turn more directly to the nature of Aristotle's critical reasoning, it is pertinent to what has just been said to start by acknowledging his insistence on separating tragic drama or poetry from its realisation in a theatrical performance (see esp. the end of ch. 6 and the start of ch. 14). This can probably be explained by a combination of theoretical and cultural factors. There is no doubt that the former is predominant, and sufficient in Aristotle's own mind. The tragedian's art is firmly centred on the design of a dramatic structure of action in poetic media, and such a structure need not be acted out for its effects to be felt: reading (by which some sort of recitation is meant) is sufficient. Aristotle can still recognise the capacity of performance to communicate the power of a dramatic work, though he is also concerned about its independent scope for effects ('the sensational', ch. 14) which would interfere with the true tragic emotions. But this theoretical position probably in turn reflects the sense that the theatrical arts of actor and producer were developing in the fourth century in a direction which might be inimical to certain kinds of dramatic value. The chief evidence for this claim comes from Aristotle's own remark, at *Rhetoric*

3.1.4, that in the theatre 'actors nowadays have more power than the poets'.

It is difficult, therefore, to convict Aristotle of sheer insensitivity to, rather than a reasoned detachment from, the theatre. By the fourth century tragic texts, as well as those of other kinds of poetry, were becoming more easily and widely available than in earlier periods; a process had started which was to lead to the much more pervasively based book-culture of the Hellenistic age. Aristotle is part of this movement, even though he also has his own coherent case for excluding theatrical considerations from a strict conception of poetic drama. Nonetheless, most Athenians in the fourth century must still have experienced tragedy primarily in performance, not through reading, and this means that the *Poetics* offers us a level of pondered criticism which can hardly have been typical of the culture as a whole. In this general respect, however, the treatise is hardly likely to strike a modern reader as unusual, since so much dramatic criticism in more recent times similarly depends on the availability of texts and the possibility of bringing to bear on them a degree of analytical attention which would not be practicable for the majority of a theatre audience.

The separation of drama from any necessary engagement with performance, and a concomitant abstraction of critical method, are, then, essential features of the *Poetics*. But if this opens up a breach between the theorist and the Athenian audience in the theatre, it is one which can partly be closed by other considerations. The abstract character of Aristotle's critical method is undeniable, but it should not be mistaken for a lack of receptiveness to the emotional experience of tragedy. It has been well said that the work's central discussion of plot-structure 'is not a "substitute" for feeling but an enquiry into the ways by which a dramatist can intensify feeling'.[7] Aristotle himself makes this explicit at many points, particularly in his comments on the potency of recognitions and reversals (tragedy's 'greatest means of emotional power', p.38). Without a deep arousal of emotion, tragedy cannot possibly be successful in Aristotle's view, and when, in ch. 14, he argues for the validity of reading as a means of experiencing tragedy, he does so significantly by reference to the emotions of pity and fear. There is for Aristotle

---

[7] Vickers, *Towards Greek Tragedy* p. 62.

no intrinsic suspicion of audience-emotion of the kind which we meet with in Plato (for example at *Republic* 10.604e), and it is certainly not this aspect of theatrical experience which is responsible for the *Poetics'* qualified stance towards performance. Moreover, the formula of pity and fear for the tragic emotions is not by any means original with Aristotle, despite the distinctive character which he gives to its interpretation.[8] Here too, then, there is no reason to treat the *Poetics* as conceived entirely outside the prevailing cultural conception of the genre.

Having so far emphasised some of the ways in which the treatise can be seen to tie up with what we can gather of the background of existing ideas on tragedy, I now need to counterbalance this with certain observations on the major concepts which run through Aristotle's treatment of the genre. Clearly our best means for evaluating these concepts are the surviving Greek tragedies, which, although much less than the corpus of plays available to Aristotle himself, at least enable us to discern where the theorist places, so to speak, his critical accents, and – equally importantly – which dimensions of tragedy he disregards or undervalues. Such a process of evaluation is far from simple, since we cannot engage in it without committing ourselves to interpretations both of individual works and of wider tendencies in the genre. I shall try at various points in the commentary to address myself particularly to the plays which Aristotle cites most often in the *Poetics*, Sophocles' *Oedipus Tyrannus* and Euripides' *Iphigeneia in Tauris*. I restrict myself here to a few concise remarks on a wide range of topics which a full consideration of Greek tragedy could obviously carry much further.

It is as well to be clear at once that, contrary to common assertion, we have no reason to suppose Aristotle's theory of tragedy has been arrived at by generalisation from chosen models of the genre. In particular, the *Poetics* does *not*, either explicitly or implicitly, put forward a view of tragedy derived directly from the plays of Sophocles, still less from the *Oedipus Tyrannus* alone. Aristotle is certainly prepared to use Sophoclean examples to illustrate his principles and injunctions, but he also commends individual dramaturgical and poetic

---

[8] For earlier occurrences of the combination of pity and fear see my book, *Aristotle's Poetics* p.170 n.3.

points in the works of many other tragedians – Aeschylus (in ch. 18), Euripides, Agathon, and Theodectes among them. This is not to deny that certain broader correlations, both positive and negative, can be detected between Aristotle's theory and individual playwrights: a relative lack of interest in Aeschylus' work, for example, probably because of the extent of its lyric element (but Aeschylean texts may well have been scarce in the fourth century); a positive admiration for the work of *both* the other major fifth-century tragedians (more qualified, but still strong, in the case of Euripides); and instances of both attraction to and disapproval for the practices of contemporary tragedy.[9]

But all these points must not be allowed to obscure the fundamental fact that Aristotle's approach to tragedy is, *au fond*, a system of theoretical premises and reasoning, incorporating ideas drawn from observation but essentially relying on and elaborating philosophical convictions about the nature of poetry and the experience which it provides. Because of the importance to Aristotle of the notion of *generic* potential, he has no need to turn directly to particular plays for the vindication of his principles. The nature of the tragic genre is discerned by him in its entire pattern of development, and can be formulated for the most part in consciously theoretical terms. References to individual works could never provide Aristotle with the full or general validity of reasoning at which he aims, for he does not conceive of tragedy as a contingent achievement of specific poets, but as a kind of cultural organism whose intrinsic essence is independent of this work or that.

Aristotle's criticism is not, in other words, primarily empirical, though it contains certain empirical elements. It is a type of prescriptive criticism which has the confidence to judge individual works by reference to the 'first principles' of poetic art. What this means is that we cannot hope in any real sense to *refute* the *Poetics* by turning to Greek tragedy for contrary examples of dramatic practice. This is a point which many modern readers and critics are likely to have difficulty with, used as they are to a climate of criticism in which a much more

[9] On fourth-century tragedy Ar.'s views are mixed: he finds contemporary plays lacking in characterisation (p.38), rhetorical in 'thought' (p.38), and failing to integrate the chorus (p.52). Ch. 13 (p.45) aligns the current choice of tragic subjects with Ar.'s own ideal, and elsewhere fourth-century plays are cited for a mixture of good and bad points: see the Glossary s.v. Astydamas, Carcinus, and Theodectes.

relative sense of literary values and standards prevails. But it must be accepted that we are confronted in the *Poetics* with a kind of theorising which it is easier to reject than to argue with on common ground. This does not, of course, absolve us from the critical responsibility of evaluating Aristotle's ideas as honestly as possible against our own considered judgements on Greek tragedy, and I would like now to mention briefly three major areas in which it seems to me that there is scope for dissenting from the *Poetics*.

The first concerns Aristotle's treatment of the subject matter of tragedy. While the Greeks had no fixed concept corresponding to our 'myth', they recognised the distinctive body of traditional stories and material which we include in this term. 'Myth' derives from *muthos* (plural *muthoi*), which means usually a 'story' or 'tale', whether traditional or otherwise; and a passage such as Plato *Republic* 2.377ff. indicates a strong association between certain *muthoi* and both epic and tragic poetry. Tragedy took its material almost universally from heroic saga or myth, and the character of the genre was deeply affected by this fact. Aristotle seems to acknowledge the heroic quality of tragedy by his formula of men 'better than us' (chs. 2, 15),[10] but he also makes it clear, particularly in ch. 9 (where he cites a rare instance of a non-mythical tragic subject), that he sees no particular necessity for traditional material to be used in tragedy. This view is nicely reflected in his use of the term *muthos* mostly to mean 'plot' or 'plot-structure': the *muthos* of a tragedy is defined in ch. 6 as a structure of events or action (from whatever source: history, myth, or sheer invention) for whose dramatic shape and design the poet is fully responsible. The poet cannot rely on tradition to give proper form to his material; it is his own artistic reponsibility. It should be noted that the precise sense of *muthos* as plot-structure is found nowhere else either in Aristotle's own writings or in other Greek criticism.

The concept of plot elaborated in the *Poetics* is a powerful critical instrument for the interpretation of dramatic structure, but it is arguable that one of its implications is a shift away from a special sort of subject-matter ('myth') towards a more neutral

---

[10] Note the reference to heroic characters ('demigods'), and a heroic style to suit them, at *Frogs* 1058-60. This expresses a view of tragedy which, comically at least, Aristophanes represents as undermined by Euripidean 'realism'.

or abstract notion of poetic form. It is certainly the case that Aristotle makes very little of the specifically mythical and heroic qualities of the tragic tradition; and even his formula of men 'better than us' is qualified, and perhaps called into question, by the argument in ch. 13 that major tragic figures should not be outstanding in virtue.[11] If it is the case that the stories of heroic saga possessed certain distinctive properties for Greek audiences – allowing a sense of universal or paradigmatic human significance to be combined with a conscious distance between the world of myth and the actuality of the present – then it is fair to ask whether Aristotle does justice to this aspect of tragedy. I would suggest that he does not, and that the reason for this lies in the wider movement of fourth-century Greek culture away from the domination of traditional mythic material and categories.[12]

The point can be carried a little further by introducing the second of my four topics, religion. Myth and religion are inextricably connected in archaic and classical Greek culture. The world of heroic saga portrayed in tragedy, as in epic, is also necessarily a world in which divine forces must always be reckoned with. It could indeed be argued that one of the particular qualities of myth is the close and intense interpenetration of the human and divine worlds to which it gives expression. Yet religion too is an aspect of tragedy to which the *Poetics* pays scant attention, and we cannot afford not to ask why this should be so. I believe that the answer lies in the fact that Aristotle's own view of the world is not, in traditional terms, a religious one, and that he deliberately reinterprets the possibilities of tragic drama so as to make the religious ideas of myth marginal to its purpose. This is, naturally, a large and complex contention, but it will account both for the negative attitude which Aristotle shows at certain points towards the impingement of the divine on dramatic action, and also for the relentlessly rational and 'secular' principles which his own theory applies to the coherence and intelligibility of such action.[13]

---

[11] On this point see p.124 below.

[12] On the diminishing influence of myth on Greek culture in this period see G. S. Kirk, *Greek Myth* (Harmondsworth 1974) ch. 12. On the significance of myth for tragedy, see Knox, *Word and Action* ch.1.

[13] On the *Poetics*' neglect of religion cf. esp. p.151. For a recent discussion of tragedy and religion, covering the Greek case, see H. A. Mason, *The Tragic Plane*

This whole question is perhaps the most intricate issue that could be raised about the relation of the *Poetics* to Greek tragedy, not least because it is likely to draw us into large problems about the nature of religious thinking. I can only indicate here that my claim about the *Poetics'* neglect of tragic religion does not depend on any precise interpretation of the latter (least of all on any fixed concept of 'fate'), but only on the fundamental proposition that the universe portrayed in all the Greek tragedies we know – including those which Aristotle himself cites most frequently – is one in which significant human action is never regarded as wholly autonomous or independent of larger, non-human powers. By contrast with this, Aristotle's own understanding of dramatic action posits, it seems to me, nothing other than intrinsic and purely human criteria of plausibility and causal intelligibility.

Part of the difficulty which some critics have in taking this feature of the *Poetics* as seriously as I wish to do, stems from the fact that much modern criticism of Greek tragedy, in moving away from naive interpretations in terms of religious fate or destiny, itself rests on an ultimately secular reading of the plays. The *Oedipus Tyrannus* provides a pertinent instance. There has been a significant modern trend towards minimising the religious dimension of the play, and *detaching* the dramatic foreground from it, in order to stress the degree to which the action is determined by human choices and intentions. But such a reading can be taken too far, and it is difficult to see how the constant presence of Apollo in both Oedipus' past and his present can simply be explained away: Oedipus' own words, 'These things were Apollo, Apollo' (*OT* 1329), give taut expression to this side of the myth. One need not suppose that a determinate, unambiguous meaning can be given to Apollo's function in order to see that it is nonetheless central to the work's dramatic force.[14]

(Oxford 1985) ch. 8. But Mason, pp. 170f., takes a different view from mine of Ar.'s position, and he seems to me to be too concerned about associations of the concept of religion which do not apply in the Greek context (thus 'standards of unquestionable truth', p. 170, are irrelevant to Greek religion).

[14] The secularising reading of the *OT* can be conveniently illustrated from the work of an outstanding Sophoclean critic, B. Knox's recent Introduction to the play in Robert Fagles' Penguin Classics translation, *Sophocles: the Three Theban Plays* (Harmondsworth 1984). Knox repeatedly emphasises Oedipus'

There is, then, a parallelism between some modern criticism of the *OT* and the view of the play implicit in the *Poetics*. The whole thrust of Aristotle's theory emphasises the internal logic of the dramatic action, the nexus of events which make up the plot-structure. It is of great importance to see how this approach to dramatic works can have implications for what counts as significant within them. Since most Greek tragedies dramatise portions of much more extended sets of events, and since the religious dimension of a story is often connected with the larger pattern of these events, Aristotle's stress on the intrinsic construction of a play is the counterpart of his neglect of the mythico-religious background which is often of great weight in the total effect of a tragedy. This question will be pursued in the commentary in connection with Aristotle's use of the notion of 'inside/outside the play' (see p.150). It is enough here to observe that the *Poetics'* treatment of dramatic logic and unity is not an autonomous doctrine of form, but brings with it a whole way of looking at the content and fabric of a play.

As a rider to this last point, it is worth adding an observation on the notion of action in Aristotle's theory. The term *praxis* in the *Poetics* is applied both to individual human actions and to the totality or complete pattern of action in a plot-structure. It is this second sense on which the stress of the theory is placed, but Aristotle can harmonise this emphasis on unified action with the need for distinctively *tragic* events only by positing a strong element of human fallibility (the doctrine of *hamartia* in ch. 13). For all its apparent clarity, the *Poetics'* concept of action remains a problematic idea with complex ramifications, including the relation of action to character (on which Aristotle pronounces in ch. 6), the relation of different agents' actions to

---

responsibility as against divine influence: e.g. 'not by divine agency ... but ... action of Oedipus himself' (p. 131), 'Oedipus ... is responsible for the catastrophe ... this discovery is *entirely due* to his action' (p. 149, my italics). This is all very Aristotelian, but ignores the following significant factors which are all independent of Oedipus' action: the plague at Thebes, the influence of Apollo's oracle, the arrival of the Corinthian messenger (especially important: cf. p.119 below), and the latter's original involvement in the exposure of the infant Oedipus. No wonder that even Knox relents enough to suggest, in a later note (p. 406), that '[Apollo's] hand is felt to be mysteriously at work' in the fulfilment of the oracle and the revelation of the truth.

one another (for example, in dramatic conflict: cf. p.134), and the relation of action – purposeful behaviour – to passive suffering (cf. p.120).

It is in the last two of these areas that the *Poetics* may be judged to raise more questions than it satisfactorily answers, and I believe that there is a link between this and the treatise's neglect of traditional religious attitudes. Tragedy does not offer simple or definitive solutions to the problems of human action and experience which it dramatises, but it does place such problems in a light where divine forces are sensed to be themselves active. Once again, what is at stake here is not an unequivocal role for these forces in the world of tragedy, but only their necessary relevance to the whole outlook and ethos of tragic material. If it is right that Aristotle constructs a model of tragedy which puts all religious ideas aside, then this may help to explain the resulting void in his own theory of tragic causation. Aristotle ultimately, I believe, locates the heart of tragedy indeterminately in the failure of human action, and this gives what I take to be a largely negative significance to his concept of *hamartia*. What my contention finally amounts to is a claim that Aristotle wishes dramatic action to be intelligible in purely human terms, and that this is a premise which none of the major Attic tragedians accepted in their work.

Action leads on to the final topic which I wish to mention in this part of my Introduction. It is again a topic which involves an undervaluation by Aristotle of a substantial dimension of tragedy, this time of the choral and lyric dimension. Action is here too at the root of the matter, because it is a concept which can be applied only with grave difficulty to the fluctuating function of the chorus in tragedy. We need not be surprised, therefore, if Aristotle's injunction near the end of ch. 18 that the chorus should be handled 'as one of the actors' remains an unassimilated and unjustified attempt to indicate a dramatic role for a choral element which has received no consideration in the central discussion of the genre. Aristotle's position certainly cannot be interpreted simply as a reflection of the diminishing importance of the chorus in contemporary tragedy, since he explicitly defines his point in opposition to this trend. Yet in a more subtle way it is plausible to see this aspect of the *Poetics* as symptomatic of fourth-century Greek culture, in which a decline in the formerly integral cultural status of music has been diagnosed.[15] If this is right, then we can hypothesise that Aristotle, while rejecting the irrelevance to which the choral component of tragedy had apparently degenerated, was hardly in a position to recapture a sense of the essential yet distinctive contribution of the choral lyrics to classical tragic drama.

That is, of course, a bold judgement, but it is compatible with the evidence of the *Poetics*. I do not, however, wish to suggest that Aristotle's neglect of the tragic chorus was culturally determined, only that the movement of cultural attitudes may have helped to shape it. But the final explanation must undoubtedly be sought within the fundamental terms of the treatise, which presupposes from the start that poetry is concerned with the representation of action. Within a framework which incorporates this view, there is little or no place for accepting the ambiguity of status which is unavoidable in the chorus of tragedy. Aristotle's is the first in a long succession of critical attempts to fix a single, essential function onto the chorus; but it is revealing that these attempts have been polarised between conceptions of dramatic integration and non-dramatic independence. What this shows is that the polarity in question is too hard-and-fast, too inflexible to cope with the special and variable nature of the chorus's relation to the action of the individual characters. In Aristotle's case, we can add that the neglect of the chorus is congruent with the underplaying of mythical and religious factors which I have already discussed, for it is especially in their use of choral lyrics that the Greek tragedians often unfold the larger background to the action which is played out in the foreground of their dramas.

There is, then, a certain continuity between the three areas where I have attempted to illustrate ways in which we may wish to question the critical approach of the *Poetics* to Greek tragedy. The purpose of this exercise has not been to show contempt for Aristotle's theory, but, on the contrary, to pay it the true respect of engaging seriously with its implications from my own, very different critical standpoint. I suggested earlier that the opportunity to do this is precisely one of the justifications for continuing to read the work. Other readers will wish to do the same, and in the process to question many of the arguments

---

[15] See I. Henderson, 'Ancient Greek Music', in E. Wellesz (ed.) *The New Oxford History of Music*, vol. 1 (Oxford 1957) pp. 339f.

which I have myself put forward. In the second part of this introduction I want now to turn directly to part of the history of others' interpretations of the *Poetics*, with particular reference to the work's role in the development of English criticism.

*

When the *Poetics* was effectively rediscovered for literary theory and criticism by the humanists of sixteenth-century Italy, it was read in an already existing and developing context of Renaissance thought. This meant that two strong elements in attitudes towards poetry (both of ancient pedigree) coloured the interpretation of Aristotle's work: the first, an assumption that poetry was akin to rhetoric in its aims of producing an effect on an audience; the second, a deep conviction that literature needed to be justified in ethical terms if its status was to be respectable. These two views could be, and often were, conveniently combined by the use of a formula borrowed from Horace's *Ars Poetica*, that the poet's task is to edify and (Horace says 'or') delight (333f.). Although other factors sometimes played a part (such as the desire to reconcile the ideas of Aristotle and Plato), it was the rhetorical and the ethical conceptions of literature which dominated Renaissance poetics and, consequently, the new interest in Aristotle's treatise.

It was Renaissance Italy which shaped the basic pattern of literary neo-classicism that was to spread and influence other parts of Europe as late as the eighteenth century. My main purpose in this section is to offer some remarks on the place of the *Poetics* in England from the sixteenth century onwards, but a wider generalisation about neo-classicism is a necessary preliminary to this.[16] Although there were certainly individual dissenters among Italian theorists, particularly regarding the relevance of the *Poetics* to vernacular literature, the neo-classical movement as a whole succeeded in combining Aristotle with Horace as twin authorities for what became widely regarded as the 'rules' of poetry. The establishment of this authoritarian

[16] For an essay on changing attitudes to the *Poetics* see the final chapter in my *Aristotle's Poetics*, with further bibliography. The present section is designed to say more about England than I had space for there. Most of the English material is surveyed, a little mechanically, in M. Herrick, *The Poetics of Aristotle in England* (New Haven 1930).

approach to criticism had a number of adverse consequences for the understanding of the *Poetics*.

One was the belief, which has never been altogether shaken off, that Aristotle's aim was to lay down practical precepts in the manner of a rhetorical handbook. The corollary of this was that the more philosophical and theoretical aspects of the *Poetics* were insufficiently grasped. Closely related to this was the widespread, if not universal, assumption that Aristotle's principles were timelessly valid, and should be enforced on all living writers, which for long made it practically impossible for anyone to regard the *Poetics* as an important *historical* document which yet need not be treated as an authority. As regards particular items of doctrine or principle, the *Poetics* also suffered from a tendency to mix classical sources indiscriminately in order to produce a uniform body of critical dogma: if a tenet could be found in, say, Horace or Cicero, then an orthodox neo-classicist could hardly fail to believe that it must also have been subscribed to by Aristotle. As a result, distinctive Aristotelian ideas were effaced or blunted for the sake of a harmonious assimilation of all authorities. Thus, the *Poetics* often had foisted on it the terms of the edification/delight principle, even though it is an important feature of Aristotle's theory of poetry that he avoids any such reductive formula.

It is not surprising, therefore, that in the first major English document of neo-classical poetics, Sidney's *Defence of Poetry*, which reworks much material from continental writings, we find fragments of Aristotelian thought often juxtaposed with ideas deriving from very different sources, yet seemingly harmonised into a consistent classicising view of poetry. Having, for example, set out an essentially neo-platonic interpretation of the poet's work as the embodiment of ideas and invention which go beyond the limits of nature, Sidney then offers his definition of poetry: 'an art of imitation, for so Aristotle termeth it in the word *mimesis* ... with this end, to teach and delight.'[17] We see, in other words, that Aristotelian mimesis (for which Sidney has various reasonable glosses, including 'fiction' and 'representing') is combined both with a much more far-reaching neo-platonic notion of poetic imagination, and with the Horatian formula for poetic purposes on which I have already commented.

---

[17] *A Defence of Poetry*, ed. J. van Dorsten (Oxford 1966) pp. 22-5.

These same two elements penetrate in a more pervasive way the interpretation of ideas drawn ultimately from Aristotle's treatise. At a number of points in his book, Sidney uses a phrase such as 'what may be and should be' to indicate the compass of poetic subject-matter, and on one occasion the phrase is directly linked to the exposition of the theory of poetic universals in *Poetics* ch. 9.[18] Now *Poetics* 9 is the original source of the notion of poetry's concern with things 'which may be' ('which *could* occur ...', p.40 below), but the point of the phrase is essentially logical: poetry's material consists of fictional and hypothetical, not actual, events. Elsewhere in the *Poetics*, in ch. 25, we encounter the criterion of things 'as they should be', but in this passage Aristotle is referring to a poet's *possible* use of an idealising level of representation, not to a necessary feature of all poetry. By contrast, Sidney (through his sources) turns the doctrine into one of fundamental poetic idealism with, moreover, a moral colouring: the poet shows us ideal images of goodness in order to move us to goodness. Elsewhere, we may feel, Sidney comes closer to the spirit of the *Poetics* in his famous remark (which is awkward to reconcile with his larger moralism) that the poet 'nothing affirms, and therefore never lieth'.[19]

Sidney's *Defence* can be used to pick out a number of features which were to remain broadly characteristic of Aristotle's place in neo-classicism: first, the mixture of elements from the *Poetics* with those from other classical authorities; second, the strong tendency towards regularising Aristotelian ideas into fixed precepts, both technical and ethical; third, the use of the *Poetics* in the growing debate over the respective merits of ancient and modern poetry. This last point was to prove especially important in England, largely on account of the robustly 'irregular' and unclassical qualities of Elizabethan and Jacobean drama. Already in Sidney (writing probably around 1580, and before the career of Shakespeare) we find English tragedy faulted for failing to adhere to the unities of time and place, which, though stemming from Castelvetro and Scaliger, are wrongly yet

---

[18] *Op. cit.* pp. 26, 35, and 53 (twice). It is interesting to note that the neo-platonist Plotinus, *Enneads* 5.8.1, uses a similar phrase to Ar.'s 'what could/might be', but to refer to the idealistic conception of Zeus's physical form conceived by the sculptor Pheidias. For more recent neo-platonic reinterpretations of *Poetics* 9 see p.23 below.

[19] *Op. cit.* p. 52.

20   *The* Poetics *of Aristotle*

confidently attributed to 'Aristotle's precept'.[20]

The pseudo-Aristotelian trio of Unities was to become a hallmark of the dominant French strain of neo-classicism in the seventeenth century, and it was consequently a necessary dogma for the few English critics who subscribed wholeheartedly to such uncompromising critical 'purity'. Of these the best known is Thomas Rymer, who was prepared to carry what he regarded as his literary Aristotelianism to the point of requiring even a chorus in tragedy, as a guarantee of unity of place. The same line of thought, though without the same authoritarian presentation, led to Milton's *Samson Agonistes* of 1671, just a few years before Rymer's main publications.[21]

But much more typical of English critical tendencies was a questioning and qualified attitude towards classical authorities which had appeared, in fact, long before the Rymerian extreme was reached. The two greatest native critics of the century, Jonson and Dryden, both, in their different ways, evince this attitude; and the work of minor critics demonstrates the wider spread of such feelings.[22] Jonson was as indebted to continental humanists as Sidney had been, or as Rymer would later be, for many of his ideas about literature; but a strong difference of literary temperament is reflected in his conviction that the ancients are not timeless or infallible legislators for art. Such, however, was the varying reliability of neo-classicism's use of Aristotle, that we find in Jonson's notebook, *Timber*, a much fuller and more accurate statement of the *Poetics*' essential doctrine of unity of action than many more conformist thinkers were able to offer.[23]

The paradox that Jonson, alive to the vital qualities of the English vernacular tradition, could yet come closer to Aristotelian doctrine than Rymer, who advocated that modern literature should be written entirely in the image of classical, is a

[20] *Op. cit.* p. 65.

[21] Rymer translated Rapin's *Reflections on Aristotle's Treatise of Poesie* in 1674, and published *Tragedies of the Last Age Considered* in 1678.

[22] For a collection of evidence see P. S. Wood, 'The Opposition to neo-Classicism in England Between 1660 and 1700', *Publications of the Modern Language Association of America* 43 (1928) 182-97.

[23] The last section of *Timber* is virtually a translation of parts of the *Poetics*: see *Ben Jonson: The Complete Poems*, ed. G. Parfitt (Harmondsworth 1975) pp. 454-8. But Jonson appears to have taken the material from the work of Daniel Heinsius, on whom see my *Aristotle's Poetics* pp. 302-4.

symptom of the fact that neo-classicism in its various manifestations was less interested in a historical interpretation of the *Poetics* than in deploying its weight of authority in debates which came increasingly to focus on contemporary literature and standards of criticism. It is not, I think, accidental that Dryden, for example, who was certainly aware of Aristotle's view that tragedy was superior to epic, could still bring himself to write: 'Heroic poetry ... has ever been esteemed ... the greatest work of human nature: in that rank has Aristotle placed it.'[24]

In the context of an 'Apology for Heroic Poetry', such a remark is a telling sign of a pressure to invoke as much classical authority as possible for one's critical position. Yet Dryden was no unthinking or automatic classiciser. His copious critical writings show as well as any other English documents the tension between a basic commitment to classical ideals, and the impetus of a living writer towards authentic poetic standards in his own time. The conflict is particularly clear in the notes which Dryden made for a reply to Rymer, where the paradigmatic status of the *Poetics* and of Greek tragedy is firmly called into question, yet notably within a framework which, in its moral suppositions as well as in much of its conceptual apparatus, remains obviously neo-classical. Dryden insists on the cultural differences ('the genius of the age and nation') which separate English from Greek tragedy, and he refuses to judge the former simply by the rules of French theorists. He diverges most strikingly from Aristotelianism in his rejection of singleness of action in favour of 'counterturn of design or episode, i.e. under-plot'. At the same time, however, he is able to echo one of the central concerns of neo-classicism by finding the *Poetics* wanting for failure to stress the moral aim of tragedy, 'to reform manners'.[25]

After Dryden, a degree of influence of French neo-classicism on English critics continued well into the eighteenth century. It would be possible to pursue the resulting engagement with elements of the *Poetics* in such documents as Addison's long series of *Spectator* papers on Milton, which particularly demonstrate how well established the critical vocabulary of Aristotle was becoming in the analysis of particular poems; or in

[24] See *John Dryden: Selected Criticism*, edd. J. Kinsley & G. Parfitt (Oxford 1970) p. 135 for the quotation, and pp. 72 and 227 for the truth about Ar.'s views.
[25] *Op. cit.* pp. 143-9.

Johnson's *Preface to Shakespeare*, which reveals once more the
tension caused by the conflicting values of classical and
vernacular tragedy.[26] But in the present limited context it is
necessary to move ahead to new tendencies and habits of
interpretation. While Johnson could still refer with approbation,
in *Rambler* no. 139, to 'the indispensable laws of Aristotelian
criticism', attitudes to the *Poetics* were by this time being
influenced by a new current in English criticism, due in part to
the stimulus of Longinian ideas of poetic greatness, passion,
imagination, and the sublime.

This can readily be illustrated by some of the writers already
mentioned. As early as Dryden's 'Apology for Heroic Poetry' we
find direct reference to Longinus' contrast between true
greatness, which can afford small mistakes or blemishes, and
sustained but mediocre correctness. This contrast evidently cuts
against the grain of normal neo-classical insistence on
conformity to 'the rules', and it entails an attitude which in time
was to alter approaches to the *Poetics*. In Addison's Milton
papers, an enterprise which is framed in basic terms taken from
Aristotle (using his categories of plot, character, thought, etc. to
analyse particular works) comes increasingly to rely on 'the
sublime' as a touchstone of epic achievement. A Longinian spirit
can be seen steadily encroaching on ostensibly Aristotelian
territory.

In the more developed, Romantic phase of this movement of
ideas and feeling, it would be misleading to suggest that the
Poetics was of more than marginal or occasional importance.
Once the grip of neo-classical authority was slackened, there was
clearly no obligation on any critic to take much note of
Aristotle's ideas. In addition to the general current of
Romanticism, which attached an unaristotelian degree of
importance to the individual poet's capacity for emotion and
imagination, it was obvious that the *Poetics* could hardly provide
any guidance with genres such as subjective lyric, or the novel,
for which Aristotle had made no provision. Against this

---

[26] Addison on Milton: *Spectator* nos. 267 seq. (weekly). These papers well
demonstrate the way in which analytical categories derived from Ar. had become
commonplace, though no longer part of a unified critical approach: on the process
by which this happened see the long n. 7 to R. S. Crane, 'The Concept of Plot and
the Plot of *Tom Jones*', in *Critics and Criticism* (Chicago 1952), also edited by
Crane. On Johnson's *Preface* see my *Aristotle's Poetics* pp. 309-11.

background, a number of newly conceived attitudes to the treatise started to define themselves, in England as on the Continent.

Simplest and most hostile was the option of outright rejection, on the grounds of the *Poetics'* association with the dominant French criticism of the seventeenth and early eighteenth centuries. The voice of this point of view can at least be heard, even if it is not directly represented, in passages of Coleridge's lectures on Shakespeare, where French notions of Aristotle as 'infallible censor' and 'dictator' in literary matters are now confidently dismissed as part of a vindication of Shakespeare against inappropriate critical strictures. Coleridge's target is of course the French misuse of Aristotle's authority, rather than Aristotle himself. In fact, Coleridge can also exemplify for us a rather different approach to the *Poetics*, one which was sympathetic but eclectic. If a systematic adherence to Aristotelian doctrine was no longer possible, at least *something* congenial to a Romantic sensibility might be salvaged.

In Coleridge's case, this remnant was taken, hardly surprisingly, from ch. 9 of the treatise. This passage had lent itself as early as the Renaissance to reinterpretation in the light of neo-platonic belief in the idealising and transcendent powers of art (cf. p.19 above on Sidney), and Coleridge represents a Romantic revival of that view. In the *Biographia Literaria* he tells us in ch. 17 that he subscribes to 'the principle of Aristotle that poetry as poetry is essentially ideal', which he qualifies in a footnote as 'an involution of the universal in the individual'. Although the elaboration of the point in the text approximates to part of Aristotle's point in mentioning universals, Coleridge's use of 'ideal' alerts us to a desire to inflate *Poetics* 9 into a much more portentous text than it really is. This is confirmed by Coleridge's later (inaccurate) paraphrase, in ch. 22, of Aristotle's comparison of poetry to philosophy: instead of 'more philosophical and more serious than history', Coleridge makes Aristotle regard poetry, altogether more gravely, as 'the most intense, weighty and philosophical product of human art'.

We can see from a minor document like the youthful J. H. Newman's review article, 'Poetry, with reference to Aristotle's *Poetics*' (1829), that the exercise of assimilating Aristotle's treatise to one kind of Romantic preconception was not a quirk of Coleridge's. Newman's piece is hardly worth considering in detail, but its strategy towards the *Poetics* is worth noting as an instance of the tensions left in attitudes towards the work by the transition from neo-classicism to Romanticism.[27] Newman sets out by criticising Aristotle's excessive concern with plot, and claims that the Greek tragedians were anyway 'not generally felicitous in the construction of their plots': he offers, in other words, a fairly routine rejection of what, against the backcloth of neo-classicism, had appeared to be the central poetic values advocated by Greek poetry and Aristotle's theory. But before long both these things have been transformed in the light of Newman's conviction that poetry entails 'the spontaneous exhibition of pathos or imagination', and 'a free and unfettered effusion of genius'. Greek tragedy, it turns out, was entirely consistent with this, and so was the *Poetics*, for Aristotle regarded poetry as 'a representation of the ideal', and the poetic mind, Newman tells us, 'is one full of the eternal forms of beauty and perfection'.

This is, of course, rampant Romantic neo-platonism (and specifically Christianised later in the essay), presented in such a way as to suggest that the *Poetics*, despite some regrettable notions on dramatic plot, can ultimately be reconciled with a more enthusiastic view of poetry. Such a curious reinterpretation of Aristotle's position would be more negligible if it did not have later and influential analogues, most notably in S. H. Butcher's *Aristotle's Theory of Poetry and Fine Art* (1895), which in its later editions has been perhaps the most influential work on twentieth-century attitudes to the *Poetics* in England and America. Butcher's treatment of Aristotle, it should be stressed, is much more responsibly argued than Newman's, and a great deal of his book can be read as a continuation of the tradition of scholarship on the treatise which had been accumulating, especially in Germany, during the nineteenth century. But Butcher, like others of his academic generation, was also influenced by modern German idealist philosophy, particularly Hegel's, and this induced him to restate another version of the idealising interpretation of the *Poetics* which we have already encountered. It will be sufficient here to note how this leads

---

[27] Newman's essay has been often reprinted. See e.g. *English Critical Essays: Nineteenth Century*, ed. E. D. Jones (Oxford 1916) pp. 223-53. My quotations will be found on pp. 226, 229, 232, 234-5.

Butcher to attribute to Aristotle the belief that poetry 'represents things which are not, and *never can be* ... it gives us ... the true idea' (my italics).[28] Unfortunately for this contention, *Poetics* 9 tells us expressly that poetry portrays 'events which *could* occur'.

Butcher's essays on the *Poetics* represent the final attempt of Romanticism in England to appropriate some of Aristotle's views for its own cause. Butcher's influence has given a certain currency to this revaluation of the *Poetics*, but it is fair to say that no single approach to the treatise has been generally subscribed to during the present century. That is largely because the great ramification of modern criticism into schools and approaches has brought with it a tendency for the *Poetics* to be treated in a piecemeal and eclectic fashion by the various writers who have thought it worthwhile to reexamine Aristotle's thinking about poetry. Some engagement with the work can be found in a wide range of modern criticism, and in many cases elements of its theory are reinterpreted in the image, so to speak, of the particular modern critic.[29] With, for example, an individual and controversial issue such as *katharsis*, we find a spectrum of interpretations running from, at one end, the interest of psychological critics in using or adapting the idea as a supposedly congenial insight into the mental experiences induced by art, to the contention of certain New Critics, at the other, that *katharsis* is just an early instance of the confusion between a poem and its putative effects ('the affective fallacy': cf. p.91). In such ways the Aristotelian doctrine, which remains conveniently obscure, is placed in relation to the modern critic's own concerns, just as in an earlier period *katharsis* was frequently aligned with the moralism of neo-classicists.[30]

After the excessive idealism of certain nineteenth-century readings of the *Poetics*, a counter-reaction, as part of a wider withdrawal from Romantic views of poetry and literature, was perhaps only to be expected. An interesting if limited example of

[28] S. H. Butcher, *Aristotle's Theory of Poetry and Fine Art*, 4th edn. (London 1907) p. 168. Butcher's claim is based on an illegitimate extrapolation from a point made by Ar. in ch. 25: cf. p.19 above on a similar flaw in Sidney's use of Ar.

[29] A mass of material, not all of equal interest or importance, has been gathered in the unpublished Ph.D. of K. J. Kerrane, *Aristotle's Poetics in Modern Literary Criticism* (Univ. of North Carolina 1968).

[30] On neo-classical views of *katharsis* see my *Aristotle's Poetics* Appendix 5.

this can be found in the early criticism of T. S. Eliot, which took a stance consciously opposed to the existing tendency to locate the author's expression of personality and personal emotion at the centre of a work of literature. Aristotle is cited on a number of occasions in *The Sacred Wood* (1920) to lend a particular kind of classical corroboration to Eliot's attitudes to poetry and to criticism. Eliot not only quotes Aristotle in support of his conception of drama as a mode of 'statement' to which the poet's personality is irrelevant, but he holds him up (after defensively putting aside the 'canonical' way he has been treated by his 'sectaries') as a model of disinterested critical intelligence, which consists in looking 'solely and steadfastly at the object' and yielding to no emotions other than those 'immediately provoked by a work of art'.[31] Eliot's idea of poetic impersonality is matched by one of critical objectivity, for which he finds Aristotle a classic precedent.

Without engaging in a direct analysis of Eliot's position, one can confidently say that, under the pressure of combatting certain Romantic habits towards literature and seeking support for his own contentions, he greatly exaggerates Aristotle's objectivity in the *Poetics.* Eliot ignores the extent to which the philosopher brings his own *a priori* assumptions and general intellectual principles to bear on the subject, and the ways in which his prescriptive approach constantly rules out alternative means of poetic success. What Eliot, however, legitimately had in mind was Aristotle's refusal to judge poetry directly by external standards as Plato and other Greek critics had done before him: there is a close parallel (once we allow for the different language of their times) between Aristotle's dictum, 'correct standards in poetry are not identical with those in politics or in any other particular art' (ch. 25), and Eliot's, 'when we are considering poetry we must consider it primarily as poetry and not another thing.'[32]

This latter principle represents a point (if perhaps the only

---

[31] *The Sacred Wood*, 7th edn. (London 1950) pp. 10-14, 67 and 70. For later references to Ar. in Eliot's criticism see especially *The Use of Poetry and the Use of Criticism*, 2nd edn. (1964) pp. 45-9 (a strange attempt to justify the Unities, sliding, under Butcher's influence, from unity of action to 'unity of sentiment'), and pp. 74f. (on the supposedly Aristotelian character of Wordsworth's view of 'mimesis').

[32] *The Sacred Wood* p. viii.

one) at which an affinity can be discerned between Eliot and the most extensive modern attempt to revive the critical system of Aristotle, namely that of the so-called Chicago critics, operative from the mid-1930s onwards.[33] This set of writers argued extensively for the value of the *Poetics* (as well as other elements of Aristotelian philosophy) in a reassessment of 'the grounds of criticism'; and in the process they cited, paraphrased, and adapted the treatise again and again. Unlike virtually all the earlier critics so far considered, therefore, the Chicago school set out effectively to offer an entire interpretative approach to the *Poetics*, as well as to introduce its ideas into the practice of modern criticism.

Two major tenets can be picked out at the heart of this combined enterprise: the first is the importance of literary genres or species; the second, the need to concentrate on literary form and structure, or the entire and internal organisation of a literary work. The stress on genres inevitably looks like a throwback to neo-classicism and a reaction against the strong Romantic tendency to dwell on the general or universal qualities of all literature and poetry, rather than features specific to certain types. There can be no argument that genres are fundamental to Aristotle's thinking about poetry, but it is equally clear that a revival of generic theory needs much more than this to justify it. Neo-classicism had, in fact, been gradually undermined by the growth of modern literary types which were unknown to Aristotle and to other ancient critics, as well as by what seemed to some to involve the mixing of genres (such as 'mongrel tragi-comedy', in Sidney's phrase) in contravention of classical purism. The long history of European literature now allows us to see that a theory of genres of the clear-cut kind put forward in the Greek context by Aristotle can scarcely be sustained.

The Chicago concern with literary form has helped to establish a widespread modern view that the concept of form defined in the *Poetics* is of an autonomous, self-contained kind. I believe, however, that this view is misguided, for reasons which will emerge in my commentary (see p.98). It is enough for the

---

[33] The most representative collection of work by the Chicago critics is the one edited by Crane and cited in n. 26 above. It should be said (as perusal of that volume will make clear) that these critics varied considerably in their degree of adherence to, or consistency with, the general principles I mention in the text.

moment to say that Aristotle's understanding of form is inextricable from his acceptance of a mimeticist model of poetry, and that from such a point of view form is not in any sense applied or superimposed, but rather built or designed into the human material (the 'action') which is the object of the poet's representation. Although, therefore, form is undeniably central to Aristotle's treatment of poetry, it is not a self-sufficient or purely 'aesthetic' notion of form which he offers. While the Chicago critics have done something to clarify the way in which the *Poetics* concentrates on the internal order and unity of a literary work, they have, I believe, underestimated the extent to which mimesis commits Aristotle to an acceptance of poetry's engagement with reality. If neo-classicism went much too far in using the *Poetics* to support its prevailing moralism, there is equally a danger, in the climate of modern criticism, of attributing to Aristotle too complete a separation of literature and 'life'.

*

These compressed and necessarily selective remarks on some of the uses made of the *Poetics* in English criticism will at least serve, I hope, to show that a wide range of writers and thinkers have thought it worthwhile to try to define certain elements of their critical outlook by reference to what they took to be Aristotelian doctrines. A relatively simple moral can perhaps be deduced from the evidence considered. If we read the *Poetics* with the expectation or intention of finding ideas congenial to our own experience of literature, the risk of distorting the balance of Aristotle's thesis, or even of wholly misinterpreting it, becomes considerable. The work should not be exploited in this way as a stock of renewable but isolated principles. To 'plead', for example, for the 'reinstatement' of Aristotle's notion of mimesis, is not only to presuppose a bizarre concept of modern critical activity, but also, and almost inevitably, to be drawn into a misconstrual of just what Aristotle's notion originally meant.[34] It is certainly legitimate and important to try to see

---

[34] Potts, *Aristotle on the Art of Fiction* p.10: the plea follows the thoroughly confused assimilation of mimesis (regrettably translated as 'imitation': see p.71 below) to 'creative imagination'.

that the *Poetics* addresses itself to many fundamental issues which are still of relevance to criticism. But it is just as important to acknowledge that the work belongs to another time and place, and therefore to engage with its arguments without losing our sense of the historical distance across which we necessarily view them.

Translation

Ch. 1

To discuss the art of poetry in general, as well as the potential of each of its types; to explain the unity of plot required for successful poetic composition; also to analyse the number and nature of the component parts of poetry; and to deal similarly with the other questions which belong to this same method of enquiry – these are my proposed topics, beginning in the natural way from first principles.

Now, epic and tragic poetry, as well as comedy and dithyramb (and most music for the pipe or lyre), are all, taken as a whole, kinds of mimesis. But they differ from one another in three respects: namely, in the *media* or the *objects* or the *mode* of mimesis. For just as there are people who produce mimetic images of many things in the media of colours and shapes (some relying on a skilled art, some on practice), and others who use the medium of the voice, so in the case of all the arts mentioned above mimesis is effected in the media of rhythm, language and melody.

But these can be employed separately or in combination, as follows:

(a) the arts of the pipe and lyre (and any other arts with a similar potential, such as that of the pan-pipes) use melody and rhythm alone;

(b) the art of dancing presents mimesis in the medium of rhythm without melody (for dancers, through the rhythms which shape their movements, engage in the mimesis of character, emotions and actions);

(c) *the art which employs language alone, or language in metrical form (whether in a combination of metres or just one kind), is still without a name. For we have no common name for the mimes of Sophron and Xenarchus and

Socratic dialogues, nor for any mimetic work which might be written in iambic trimeters or elegiac couplets or something else of this kind. It is of course true that people attach the verbal idea of 'poetry' (*poiein*) to the name of the metre, and so call these writers 'elegiac poets' (*elegopoioi*), 'epic poets' (*epopoioi*), and so on; but the categories refer not to their status as poets in virtue of mimesis, but to the metre they have in common: since, if a work of medicine or natural philosophy is written in metre, people still use these same descriptions. But Homer and Empedocles have nothing in common except their metre; and so, while one must call the former a poet, the latter should be called a natural philosopher rather than a poet. A corollary is that even if someone should produce a mimesis in a mixture of all the metres (as Chairemon did in his mixed rhapsody, *Centaur*), he too must be called a poet. So let distinctions of these kinds be drawn in these matters.

(d)   Finally, there are some poetic arts which employ all the stated media (that is, rhythm, melody and metre), such as dithyramb, nome, tragedy and comedy: they differ, though, in that some use all throughout, some only in parts. These, then, are the distinctions between the arts as regards the media of their mimesis.

Ch. 2

Since mimetic artists portray people in action, and since these people must be either good or bad (for men's characters practically always conform to these categories alone*), they can portray people better than ourselves, worse than ourselves, or on the same level. The same is true in painting: Polygnotus portrayed men who are superior, Pauson worse, and Dionysius on the same level. And it is evident that each of the stated types of mimesis will exhibit these differences, and will thus be distinguishable according to the variations in the objects which it represents. For such differences are possible in dancing, and in music for the pipe and lyre, as well as in the arts which use language alone or language in metre: for instance, Homer represented superior men, Cleophon men like us, Hegemon of Thasos (the first writer of parodies) and Nicochares (author of the *Deiliad*) inferior men. The same principle applies in dithyramb and the nome, *as one sees ... and from the possibility of portraying the Cyclopes in the manner of Timotheus and Philoxenus. This very distinction also separates tragedy from comedy: the latter tends to represent men worse than present humanity, the former better.

Ch. 3

Beside the two already cited, there is a third distinction: namely, the mode in which the various objects are represented. For it is possible to use the same media to offer a mimesis of the same objects in any one of three ways: first, by alternation between narrative and dramatic impersonation (as in Homeric poetry); second, by employing the voice of narrative without variation; third, by a wholly dramatic presentation of the agents.

So then, as indicated at the outset, mimesis can be distinguished in these three respects: by its *media*, its *objects*, and its *modes*. Consequently, in one respect Sophocles uses the same mimesis as Homer, for in both cases the objects are good men; while in another respect, Sophocles and Aristophanes are parallel, since both use the mimetic mode of dramatic enactment.

It is because of this that some people derive the term *drama* itself from the enactive mimesis of agents (*drôntas*). And for this reason, the Dorians even lay claim to both tragedy and comedy: in the case of the latter, the Megarians here on the mainland claim that it was invented during their democratic period, while the Megarians in Sicily think it theirs because the poet Epicharmus, who greatly predated the Athenians Chionides and Magnes, came from there; and as for comedy, some of the Dorians in the Peloponnese lay claim to it. The Dorians regard the terminology as evidence, since they assert that their own name for rural districts is *kômai*, while the Athenians call them 'demes'; and they suppose that the name for comic actors, *kômôdoi*, was derived not from revelling (*kômazein*) but from the fact that, when barred as unrespectable from the town, they toured through the villages (*kômai*). Similarly, the Dorians say that their verb for activity is *dran*, while the Athenians use *prattein*.

So then, let these remarks suffice to cover the number and nature of the mimetic distinctions.

Ch. 4

Poetry in general can be seen to owe its existence to two causes, and these are rooted in nature. First, there is man's natural propensity, from childhood onwards, to engage in mimetic activity (and this distinguishes man from other creatures, that he is thoroughly mimetic and through mimesis takes his first steps in understanding). Second, there is the pleasure which all men take in mimetic objects.

An indication of the latter can be observed in practice: for we take pleasure in contemplating the most precise images of things whose sight in itself causes us pain – such as the appearance of the basest animals, or of corpses. Here too the explanation lies in the fact that great pleasure is derived from exercising the understanding, not just for philosophers but in the same way for all men, though their capacity for it may be limited. It is for this reason that men enjoy looking at images, because what happens is that, as they contemplate them, they apply their understanding and reasoning to each element (identifying this as an image of such-and-such a man, for instance). Since, if it happens that one has no previous familiarity with the sight, then the object will not give pleasure *qua* mimetic object but because of its craftmanship, or colour, or for some other such reason.

Given, then, that mimetic activity comes naturally to us – together with melody and rhythm (for it is evident that metres are species of rhythm) – it was originally those with a special natural capacity who, through a slow and gradual process, brought poetry into being by their improvisations. And poetry was split into two types according to the poets' own characters: the more dignified made noble actions and noble agents the object of their mimesis; while lighter poets took the actions of base men and began by composing invectives, just as the other group produced hymns and encomia. Now, we cannot cite an invective by any individual poet before Homer's time, though it is likely there were many such poets; their known history starts with Homer, with his *Margites* and other such works. It was appropriate that in these works the iambic metre came to find its place – and this is why it is called 'iambic' now, because it was in this metre that they abused one another (in the manner called *iambizein*).

Of the old poets, some composed in epic hexameters, others in iambics. Just as Homer was the supreme poet of serious subjects (for he was unique both in the quality and in the *dramatic* nature of his poetry), similarly he was the first to reveal the form of comedy, by producing dramatic poetry which dealt not with invective but with the ridiculous. For the *Margites* stands in the same relation to later comedies as do the *Iliad* and *Odyssey* to tragedies. And when the possibility of tragedy and comedy had been glimpsed, men aspired to either type of poetry according to their personal capacities; so some became poets of comedy instead of iambic verses, while others abandoned epic for tragedy, because the latter's forms were greater than, and superior to, epic's.

To consider whether tragedy is by now sufficiently developed in its types – judging it both in itself and in relation to audiences – is a separate matter. At any rate, having come into being from an improvisational origin (which is true of both tragedy and comedy, the first starting from the leaders of the dithyramb, the second from the leaders of the phallic songs which are still customary in many cities), tragedy was gradually enhanced as poets made progress with the potential which they could see in the genre. And when it had gone through many changes, tragedy ceased to evolve, since it had attained its natural fulfilment.

It was Aeschylus who first increased the number of actors from one to two, reduced the choral parts, and gave speech the leading role; the third actor and scene-painting came with Sophocles. A further aspect of change concerns scale: after a period of slight plots and humorous diction, it was only at a late stage that tragedy attained dignity by departing from the style of satyr-plays, and that the iambic metre replaced the trochaic tetrameter. To begin with, poets used the tetrameter because the poetry had more of the tone of a satyr-play and of dance; and it was only when speech was brought in that the nature of the genre found its appropriate metre (the iambic is the most colloquial of metres, as we see from the fact that we frequently produce the rhythm of iambic lines in our conversation, while we rarely produce hexameters and only by departing from the register of ordinary speech).

There were further developments concerning the number of

episodes, and we shall take as read the other particular elaborations which are said to have been effected, since it would be a large task to give a thorough account of every detail.

Ch. 5

Comedy, as I earlier said, is a mimesis of men who are inferior, but not in a way which involves complete evil: the comic is one species of the shameful. For the comic is constituted by a fault and a mark of shame, but lacking in pain or destruction: to take an obvious example, the comic mask is ugly and misshapen, but does not express pain. Now, while the stages of tragedy's development, and those responsible for them, have been preserved, comedy's have not been, because it was not originally given serious attention: the archon first granted a comic chorus at quite a late date; before that, the performers were volunteers. The first recorded comic poets belong to the era when the genre already possessed some established forms. We are simply ignorant about such matters as who invented masks, or introduced prologues, or increased the number of actors, and other such details. But as for the use of poetic plot-structures, that originally came from Sicily; and of Athenian poets Crates was the first to abandon the iambic concept and to compose generalised stories and plots.

Epic conforms with tragedy insofar as it is a mimesis, in spoken metre, of ethically serious subjects; but it differs by virtue of using *only* spoken verse and of being in the narrative mode. There is also a difference of scale: whereas tragedy strives as far as possible to limit itself to a single day, epic is distinctive by its lack of a temporal limit, although in the early days poets of tragedy were as free in this respect as those of epic. The parts of epic are all common to tragedy, but the latter has some peculiar to itself. Consequently, whoever knows the difference between a good and a bad tragedy knows the same for epic too; for epic's attributes all belong to tragedy as well, though not all of tragedy's are shared by epic.

Ch. 6

I shall discuss epic mimesis and comedy later. But let us deal with tragedy by taking up the definition of its essential nature which arises out of what has so far been said.

Tragedy, then, is a representation of an action which is serious, complete, and of a certain magnitude – in language which is garnished in various forms in its different parts – in the mode of dramatic enactment, not narrative – and through the arousal of pity and fear effecting the *katharsis* of such emotions.

By 'garnished' language I mean with rhythm and melody; and by the 'various forms' I mean that some parts use spoken metre, and others use lyric song. Since the mimesis is enacted by agents, we can deduce that one element of tragedy must be the adornment of visual spectacle, while others are lyric poetry and verbal style, for it is in these that the mimesis is presented. By 'style' I mean the composition of the spoken metres; the meaning of 'lyric poetry' is entirely evident.

Since tragedy is a representation of an action, and is enacted by agents, who must be characterised in both their character and their thought (for it is through these that we can also judge the qualities of their actions, and it is in their actions that all men either succeed or fail), we have the plot-structure as the mimesis of the action (for by this term 'plot-structure' I mean the organisation of the events) while characterisation is what allows us to judge the nature of the agents, and 'thought' represents the parts in which by their speech they put forward arguments or make statements.

So then, tragedy as a whole must have six elements which make it what it is: they are plot-structure, character, style, thought, spectacle, lyric poetry. Two of these are the media, one the mode, and three the objects, of the mimesis – and that embraces everything. *Many poets have exploited these parts in order to produce certain types of play [...].

The most important of these elements is the structure of events, because tragedy is a representation not of people as such but of actions and life, *and both happiness and unhappiness rest on action. The goal is a certain activity, not a qualitative state; and while men do have certain qualities by virtue of their character, it is in their actions that they achieve, or fail to achieve, happiness. It is not, therefore, the function of the agents' actions to allow the portrayal of their characters; it is, rather, for the sake of their actions that characterisation is included. So, the events and the plot-structure are the goal of tragedy, and the goal is what matters most of all.

Besides, without action you would not have a tragedy, but one without character would be feasible, for the tragedies of most recent poets are lacking in characterisation, and in general there are many such poets. Compare, among painters, the difference between Zeuxis and Polygnotus: while Polygnotus is a fine portrayer of character, Zeuxis' art has no characterisation. Furthermore, if a poet strings together speeches to illustrate character, even allowing he composes them well in style and thought, he will not achieve the stated aim of tragedy. Much more effective will be a play with a plot and structure of events, even if it is deficient in style and thought.

In addition to these considerations, tragedy's greatest means of emotional power are components of the plot-structure: namely, reversals and recognitions. Moreover, it is symptomatic that poetic novices can achieve precision in style and characterisation before they acquire it in plot-construction – as was the case with virtually all the early poets. And so, the plot-structure is the first principle and, so to speak, the soul of tragedy, while characterisation is the element of second importance. (An analogous point holds for painting: a random distribution of the most attractive colours would never yield as much pleasure as a definite image without colour.) Tragedy is a mimesis of action, and only for the sake of this is it mimesis of the agents themselves.

Third in importance is thought: this is the capacity to produce pertinent and appropriate arguments, which is the task in prose speeches of the arts of politics and rhetoric. The older poets used to make their characters speak in a political vein, whereas modern poets do so in a rhetorical vein. Character is the element which reveals the nature of a moral choice, in cases where it is not anyway clear what a person is choosing or avoiding (and so speeches in which the speaker chooses or avoids nothing at all do not possess character); while thought arises in passages where people show that something is or is not the case, or present some universal proposition.

The fourth element is style: as previously said, I mean by this term the verbal expression achieved through the choice of words, which has the same force whether in verse or in prose. Of the remaining elements, lyric poetry is the most important of garnishings, while spectacle is emotionally powerful but is the least integral of all to the poet's art: for the potential of tragedy does not depend upon public performance and actors; and, besides, the art of the mask-maker carries more weight than the poet's as regards the elaboration of visual effects.

Ch. 7

Given these definitions, my next topic is to prescribe the form which the structure of events ought to take, since this is the first and foremost component of tragedy. We have already laid down that tragedy is a representation of an action which is complete, whole and of a certain magnitude (for something can be whole but of no magnitude).

By 'whole' I mean possessing a beginning, middle and end. By 'beginning' I mean that which does not have a necessary connection with a preceding event, but which can itself give rise naturally to some further fact or occurrence. An 'end', by contrast, is something which naturally occurs after a preceding event, whether by necessity or as a general rule, but need not be followed by anything else. The 'middle' involves causal connections with both what precedes and what ensues. Consequently, well designed plot-structures ought not to begin or finish at arbitrary points, but to follow the principles indicated.

Moreover, any beautiful object, whether a living creature or any other structure of parts, must possess not only ordered arrangement but also an appropriate scale (for beauty is grounded in both size and order). A creature could not be beautiful if it is either too small – for perception of it is practically instantaneous and so cannot be experienced – or too great, for contemplation of it cannot be a single experience, and it is not possible to derive a sense of unity and wholeness from our perception of it (imagine an animal a thousand miles long). Just, therefore, as a beautiful body or creature must have some size, but one which allows it to be perceived all together, so plot-structures should be of a length which can be easily held in the memory.

An artistic definition of length cannot be related to dramatic competitions and the spectators' concentration. For if a hundred tragedies had to compete, they would measure them by the water-clock (as people say they once did). The limit which accords with the true nature of the matter is this: beauty of size favours as large a structure as possible, provided that coherence is maintained. A concise definition is to say that the sufficient limit of a poem's scale is the scope required for a probable or necessary succession of events which produce a transformation either from affliction to prosperity, or the reverse.

Ch. 8

A plot-structure does not possess unity (as some believe) by virtue of centring on an individual. For just as a particular thing may have many random properties, some of which do not combine to make a single entity, so a particular character may perform many actions which do not yield a single 'action'. Consequently, all those poets who have written a *Heracleid* or *Theseid*, or the like, are evidently at fault: they believe that because Heracles was a single individual, a plot-structure about him ought thereby to have unity. As in other respects, Homer is exceptional by the fineness of his insight into this point, whether we regard this as an acquired ability or a natural endowment of his: although composing an *Odyssey*, he did not include everything that happened to the hero (such as his wounding on Parnassus or his pretence of madness at the levy – events which involved no necessary or probable connection with one another). Instead, he constructed the *Odyssey* around a single action of the kind I mean, and likewise with the *Iliad*.

So then, just as in the other mimetic arts a unitary mimesis is a representation of a unitary object, so the plot-structure, as the mimesis of action, should be a representation of a unitary and complete action; and its parts, consisting of the events, should be so constructed that the displacement or removal of any one of them will disturb and disjoint the work's wholeness. For anything whose presence or absence has no clear effect cannot be counted an integral part of the whole.

Ch. 9

It is a further clear implication of what has been said that the poet's task is to speak not of events which have occurred, but of the kind of events which *could* occur, and are possible by the standards of probability or necessity. For it is not the use or absence of metre which distinguishes poet and historian (one could put Herodotus' work into verse, but it would be no less a sort of history with it than without it): the difference lies in the fact that the one speaks of events which have occurred, the other of the sort of events which could occur.

It is for this reason that poetry is both more philosophical and more serious than history, since poetry speaks more of universals, history of particulars. A 'universal' comprises the *kind* of speech or action which belongs by probability or necessity to a certain *kind* of character – something which poetry aims at *despite* its addition of particular names. A 'particular', by contrast, is (for example) what Alcibiades did or experienced.

This point has become clear in the case of comedy, where it is only after constructing a plot in terms of probable events that they give the characters ordinary names, so diverging from the iambic poets' practice of writing about individuals. In tragedy, on the other hand, the poets hold to the actual names. (The reason for this is that people are ready to believe in what is possible; and while we may not yet believe in the possibility of things that have not already happened, actual events are evidently possible, otherwise they would not have occurred.) Even so, there are some tragedies in which one or two of the familiar names are kept, while others are due to the poet; and some plays in which all are new, as in Agathon's *Antheus*: for in this play both the events and the names are equally the poet's work, yet the pleasure it gives is just as great. So, fidelity to the traditional plots which are the subject of tragedies is not to be sought at all costs. Indeed, to do this is absurd, since even familiar material is familiar only to a minority, but it can still afford pleasure to all.

It is clear, then, from what has been said that the poet should be a maker of plot-structures rather than of verses, in so far as his status as poet depends on mimesis, and the object of his mimesis is actions. And he is just as much a poet even if the material of his poetry comprises actual events, since there is no reason why *some* historical events should not be in conformity with probability, and it is with respect to probability that the poet can make his poetry from them.

*Of simple plot-structures and actions the worst are episodic. I call an 'episodic' plot-structure one in which the episodes follow in a succession which is neither probable nor necessary. Such plays are produced by bad poets through their own fault, and by good poets because of their actors: for in composing declamatory set-pieces, and straining the plot-structure to excess, they are often compelled to distort the dramatic sequence.

Since, tragic mimesis portrays not just a whole action, but events which are fearful and pitiful, this can best be achieved when things occur contrary to expectation yet still on account of one another. A sense of wonder will be more likely to be aroused in this way than as a result of the arbitrary or fortuitous, since even chance events make the greatest impact of wonder when they *appear* to have a purpose (as in the case where Mitys's statue at Argos fell on Mitys's murderer and killed him, while he was looking at it: such things do not *seem* to happen without reason). So then, plot-structures which embody this principle must be superior.

Ch. 10

Plot-structures can be divided into the simple and the complex, for the actions which they represent consist naturally of these types. By a 'simple' action I mean one which is, as earlier defined, continuous and unitary, but whose transformation occurs without reversal or recognition. A 'complex' action is one whose transformation involves recognition or reversal, or both. Reversal and recognition should arise from the intrinsic structure of the plot, so that what results follows by either necessity or probability from the preceding events: for it makes a great difference whether things happen because of one another, or only *after* one another.

Ch. 11

Reversal, as indicated, is a complete swing in the direction of the action; but this, as we insist, must conform to probability or necessity. Take, for example, Sophocles' *Oedipus Tyrannus*,[1] where the person comes to bring Oedipus happiness, and intends to free him from his fear about his mother; but he produces the opposite effect, by revealing Oedipus' identity. And in *Lynceus* the one person is led off to die, while Danaus follows to kill him;

[1] *OT* 924ff.

yet it comes about that the latter's death and the former's rescue result from the chain of events.

Recognition, as the very name shows, is a change from ignorance to knowledge, bringing the characters into either a close bond, or enmity, with one another, and concerning matters which bear on their prosperity or affliction. The finest recognition occurs in direct conjunction with reversal – as with the one in the *Oedipus*. There are, of course, other kinds of recognition, for recognition can relate to inanimate or fortuitous objects, or reveal that someone has, or has not, committed a deed. But the type I have mentioned is the one which is most integral to the plot-structure and its action: for such a combination of recognition and reversal will produce pity or fear (and it is events of this kind that tragedy, on our definition, is a mimesis of), since both affliction and prosperity will hinge on such circumstances. And since recognition involves people, there are cases where one person's recognition by another takes place (when this other's own identity is clear), and cases where the recognition must be reciprocal: for instance, Iphigeneia was recognised by Orestes through the sending of the letter, but another means of recognition was needed for Iphigeneia's identification of *him*.[2]

Well then, reversal and recognition form two components of the plot-structure; the third is suffering. To the definitions of reversal and recognition already given we can add that of suffering: a destructive or painful action, such as visible deaths, torments, woundings, and other things of the same kind.

Ch. 12

Having earlier given the parts of tragedy which determine its qualities, the quantitative divisions of the genre can be listed as: prologue, episode, *exodos*, choral unit. The latter can be divided into the choral entry (*parodos*) and the choral ode (*stasimon*), which are common to all plays, while actors' songs and lyric exchanges (*kommoi*) are peculiar to only certain plays.

The prologue is the entire portion of a tragedy preceding the choral entry. An episode is an entire portion of a tragedy lying

---

[2] Euripides, *Iphigeneia in Tauris* 727-841.

between complete choral odes. The *exodos* is the entire portion of a tragedy which follows the final choral ode. Of the choral elements, the *parodos* is the first entire choral utterance; a *stasimon* is a choral song in a metre other than anapaestic or trochaic; while a *kommos* is a lamentation shared between chorus and actors.

The parts of tragedy which determine its qualities were given earlier, while those above are the divisions of a quantitative analysis.

Ch. 13

It follows on from my earlier argument that I should define what ought to be aimed at and avoided in plot-construction, as well as the source of tragedy's effect. Since, then, the structure of the finest tragedy should be complex, not simple, and, moreover, should portray fearful and pitiful events (for this is the distinctive feature of this type of mimesis), it is to begin with clear that:

(a) good men should not be shown passing from prosperity to affliction, for this is neither fearful nor pitiful but repulsive;

(b) wicked men should not be shown passing from affliction to prosperity, for this is the most untragic of all possible cases and is entirely defective (it is neither moving nor pitiful nor fearful);

(c) the extremely evil man should not fall from prosperity to affliction, for such a plot-structure might move us, but would not arouse pity or fear, since pity is felt towards one whose affliction is undeserved, fear towards one who is like ourselves (so what happens in such a case will be neither pitiful nor fearful).

We are left, then, with the figure who falls between these types. Such a man is one who is not preeminent in virtue and justice, and one who falls into affliction not because of evil and wickedness, but because of a certain fallibility (*hamartia*). He will belong to the class of those who enjoy great esteem and prosperity, such as Oedipus, Thyestes, and outstanding men from such families.

It is imperative that a fine plot-structure be single and not double (as some assert), and involve a change from prosperity to affliction (rather than the reverse) caused not by wickedness but by a great fallibility on the part of the sort of agent stipulated, or one who is better, not worse, than indicated. Actual practice tends to confirm my thesis. For in the beginning the poets' choice of stories was arbitrary, whereas now the finest tragedies are constructed around a few families – Alcmaeon, for example, Oedipus, Orestes, Meleager, Thyestes, Telephus, and others who have suffered or committed terrible deeds.

This, then, is the plot-pattern for the tragedy which best fulfils the standards of poetic art. Those who fault Euripides for following this, and for ending many of his plays with affliction, make the same mistake as mentioned above. For such an ending is legitimate, as argued, and the greatest confirmation is that such plays make the most tragic impression in acted competition (provided they are staged effectively), and Euripides, whatever other faults of organisation he may have, at least makes the most tragic impression of all poets.

The second-best pattern (which some hold to be the best) is the kind which involves a double structure (like the *Odyssey*) and contrasting outcomes for good and bad characters. It is the weakness of audiences which produces the view of this type's superiority; poets are led to give the spectators what they want. But this is not the proper pleasure to be derived from tragedy – more like that of comedy: for in that genre people who are outright foes in the plot (say, Orestes and Aegisthus) go off as friends at the end, and nobody is killed.

Ch. 14

The effect of fear and pity can arise from theatrical spectacle, but it can also arise from the intrinsic structure of events, and it is this which matters more and is the task of a superior poet. For the plot-structure ought to be so composed that, even without seeing a performance, anyone who hears the events which occur will experience terror and pity as a result of the outcome; this is what someone would feel while hearing the plot of the *Oedipus*. To produce this effect through spectacle is not part of the poet's art, and calls for material resources; while those who use spectacle to produce an effect not of the fearful but only of the sensational fall quite outside the sphere of tragedy: for it is not every pleasure, but the appropriate one, which should be sought from tragedy. And since the poet ought to provide the pleasure which derives from pity and fear by means of mimesis, it is evident that this ought to be embodied in the events of the plot.

Let us, then, take up the question of what sort of circumstances make an impression of terror or pity. These are the only possibilities: such actions must involve dealings between those who are bonded by kinship or friendship; or between enemies; or between those who are neither. Well, if enemy faces enemy, neither the deed nor the prospect of it will be pitiful (except for the intrinsic potential of visible suffering); and the same is true of those whose relations are neutral. What must be sought are cases where suffering befalls bonded relations – when brother kills brother (or is about to, or to do something similar), son kills father, mother kills son, or son kills mother. Now, one cannot alter traditional plots (I mean, Clytemnestra's death at Orestes' hands, or Eriphyle's at Alcmaeon's) but the individual poet should find ways of handling even these to good effect.

I should explain more clearly what I mean by 'to good effect'. It is possible

(a) for the deed to be done with full knowledge and understanding, as the old poets used to arrange it, and in the way that Euripides too made Medea kill her children;

(b) for the deed to be done, but by agents who do not know the terrible thing they are doing, and who then later recognise their bond-relationship to the other, as with Sophocles' *Oedipus* (that is an instance where the deed occurs outside the drama, but Astydamas' *Alcmaeon*, and Telegonus in *Odysseus Wounded*, supply examples within the play itself);

(c) alternatively, for one who is on the point of committing an incurable deed in ignorance to come to a recognition before he has done it.

These are the only possibilities, for either the deed is done or it is not, and the agents must either know the facts or be ignorant of them. Of these cases, the worst is where the agent, in full knowledge, is on the point of acting, yet fails to do so: for this is repulsive and untragic (as it lacks suffering). Consequently, poets only rarely do this (for instance, Haemon's intention against Creon in *Antigone*).[1] Not much better is for the deed to be executed in such a case. A superior arrangement is where the agent acts in ignorance, and discovers the truth after acting: for here there is nothing repulsive, and the recognition produces a powerful effect. But the best case is the last I have listed – for example, where Merope is about to kill her son in the *Cresphontes*, but does not do so because she recognises him; likewise with sister and brother in *Iphigeneia*,[2] and in the *Helle*, where the son, on the point of handing her over, recognises his mother. Hence, as said before, tragedies concentrate on a few families. Luck not art led poets to find how to achieve such an effect in their plots; so they have to turn to the families in which such sufferings have occurred.

Enough, then, about the structure of events and the required qualities of plots.

Ch. 15

Regarding characterisation, there should be four aims:

(a)   first and foremost, that the characters be good. Characterisation will arise, as earlier explained (ch.6), where speech or action exhibits the nature of an ethical choice; and the character will be good when the choice is good. But this depends on each class of person: there can be a good woman and a good slave, even though perhaps the former is an inferior type, and the latter a wholly base one.

(b)   that the characters be appropriate. For it is *possible* to have a woman manly in character, but it is not appropriate for a woman to be so manly or clever.

(c)   likeness of character – for this is independent of making character good and appropriate, as described.

(d)   consistency of character. For even where an inconsistent person is portrayed, and such a character is presupposed, there should still be consistency in the inconsistency.

An illustration of unnecessary wickedness of character is

---

[1] Sophocles, *Antigone* 1231ff.
[2] Euripides, *Iphigeneia in Tauris* (ch.11, n. 2 above).

Menelaus in *Orestes*;[1] of unbecoming and inappropriate character, the lament of Odysseus in *Scylla*, or Melanippe's speech; and of inconsistency, *Iphigeneia in Aulis* (for the girl who beseeches bears no resemblance to the later girl).[2] In characterisation just as in plot-construction, one should always seek the principle of necessity or probability, so that a necessary or probable reason exists for a particular character's speech or action, and similarly for the sequence of events.

*It is evident that the dénouements of plot-structures should arise from the plot itself, and not, as in *Medea*, from a *deus ex machina*, or in the episode of the departure in the *Iliad*.[3] But the *deus ex machina* should be used for events outside the play, whether earlier events of which a human cannot have knowledge, or future events which call for a prospective narrative; for we attribute to the gods a vision of all things. No irrational element should have a part in the events, unless outside the tragedy (as, for example, in Sophocles' *Oedipus*).

Since tragedy is a mimesis of men better than ourselves, the example set by good portrait-painters should be followed: they, while rendering the individual physique realistically, improve on their subjects' beauty. Similarly, the poet, while portraying men who are irascible or lazy or who have other such faults, ought to give them, despite such traits, goodness of character. *An example of this is Homer's presentation of Achilles as good, despite his harshness. *In addition to observing these points, the poet must guard against contraventions of the perceptions which necessarily attach to poetic art, since there are many ways of making mistakes in relation to these. But I have discussed these matters adequately in my published writings.

Ch. 16

I earlier defined the nature of recognition, but of the kinds of recognition there is, firstly, the least artistic and the one which is used most out of inadequacy: recognition through signs. These signs can be either congenital (as with [...] the starred birthmarks used by Carcinus in *Thyestes*) or acquired; and the latter can be subdivided into the physical (e.g. scars) and the external, such as necklaces or the use of the boat in *Tyro*. These

---

[1] Euripides, *Orestes* 356ff., 1554ff.
[2] Euripides, *Iphigeneia in Aulis* 1211ff and 1368ff.
[3] Euripides, *Medea* 1317ff; Homer, *Iliad* 2.155ff.

means can be employed either well or badly: for instance, through his scar Odysseus was recognised in different ways by his nurse and by the swineherds.[1] Those recognitions which occur for the sake of confirmation, and all similar sorts, are less artistic; while those which accompany a reversal, like the one in the washing scene of the *Odyssey*,[2] are superior.

The second kind are those contrived by the poet (and consequently inartistic). An example is the way in which Orestes makes himself known in *Iphigeneia*, for Iphigeneia is recognised through the letter, while Orestes himself says what the poet, but not the plot, requires:[3] the result is close to the fault mentioned above, since producing tokens would be equivalent. Another instance is the voice of the shuttle in Sophocles' *Tereus*.

The third kind is recognition through memory. The experience may depend on the sight of something: for example, the case in Dicaeogenes' *Cyprians*, where the person wept on seeing the painting. Or there is the example in Odysseus' speech to Alcinous, where he heard the singer and wept at the memory.[4] Recognition resulted in both instances.

The fourth kind of recognition results from reasoning: for example, in *Choephori* (someone like Electra has come, and there is no one like her other than Orestes, so it is he who has come).[5] Also the example from Polyidus the sophist's work on Iphigeneia: he said it was plausible for Orestes to reason that he was to be sacrificed just as his sister had been. Another example in Theodectes' *Tydeus*: the character reasons that it is by coming to find his son that he is facing death. And the instance in the *Phineidai*: upon seeing the place, they reasoned that it was their destiny to die there, since it was also the place where they had been exposed.

*It is also possible to make a recognition depend on the audience's false reasoning, as in *Odysseus the False Messenger*: the fact that he alone could bend the bow is a premise contrived by the poet, as is his statement that he would recognise the bow (which he had never seen); and it is false reasoning to suppose that he will reveal himself through this.

The best of all recognitions is the type which arises from the

---

[1] Homer, *Odyssey* 19.386ff. and 21.205ff.
[2] *Odyssey* 19.392ff.
[3] The same refs. as in ch.11, n.2.
[4] *Odyssey* 8.521ff.
[5] Aeschylus, *Choephori* 168ff.

events themselves, where the emotional impact comes about through a probable sequence of action. There are examples in Sophocles' *Oedipus*, and in *Iphigeneia* (for it is in conformity with probability that she should want to entrust a letter).[6] Such instances alone avoid contrived tokens.* Next best are those resulting from reasoning.

Ch. 17

A poet ought to imagine his material to the fullest possible extent while composing his plot-structures and elaborating them in language. By seeing them as vividly as possible in this way – as if present at the very occurrence of the events – he is likely to discover what is appropriate, and least likely to miss contradictions. (One can see this from the criticism brought against Carcinus: for Amphiaraus was returning from the shrine, but the poet missed the point by not visualising it, and the play failed in the theatre on account of the spectators' annoyance.) So far as possible, the poet should even include gestures in the process of composition: for, assuming the same natural talent, the most convincing effect comes from those who actually put themselves in the emotions; and the truest impression of distress or anger is given by the person who experiences these feelings. Consequently, it is the imaginative man, *rather than the manic, who is the best composer of poetry: since, of these types, the former can mould their emotions, while the latter are carried away.

Whether it exists already or is his own invention, the poet should lay out the general structure of his story, and then proceed to work out episodes and enlarge it. What I mean by contemplating the general structure can be illustrated from *Iphigeneia*. A girl was sacrificed and mysteriously vanished from her sacrificers; she was planted in another land, where strangers were traditionally sacrificed to the goddess whose priesthood the girl came to hold. Subsequently, it happened that the priestess's brother came to the place (the fact that a god's oracle sent him, and the reason for this, are outside the plot). Captured on his arrival, he was on the point of being sacrificed when he caused his own recognition (whether according to Euripides' version, or,

[6] Euripides, *Iphigeneia in Tauris* 578ff.

as in Polyidus', by saying – as was plausible – that it was his own as well as his sister's destiny to be sacrificed). The upshot was his rescue.

The next stage is to supply names and work out the episodes. But care must be taken to make the episodes integral – as with the fit of madness which occasions Orestes' capture, and his rescue through the purification-rite.[1] Now, in drama the episodes are concise, while epic gains extra length from them. For the main story of the *Odyssey* is short: a man is abroad for many years, is persecuted by Poseidon, and is left desolate; further, circumstances at home mean that his property is consumed by suitors, and his son is a target for conspiracy; but the man survives shipwreck to reach home again, reveals his identity to certain people, and launches an attack – his own safety is restored, and he destroys his enemies. This much is essential; the rest consists of episodes.

Ch. 18

For every tragedy there is a complication and a dénouement: the complication consists of events outside the play, and often some of those within it; the dénouement comprises the remainder. By the 'complication' I mean everything from the beginning as far as the part which immediately precedes the transformation to prosperity or affliction; and by 'dénouement' I mean the section from the start of the transformation to the end. For example, in Theodectes' *Lynceus* the complication covers the earlier events, the seizure of the baby and ..., while the dénouement runs from the accusation of murder up to the end.

There are four kinds of tragedy (*in accordance with the parts earlier enumerated):

(a) the complex tragedy, the essence of which is reversal and recognition;

(b) the tragedy of suffering – for example, plays about Ajax or Ixion;

(c) the tragedy of character – for example, *Phthiotides* and *Peleus*;

(d) the *simple tragedy, such as *Phorcides*, *Prometheus*, and all works set in Hades.

[1] Euripides, *Iphigeneia in Tauris* 281ff. and 1029ff.

Now, ideally one should strive for all these elements, but, failing that, for the best and for as many of them as possible, especially in view of the criticisms now levelled against poets: since there have been good poets in each category, people expect the individual poet to surpass the particular quality of each.

It is right to contrast and compare tragedies largely in terms of plot-structure; so comparable plays are those with the same kind of complication and dénouement. There are many who contrive the complication well, but handle the dénouement badly: precision is called for in both respects. As noted more than once, the poet must remember to avoid making a tragedy into a quasi-epic structure (by which I mean a multiple plot-structure): which would happen, for example, if one were to dramatise the entire plot of the *Iliad*. The length of this poem allows the various parts to assume an appropriate scale, but in plays the result completely defeats expectations. We can see this from the failure or poor impression of plays by poets who have handled the whole sack of Troy, rather than portions of it (like Euripides); or likewise with the story of Niobe, where they fail to follow Aeschylus' example. This fault accounted even for Agathon's one failure with his audience.

*In the case both of reversals and of simple dramatic actions, poets use wonder to achieve their aim; for the effect gained arouses the tragic emotions as well as humane sympathy. Examples of this are the outwitting of a clever man who is flawed by evil (like Sisyphus), or the worsting of one who is manly but unjust. Such things conform to probability, on Agathon's principle that probability allows for the occurrence of many *im*probabilities.

The chorus too should be handled as one of the actors; it should form an integral part of the whole and should be actively involved – not as in Euripides, but as in Sophocles. The lyrics of other poets have no more connection with their own plot-structure than with any other tragedy. Hence the practice, started by Agathon, of singing interlude-odes. Yet what is the difference between singing interlude-odes and transferring a set-speech, or a whole episode, from one work to another.

Ch. 19

Having discussed the other elements, it remains for me to discuss style and thought. The details of thought can be left to my discourses on rhetoric, since they belong more integrally to that subject. Thought pertains to all those effects which must be produced by the spoken language; its functions are demonstration, refutation, the arousal of emotions such as pity, fear, anger, and such like, and arguing for the importance or unimportance of things. (It is clear that the same basic principles underlie the achievement of effects of pity, terror, importance, probability, in the dramatic events; but the difference is that these must appear without explicit statement, whereas in the spoken language it is the speaker and his words which produce the effect. For what would be the point of a speaker, if the desired effect were evident even without his words?)

In matters of verbal style, one kind of study concerns figures of speech. Knowledge of these (for instance, the difference between a command, a prayer, a narrative, a threat, a question, an answer, and so on) belongs to the art of rhetorical delivery and to anyone with such expertise. For no serious charge can be brought against poetry on the basis of knowledge or ignorance of these matters. Why should anyone follow Protagoras in finding fault with Homer for purporting to address a prayer, but in fact delivering a command, by saying 'Sing, Goddess, of the wrath ...'[1]? According to Protagoras, to enjoin someone to do or avoid something is a command. Let this consideration be left for some other enquiry, not for poetry.

Ch. 20

Verbal style in general can be analysed into the following categories: element, syllable, connective, noun, verb, conjunction, inflection, proposition.

An element is an indivisible sound – not of any kind, but one from which a composite sound can naturally arise. (There are also indivisible animal sounds, none of which do I call an

---

[1] *Iliad* 1.1.

element.) Its types are: vowels, continuants, and stops. 'Vowel' means an audible sound without any contact of the tongue; 'continuant' an audible sound *with* contact (e.g. *s* and *r*), and 'stop' refers to something which involves contact but does not produce an audible sound on its own, only in conjunction with others which do produce one (examples are *g* and *d*). These sounds are distinguishable by the shape of the mouth, the points of contact, the presence or absence of an aspirate, length and shortness, and pitch-accent (acute, grave, or intermediate): detailed consideration of all these points belongs to works on metre.

A syllable is a non-significant articulate sound, combining a stop and a vowel: *gr*, for example, only makes a syllable with the addition of *a* (*gra-*). But the study of these distinctions too belongs to metric.

A connective is a non-significant sound which neither prevents nor produces a single, semantic utterance from a combination of several sounds; it is usually placed at the end or within, but not at the start, of a proposition: [...]. Alternatively, a non-significant sound which usually produces a single, semantic utterance from a combination of sounds that signify one thing.

*A conjunction is a non-significant sound which marks the beginning, end, or division of a proposition [...]. Alternatively, a non-significant sound which can be placed at various points in a proposition, but which neither prevents nor produces a single semantic utterance from a combination of several sounds.

A noun is a non-temporal compound semantic sound, whose parts do not carry their own meaning: for instance, in the name 'Theodorus' the '-dorus' element lacks meaning.

A verb is a compound semantic sound, whose parts (just as with nouns) do not carry their own meaning, but which does have a temporal sense: for example, 'man' or 'white' has no temporal significance, but 'is walking' or 'has walked' does (present and past time, respectively).

An inflection is the aspect of a noun or verb which signifies (a) differences of case, (b) differences of number ('men' or 'man'), (c) points relevant to oral delivery (e.g. a question, command). 'Did he walk?' and 'Walk!' are instances of the inflection of a verb in these categories.

A proposition is a compound semantic utterance, some of whose parts have their own significance: for example, the name

'Cleon' in 'Cleon is walking'. But not every proposition comprises verbs and nouns (e.g. the definition of man):[1] a proposition can lack a verb, but some part of it will always have its own significance. A proposition can be unitary in either of two ways: by virtue of signifying a single concept; or by virtue of connecting several elements. For example, the *Iliad* is unitary in the latter respect, but the definition of man is unitary because of its single meaning.

Ch. 21

Nouns can be divided into the categories of single (i.e. not made up of significant elements: e.g. 'earth', *gê*) and double. The latter can be subdivided into those which comprise signifying and non-signifying elements (though this does not apply to their status *within* the noun), and those which comprise only signifying elements. One could also add triple, quadruple and polysyllabic words [...].

All nouns can be distributed into the following categories: standard terms, foreign terms, metaphors, ornaments, neologisms, lengthened terms, abbreviated terms, altered terms.

By a 'standard term' I mean one in the usage of a particular group, and by 'foreign term' one borrowed from others; it is consequently obvious that the same word can be both standard and foreign, but not for the same speakers [...].

Metaphor is the transference of a term from one thing to another: whether from genus to species, species to genus, species to species, or by analogy. Genus to species: e.g. 'My ship stands here' (since being moored is a type of standing). Species to genus: e.g. 'ten thousand noble deeds has Odysseus performed' (for 'ten thousand' is one type of multiplicity and stands here for the latter). Species to species [...].[1]

Metaphor 'by analogy' is a case where the relation of *b* to *a* is the same as that of *d* to *c*: the poet will use *d* instead of *b*, or the reverse. Sometimes they add to the metaphor something to which it is related: for instance, the wine-cup is to Dionysus what the shield is to Ares, so the poet will call the wine-cup 'Dionysus' shield' and the shield 'Ares' wine-cup'. Again, old age is to life

---

[1] Ar. means a verbless phrase such as 'rational animal'.

[1] Ar. here gives two barely intelligible poetic quotations.

what the evening is to the day: so the poet will call evening 'day's old age', or, like Empedocles, call old age 'the evening of life' or 'the dusk of life'. For some analogies there is a missing term, but the metaphor will still be used. For example, scattering seed is 'sowing', while the sun's scattering of fire lacks a name; but the latter parallels the sowing of seed, hence the poet's phrase, 'sowing his divine fire'. It is possible to use this type of metaphor with a difference, by applying the borrowed term but with a denial of one of its attributes: e.g. saying not 'the wine-cup of Ares' but 'his wineless wine-cup'.

A neologism is a term without any currency but invented by the poet himself [...].

A lengthened term is one with a longer vowel than usual, or an additional syllable [...] an abbreviated term is one with something removed [...].

An altered term is one where part of the usual word is kept, and part added [...].

Nouns can also be divided into masculine, feminine and neuter [...].*

Ch. 22

Excellence of style consists in clarity without banality. Now, the greatest clarity comes from the use of standard terms, but this involves banality: examples of this are the poetry of Cleophon and Sthenelus. Grandeur and avoidance of the ordinary, by contrast, can be achieved by the use of alien language (by which I mean foreign terms, metaphor, lengthened terms, and everything which goes beyond the standard). But the result of writing entirely in such a style will be either a riddle or barbarism: where metaphors are involved, it will be a riddle, and where foreign terms, it will be barbarism. For the form of a riddle consists in speaking of realities while attaching impossibilities to them. One cannot do this with other types of language, only with metaphor: for instance, 'I saw a man using fire to weld bronze to a man',[1] and other such things. And the result of foreign words is a barbaric style. So it is some sort of *admixture* of these things which is required: then the ordinary and commonplace will be avoided (by the use of foreign terms, metaphor, ornament, and the other earlier mentioned types), while clarity will be

[1] The riddle refers to a form of the medical procedure known as 'cupping'.

preserved by the standard component.

No small contribution is made to both clarity of style and the avoidance of the ordinary by lengthenings, abbreviations and alterations of words: the divergence from standard and usual usage will produce a heightened effect, but the presence of an element of the customary will ensure clarity. Accordingly, those who criticise this type of speech, and ridicule the poet for it, find fault without good reason – for instance, Eucleides the elder, with his satirical parodies [...] purporting to show how easy it would be to write poetry if one is allowed to lengthen words according to whim. Now, conspicuous exploitation of this device is absurd, and moderation is equally needed in all elements of style: one would produce the same result by employing metaphors, foreign words, and other types inappropriately and for deliberately comic effect. (The importance of appropriateness in epic verses could be seen by introducing such words into the metre.)

Where the foreign term, metaphors, and the other types are concerned, the truth of my argument can be seen by substituting standard words. For example, Aeschylus and Euripides composed the same iambic line with just one word's difference – a foreign term for a standard: so the one verse has beauty, while the other is vulgar. In his *Philoctetes* Aeschylus wrote:

the cancer that eats the flesh of my foot,

but Euripides replaced 'eats' by 'feasts on' [...]. Again, Ariphrades satirised the tragedians for using phrases which no one would ever speak in ordinary discourse [...]. But he failed to realise that it is just because of their absence from ordinary language that all such things produce a heightened effect in poetic diction.

While it is of importance to use each of the mentioned types appropriately, including compound and foreign terms, by far the most important point is facility with metaphor. This alone is a sign of natural ability, and something one can never learn from another: for the successful use of metaphor entails the perception of similarities. Of nouns, double terms are particularly appropriate for dithyramb, foreign terms for epic verse, and metaphors for iambic lines. In epic, all the types I have mentioned have their usefulness, while in iambics, because of the close reproduction of ordinary speech, it is appropriate to employ what one would also use in prose – namely, standard terms, metaphors and ornaments.

This brings to completion my discussion of tragedy and enacted mimesis.

Ch. 23

As for the narrative art of mimesis in spoken verse, it is evident that its plot-structures should have a dramatic coherence, just as in tragedy, and that they should concern an action which is unitary and complete (with beginning, middle and end), so that, as with a living creature, the single and entire structure may yield the pleasure which belongs to it. The corollary of this is that plots should not resemble histories, in which one need not find the exposition of a unitary action but of all the contingently connected events which happened to one or more persons in a particular period of time. For just as the battle of Salamis and the Sicilian battle against the Carthaginians occurred at the same time, but without contributing to a common end, so events can sometimes succeed one another in time without yielding any particular end.

Yet this is what probably a majority of epic poets do, and, as I earlier said (ch. 8), this is one respect in which Homer's inspired superiority is evident, because of his refusal to attempt to make a poem about the entire war (despite its clear beginning and end): such a plot would be too bulky, and could not be perceived as a unity; or, if moderate in size, would be too intricately detailed. As it is, Homer has selected a unitary portion of the war, and has used many episodes – the catalogue of ships, and others – to expand his poetry. But other poets, such as the authors of the *Cypria* and the *Little Iliad*, compose about an individual or a single period of time, or an action of many parts. Consequently, the *Iliad* and *Odyssey* provide material for only one or two tragedies each, while the *Cypria* and *Little Iliad* would yield many [...].*

Ch. 24

Moreover, epic should have the same types as tragedy – the simple, the complex, the character-poem, the poem of suffering. (And epic shares all the same elements, apart from lyrics and spectacle.) For epic has equal need of reversals, recognitions and scenes of suffering. In addition, excellence of thought and diction is called for. All of which Homer has achieved with supreme perfection. Each of his poems is a unified plot – the *Iliad* in the categories of the 'simple' and the poem of suffering, the *Odyssey* in those of the complex (using recognition throughout) and the poem of character. Furthermore, Homer has excelled all other epics in diction and thought.

Epic differs from tragedy in length of plot-structure and in metre. As for length, a sufficient definition has already been given: it should be possible to perceive the beginning and the end as a unity. This condition would be satisfied by structures which are shorter than the old epics but which match the length of the tragedies given at a single hearing. But the scope for considerable extension of length is a particular attribute of epic's. This is because tragedy will not permit the representation of many simultaneous parts of the action, but only the one on stage involving the actors; while epic, on account of its use of narrative, can include many simultaneous parts, and these, provided they are integral, enhance the poem's dignity. This lends epic an advantage in grandeur, in changes of interest for the hearer, and in variety of episodes (lack of variety soon becomes cloying and causes the rejection of tragedies).

Epic's metre, the hexameter, has been found appropriate by experience. If someone were to compose a narrative mimesis in some other metre, or in a mixture of many, the inappropriateness would be apparent. For the hexameter is the most stately and dignified of metres (hence its special openness to foreign terms and metaphors: narrative mimesis is more out-of-the-ordinary than other kinds), while the iambic trimeter and trochaic tetrameter have a greater sense of movement: the tetrameter suits dancing, the trimeter action. And a mixture of these metres, like Chairemon's, would be even more absurd. Consequently, no one has composed a long epic structure in anything other than the hexameter, but, as I said, nature herself teaches poets to choose what is appropriate for epic.

Among Homer's many other laudable attributes is his grasp – unique among epic poets – of his status as poet. For the poet himself should speak as little as possible, since when he does so he is not engaging in mimesis. Now, other epic poets participate persistently, and engage in mimesis only to a limited extent and infrequently. But Homer, after a short preamble, at once 'brings onto stage' a man, woman or some other figure (and his agents are always fully characterised).

While the marvellous is called for in tragedy, it is epic which gives greater scope for the irrational (which is the chief cause of the marvellous), because we do not actually see the agents. The circumstances of the pursuit of Hector would be patently absurd if put on the stage, with the men standing and refraining from pursuit, and Achilles forbidding them;[1] but in epic the effect is not noticed. The marvellous gives pleasure: this can be seen from the way in which everyone exaggerates in order to gratify when recounting events.

It is above all Homer who has taught other epic poets the right way to purvey falsehoods. What is involved here is a kind of fallacy: if one thing follows from the existence or occurrence of another, people quite erroneously suppose that, where the second fact obtains, the former also must be true. If, therefore, something is false, but, were it true, something else would necessarily follow from it, the poet ought to add this second fact: because, when it knows that *this* is true, our mind fallaciously infers the existence of the first fact also. There is an instance of this in the *Odyssey*'s bath scene.[2]

Events which are impossible but plausible should be preferred to those which are possible but implausible. Plots should not consist of parts which are irrational. So far as possible, there should be no irrational component; otherwise, it should lie outside the plot-structure, as with Oedipus' ignorance of how Laius died,[3] rather than inside the drama, as with the report of the Pythian games in *Electra*,[4] or with the silent character's arrival at Mysia from Tegea in the *Mysians*. To say that otherwise the plot-structure would be ruined is a ridiculous defence: such plot-construction should be avoided *from the start*. But even absurdity can sometimes be handled more or less reasonably. It would be obvious, if they were handled by an inferior poet, just how intolerable the absurdities regarding the disembarkation in the *Odyssey* could be: as it is, Homer uses his

---

[1] Homer, *Iliad* 22.205ff.

[2] 19.220ff.

[3] Cf. Sophocles, *Oedipus Tyrannus* 112-13.

[4] Sophocles, *Electra* 680ff.

other virtues to disguise the absurdity and to make it enjoyable.[5]

Verbal style should be used intensively in portions of the poem which are static and involve no characterisation or statement of thought. By contrast, characterisation and thought can be thrown into shade by an excessively brilliant style.

Ch. 25

On the subject of problems and their solutions, a clear idea of the number and types of issue can be gained from the following considerations. Since the poet, like the painter or any other image-maker, is a mimetic artist, he must in any particular instance use mimesis to portray one of three objects: the sort of things which were or are the case; the sort of things men say and think to be the case; the sort of things that should be the case. This material is presented in language which has foreign terms, metaphors, and many special elements; for we allow these to poets.

Furthermore, correct standards in poetry are not identical with those in politics or in any other particular art. Two kinds of failure are possible in poetry – one intrinsic, and the other contingent. *If a poet lacks the capacity to achieve what he sets out to portray, the failure is one of poetic art. But this is not so if the poet *intends* to portray something which is erroneous, such as a horse with its two right legs simultaneously forward, or something which is a technical mistake in medicine or any other field. So, it is from these premises that the solutions to the charges contained in problems must be found.

Firstly, points concerning poetic art itself. Suppose the poet has produced impossibilities, then granted he has erred. But poetic standards will be satisfied, provided he achieves the goal of the art (which has been earlier discussed): that is, if by these means he increases the emotional impact either of the particular part or of some other part of the work. (An example is the pursuit of Hector.)[1] If, however, the goal could be achieved better, or just as successfully, without the particular technical error, then the mistake is not acceptable: for, if possible, poetry should be altogether free of mistakes.

---

[5] *Odyssey* 13.116ff.

[1] See n.1 to ch. 24.

One must also ask whether the error concerns the poetic art or something extrinsic to it. For if, out of ignorance, a painter portrays a female deer *with* horns, this has less significance than attaches to a failure in mimesis.

Next, if the charge is one of falsehood, a possible defence is that things are being portrayed as they *should* be, just as Sophocles said that his poetic characters were as they should be, while Euripides' reflected ordinary reality. If neither category applies, then a solution may appeal to what people say, for instance in matters concerning the gods: as, while it may satisfy neither morality nor truth to say such things (and Xenophanes' criticisms may be justified), nevertheless people *do* say them.

Another possible defence is that something may be imperfect but does represent how things once were. Take the example concerning weapons ('Their spears stood upright on the butt-end'):[2] this used to be the practice at the time, as it still is with the Illyrians. When asking whether someone has spoken or acted morally or otherwise, one should look to see not just if the deed or utterance is good or evil, but also to the identity of the agent or speaker, to the person with whom he deals, and to the occasion, means and purpose of what is done (e.g. whether the aim is to effect a greater good, or prevent a greater evil).

Other points must be resolved by consideration of style, for example by reference to a foreign term [...]. A passage may involve metaphor: for instance, 'All gods and men slept through the night', while in the same passage Homer says 'whenever Agamemnon gazed across to the Trojan plane and the din of flutes and pipes'.[3] 'All' stands by metaphor for 'many', since all is a species of many [...]. Accentuation may be relevant, as with the solutions proposed by Hippias of Thasos [...] or punctuation [...] or double meaning [...] or verbal usage [...].

Whenever a word appears to entail a contradiction, one should consider how many meanings are possible in the linguistic context [...]. One should adopt the opposite procedure to the one which Glaucon describes by saying that some people make an unreasonable assumption and proceed to base their argument on acceptance of it; then, if something contradicts their own preconception, they criticise the poet as though *he* had made the

---

[2] Homer, *Iliad* 10.152.
[3] *Iliad* 10.1-2 and 11-13 (both quotations garbled).

initial assumption. This has happened in the case of Icarius: people presuppose that he was a Laconian, so they find it absurd that Telemachus did not meet him when he went to Sparta.[4] But perhaps the Cephallenians' version is correct, for they claim that Odysseus married one of theirs, and that the father was called Icadius not Icarius. It is plausible that the problem is due to a mistake.

In general, cases of impossibility should be resolved by reference to the requirements of poetry, or to a conception of the superior, or to people's beliefs. Poetic requirements make a plausible impossibility preferable to an implausible possibility ...* not such as Zeuxis painted them, but better, for the artist should surpass his model. Irrationalities should be referred to 'what people say', or shown not to be irrational (since it is likely that some things should occur contrary to likelihood). Contradictory utterances should be examined according to the same principles as verbal refutations, to see whether the sense is the same and has the same reference, and in the same way – if a poet is to be convicted of actually contradicting either himself or something which can be sensibly assumed. But it is correct to find fault with both illogicality and moral baseness, if there is no necessity for them and if the poet makes no use of the illogicality (as with Euripides and the case of Aegeus)[5] or the baseness (as with Menelaus's in *Orestes*).[6]

The charges brought against poets fall under five headings: impossibilities, irrationalities, morally harmful elements, contradictions, and offences against the true standards of the art. The solutions should be sought from the categories discussed above.*

Ch. 26

It is reasonable to consider whether epic or tragic mimesis is the superior. If the superior is the less vulgar, and this is the one addressed to the better kind of spectators, it is unarguable that the art which consists entirely of impersonation must be vulgar: for here the performers use a great deal of physical action, as

[4] Telemachus' visit to Sparta in *Odyssey* Bk.4.
[5] Euripides, *Medea* 663ff.
[6] See n.1 to ch.15.

though the audience would not appreciate the point without this emphasis (for instance, with the wheeling motion of bad pipe-players, when portraying a discus, or their hauling around of the chorus-leader, when playing Scylla's music). Now, tragedy is of this kind, and the point is similar to the opinion which earlier actors held of their successors: Mynniscus used to call Callippides an 'ape', on the grounds of his excesses, and such was also the view held of Pindarus. The relation of the whole art of tragedy to epic is analogous to that between these actors and their predecessors. So people say that epic is for good spectators who require no gestures, while tragedy is for vulgar spectators. Consequently, if tragedy is vulgar, its inferiority would be evident.

But in the first place, the charge pertains not to poetry but to acting, since it is equally possible to use excessive gestures in an epic recitation, like Sostratus, or in a singing contest, which Mnasitheos the Opountian used to do. Secondly, it is not *all* movement (any more than all dancing) which should be rejected, but that of base types – as with the charge made against Callippides, and now made against others, of impersonating non-citizen women. Besides, tragedy, just like epic, achieves its aim even without enactment: for its qualities become apparent through a reading. Therefore, if tragedy is superior in other respects, this particular defect need not be attached to it.

Next there is the fact that tragedy possesses all epic's attributes (it can even use its metre), and in addition it has music and spectacle, which produce very vivid pleasures; so it can achieve vividness either in a reading or in performance. Furthermore, tragedy is superior by achieving the aim of its mimesis in a shorter scope: the relative compression gives greater pleasure than dilution over a long period (consider the hypothetical case of someone setting Sophocles' *Oedipus* in as many verses as the *Iliad*). Also, epic mimesis is less unified (an indication is that several tragedies can be extracted from any epic): consequently, if epic poets produce a single plot-structure, it appears incomplete because of the short exposition, or else diluted if it keeps to the length which suits the metre. What I mean by the latter is, for example, a construction of several actions, like the *Iliad*'s and *Odyssey*'s possession of many parts which are individually substantial. Yet these latter poems are constructed as well as is possible, and come as close as possible to the mimesis of a unitary action.

Therefore, if tragedy differs in all these respects, as well as in the effect of the art (for these genres should yield no ordinary pleasure, but the one stipulated), its superiority over epic in achieving the goal of poetry should be evident.

This completes my discussion of tragedy and epic, their forms and the number and variations of their components, the reasons for success or the reverse, and objections against poetry, with their solutions.*

Textual notes

The purpose of these notes (which cannot pretend to offer a serious introduction to the great textual difficulties connected with the work) is, firstly, to alert the reader of the *Poetics* in translation to those textual corruptions and problems which are likely to make a material difference to understanding of the work; secondly, to note my main divergences from the Greek text of Kassel, on which the translation is based. The passages in question are all asterisked * in the translation.

ch.1 (p.31) 'the art which employs ... without a name': Kassel accepts an emendation of the transmitted text (which certainly contains at least one corruption hereabouts) so as to make Ar. refer to *two* arts (i.e. separate prose and verse mimesis). Strict consistency calls for the latter, but Ar. is sometimes a little lax in such matters, and it becomes clear that the prose/verse distinction is not important to his argument.

ch.2 (p.32) '...categories alone': the Greek contains a further phrase which repeats the point, and which I suspect of being an interpolation.

ch.2 (p.33) 'as one sees...': the Greek text of this sentence is unintelligibly corrupt here. My translation offers one rather hypothetical reconstruction of Ar.'s original meaning.

ch.6 (p.37) 'Many poets...types of play': the text is here undoubtedly corrupt, and the translation is conjectural. I also exclude as probably spurious a sentence which repeats the list of six components.

ch.6 (p.37) 'and both happiness...achieve happiness': this passage has sometimes been suspected; it is bracketed by Kassel. I regard it as genuine and important, since it makes a clear link between Ar.'s view of dramatic action and his general ethical philosophy. For a recent discussion see Nussbaum, *Fragility of Goodness* pp.378f. with nn. 2-3. .

ch.9 (p.41) 'Of simple plot-structures...dramatic sequence': this passage has conceivably become misplaced in the Greek text. Ar. only defines 'simple' plots in ch. 10. It has been variously suggested that the passage should belong at the end of ch. 8 or the end of ch. 10.

ch.15 (p.48) 'It is evident ... *Oedipus*': another example of a possibly misplaced passage (the term 'dénouement' is only defined in ch. 18), but it may stand as a digression.

ch.15 (p.48) 'an example ... harshness': this is a conjectural translation of a corrupt passage.

ch.15 (p.48) 'In addition ... in relation to these': the Greek looks sound here, but it is impossible to say just what Ar. is talking about.

ch.16 (p.49) 'It is also possible ... through this': the sense and reference of this passage are entirely unclear.

ch.16 (p.50) ' ... contrived tokens': the Greek adds 'and necklaces', which is either a crass addition by a later hand or, just conceivably, a piece of Aristotelian drollery.

ch.17 (p.50) 'rather than the manic': the Greek text reads 'or the manic'. See pp.145-6 for the case for emending.

ch.18 (p.51) 'in accordance ... enumerated': the Greek is unambiguous, but it is hard to make full sense of this back-reference as it stands.

ch.18 (p.51) 'simple tragedy': this is one possible restoration of the damaged text at this point. The best argument for it is consistency with the start of ch. 24.

ch.18 (p.52) 'in the case ... unjust': the whole of this passage is vexed, and almost certainly missing something.

ch.20 (p.54) 'A conjunction ... ': it is far from clear which part of speech Ar. is defining (the Greek term is that which later meant 'article'). The omitted part of the sentence bizarrely contains examples of *prepositions*.

ch.21 (p.56) ' ... neuter': the omitted passage distributes Greek nouns into the three given genders. The way in which it does so has cast suspicion on its authenticity.

ch.23 (p.58) ' ... yield many': there follows a very doubtful sentence in which a series of tragic titles or subjects is listed.

ch.25 (p.61) 'If a poet ... poetic art': this is quite likely to have been Ar.'s point, but it does depend on conjectural restoration of the Greek text.

ch.25 (p.63) ' ... not such as Zeuxis': in the lacuna at this point Ar. appears to have moved from 'impossibilities' to the issue of artistic idealisation of character.

ch.25 (p.63) ' ... categories discussed above': the Greek adds 'there are twelve of them', which has kept arithmetically-minded interpreters busy.

ch.26 (p.65) one manuscript of the *Poetics* contains at this point a few damaged words in which some have deciphered a reference to comedy. We know in any case from the start of ch. 6 that Ar. must originally have gone on to discuss comedy.

Commentary

Ch. 1

The greatest problem facing many readers of the Poetics today is an inevitable lack of sympathy with the spirit of Ar.'s enterprise. The work's very first sentence is likely to reveal the problem at once, by the characteristic confidence which it shows in the rational, methodical and objective character of the philosopher's quest for a comprehension of poetry and its values. The modern reader, by contrast, may well find it hard to escape the essentially Romantic idea of the poet's activity as a matter of deeply subjective expression, which can hardly be amenable to discursive analysis. It is in fact Romanticism, and all that it has brought in its wake, which has opened up a great gulf between modern approaches to literature and the whole of the earlier tradition of classical and neo-classical criticism. That is not to imply that this tradition was itself uniform and unchanging, but it was at least broadly sustained by a shared belief in the possibility of gaining rational access, through an objective framework of concepts, to the nature of poetry. For most of us now, therefore, a serious effort of historical understanding and imagination is needed if we are to make much sense of the first systematic document of European literary criticism and theory.

The rational confidence exhibited and embodied in the *Poetics* – which we see immediately in the prescriptive note struck at the start, and in the invocation of 'first principles' – derives a special colouring from Ar.'s philosophical temperament, and from his profound aspiration to reach a comprehensive view of all aspects of the human as well as the natural world. But, in addition, Ar. was influenced by two factors in Greek culture. Firstly, and generally, by the range of ideas on poetry, language and rhetoric produced by intellectuals during the preceding century, which gave collective encouragement to attempts to study cultural phenomena systematically. The second and more specific influence was the intense stimulus of Plato, Ar.'s own teacher. Plato had recognised the power and importance of poetry in Greek society, but he had been driven by his own complex philosophy to the condemnation of most existing poetry as morally and psychologically pernicious. Ar.'s response to Plato will have to be allowed to emerge gradually from the *Poetics*, for it amounts to a subtle, unpolemical yet firm set of qualifications on his teacher's view of poetry.

The opening of the treatise at once allows us to discern both a link with, and a distancing from, Plato. Ar. here uses logical methods of definition and analysis which owed something in origin to Plato, and he also employs the concept of 'art' or 'artistry' (*technê*) which had greatly interested the earlier philosopher. A *technê* can roughly be defined as a productive skill or activity, which matches rational and knowledgeable means to the achievement of predetermined ends. This concept had already been applied for some time to poetry within Greek culture, but Plato had found poetry incapable of satisfying the criteria of knowledge attached to the notion of 'art'. By *accepting* poetry as a rational art, Ar. signals a basic departure from Plato, and at the same time indicates how poetry can merit the serious interest of a philosopher: if poetry really is a knowledgeable art, then it is the philosopher's legitimate task to expound the principles and values on which it rests.

Although the *Poetics* is devoted to poetry, the first chapter indicates that Ar. possessed at least the outlines of a theory of the mimetic arts in general - music, painting, sculpture, dancing, poetry and certain vocal arts (by which Ar. probably has acting in mind, though the point is unclear). This will be confirmed particularly by the references to painting later in the treatise (chs. 2, 4, 6, 15, 25), as well as by general principles such as the canon of unity formulated at the end of ch. 8. The *Poetics* therefore broadly anticipates the later systems of the 'fine arts' elaborated especially in the eighteenth century, and these systems have in turn influenced our own loose but pervasive concept of art. But whereas beauty and expression are probably the two chief associations of this modern concept, the eighteenth century was still sufficiently close to the neo-classical tradition to retain, in its notion of 'imitation', a (distant) connection with the idea of mimesis which for Ar. was the common feature of the group of arts to which poetry belongs.

It must at once be said, however, that 'imitation' is now the least adequate (though still a regrettably common) translation of 'mimesis'. Our difficulties in understanding this concept arise in part from the fact that Ar. nowhere offers a definition of it; and this is one reason why my translation often leaves the term simply transliterated. Elsewhere, I usually favour the translation 'representation' (or alternatively 'portrayal'), because the English usage of this word (and cognate forms) comes closest to the range of meanings covered by the mimesis word-group in Greek. Thus a picture can represent a subject, an actor represent a character, a play represent an action, event or story ('imitate' has none of these senses in modern English), and in each of these cases Greek can similarly use the mimesis family of words. Visual resemblance, dramatic enactment, fictional story-telling – these are among the many meanings of mimesis, and the careful reader of the *Poetics* will need to pay particular attention to the various hints and comments which Ar. makes in elucidation of the concept. If the problems and ambiguities which may emerge in this connection perhaps show a lack of the supreme assurance which is to be found in many areas of Aristotelian philosophy, it is nonetheless salutary to reflect on the comparable uncertainties which attach to the widespread and seemingly indispensable use of a term such as 'expression' in modern criticism and aesthetics.

One important aspect of Ar.'s understanding of mimesis can be gathered from the distinction which he draws in this opening chapter between Homer and Empedocles. Negatively, this distinction belongs to the insistence that metre is not a sufficient (or even a necessary) condition for poetry. This is in itself significant, since it marks a departure from standard Greek attitudes. But Ar. is also making a positive point, by citing Empedocles' verse writings to represent the use of language for directly *affirmative* purposes – any use of language, that is, which purports to offer true statements or propositions about some aspect of reality. The further fact that Empedocles' 'natural philosophy' fails to satisfy Ar.'s requirement (see ch. 2) that poetry should deal with human action, is perhaps less important than this basic separation of mimetic (representational) from non-mimetic (affirmative) types of discourse.

Without providing a definitive criterion by which this distinction could be applied, Ar. implies what can best be described as the *fictional* status of works of mimesis:[1] their concern with images, representations, simulations or enactments of human life, rather than with direct claims or arguments about reality. This implicit recognition (or perhaps assumption) of the fictional standing of mimetic works will appear again at certain critical junctures of the *Poetics* (esp. chs. 9 and 25). Some further, brief comments can be helpfully made on its first appearance here.

First, it is worth contrasting Ar.'s distinction with the dichotomy between referential and emotive uses of language which has been drawn by some modern theorists (notably by I. A. Richards)[2] and employed in attempts to explain the special character of poetry. The referential/emotive dichotomy certainly has a superficial resemblance to Ar.'s separation of the mimetic from the non-mimetic, but the two sets of categories cannot be fully equated. The resemblance, so far as it goes, is essentially negative: Ar.'s principle (for which see ch. 25) that mimesis is exempted from the direct requirements of truth (historical, technical, philosophical, and so forth) matches one part of the separation of poetic from referential or 'scientific' language. But there is no positive correspondence between Ar.'s concept of mimesis and the category of 'emotive' language, and he would see no reason why certain uses of language should not be *both* referential and emotive: whereas Richards believes in two fundamentally different kinds of language or meaning, Ar.'s concern is with the different purpose and status of two uses of a common language. In fact, we shall see that in *Poetics* 9 Ar.'s doctrine of poetic universals does after all attribute a kind of referential status to poetic mimesis.

If poetry is not to be taken simply as a purveyor of truth in the way in which, say, historical or philosophical discourses strive to be, Ar. is not prepared to follow Plato in condemning mimesis as a species of falsehood or lies. It will emerge that the *Poetics* places constraints on the poet's freedom of fictional invention by

[1] The association between mimesis and fiction appears early in the neo-classical tradition: see, for example, Sidney, *Defence of Poetry* p. 24, 'imitation or fiction' (cf. my Introduction p.18).

[2] See e.g. *Principles of Literary Criticism* (reset edn., London 1967) ch. 34 (where Ar. is quoted on p. 211).

requiring conformity to the standards of 'probability or necessity' (ch. 7 etc.). By so doing, he opens up the possibility that poetry may offer material which, if not describable in terms of truth, can at any rate be argued to make some contribution to the understanding of human realities. In historical terms, this Aristotelian line of thought is of great significance because it represents an attempt to find a poised position between the popular Greek conception of poetry as a vehicle of truth (moral, historical and otherwise), and the outright Platonic condemnation of poetry as falsehood and deception.

Ch. 2

This chapter introduces us, with a brevity which should provoke careful scrutiny, to Ar.'s categorisation of the subject-matter (the 'objects') of poetry. Ch. 1 has already placed certain technical fields outside the proper domain of the poet, thereby eschewing the sorts of claims, and equally avoiding the criticisms of them, to be found in a work such as Plato's *Ion*: Ar. will have nothing to do with the idea (apparently quite widespread in the classical period) that poets speak as 'experts' in many different areas of skill and knowledge; but, by the same token, he will refuse to admit that a technical error found in a poem necessarily amounts to a poetic fault (ch. 25).

Poetics 2 announces the true subject-matter of poetry as 'people in action'. This formula in part depends on the strong association of the term 'mimesis' with some form of enactment or behavioural representation (cf. p.71 above) – a fact which will prove relevant to certain other passages in the work as well (esp. ch. 24). If, as Ar. will tend to assume, poetic mimesis ideally takes a dramatic or enactive form, then 'the mimesis of people in action' acquires something of the character of a tautology. Moreover, the poet's mode of discourse commits him, in Ar.'s terms, to dealing with the life of men in its essential dimension, which the philosopher considers to be the active pursuit of goals (cf. ch. 6). But if this point of view is presented in ch. 2 as if it were axiomatic and unquestionable, we need to note just how much Ar. is already effectively excluding from poetry's sphere. On the one side, it seems to rule out poetry which moves beyond the strictly human (into the realm of the divine, for example).

On the other, it looks inhospitable to the idea of poetic genres which use non-narrative statement, argument and discursive reflection as basic resources. Both these implications will be largely borne out by the remainder of the work.

On the first, I shall have various occasions later to stress that Ar.'s theory of tragedy and epic pays scant attention to these genres' religious dimension, and interprets poetic action in purely human terms. On the second, it needs only to be mentioned that the *Poetics* almost entirely omits all forms of Greek poetry which are primarily *non-dramatic*: namely, Hesiodic didactic (which Ar. would probably bracket with Empedoclean verse, on the principle given in ch. 1); elegiac and iambic poetry (Archilochus, Solon, Theognis, and others); and various types of lyric (Sappho, Alcaeus, Simonides, Pindar, etc.). Ar. would have had great difficulty in reconciling most of the works in these categories with his basic principle that the poet is a 'maker of plot-structures' (ch. 9), or with its negative corollary, that the poet should not speak (or even seem to speak, we might add) in his own person (ch. 24). Related considerations will also later help to explain why the *Poetics* shows so little interest in the chorus of tragedy (see comm. on ch. 18).

Ar.'s restriction of the scope of poetry, both in its subject-matter and in its modes of language (ch. 3), can best be seen as a response to two pressures on his thinking: first, the need to define a more precise role for poetry in a culture which was rapidly developing other types of discourse (history, philosophy, rhetoric, science etc.); secondly, the determination of Plato to judge poetry by strict standards of veracity. If Plato's charge is that poets purvey falsehoods about reality, Ar.'s reaction is to assert both that many aspects of reality lie anyway outside the reach of poetry proper, and that when a poet does deal with his legitimate object (human action) he is not to be understood as making truth-bearing statements or claims, but as offering plausible yet fictional structures of possible (rather than actual) events. The poet is a dramatiser, not an interpreter, of human life. And where interpretation or judgement takes over from mimetic representation, Ar. does not consider the result as 'poetry' but as some other kind of discourse, needing to be assessed by a different set of criteria.

But in firmly asserting human action to be the province of poetry, Ar. is also laying the basis for a theory of poetic value. In

Aristotelian philosophy, 'action' denotes intrinsically *purposive* behaviour: in their actions, men engage in the distinctively human pursuit of aims, the realisation of their intentions. So ch. 2's formula, 'people in action', implies that poetry is capable of treating, if only in fictional form, the fundamental patterns of life. While, therefore, Ar. draws back from traditional Greek conceptions of the poet as an 'expert' or a teacher in possession of all important knowledge, he does nevertheless leave poetry with the possibility of real seriousness and significance.

Ar.'s position is elucidated by the way in which he stipulates the ethical characterisation of poetic agents as a premise immediately attached to, or even inherent in, the idea of action. The active strivings of human agents are differentiated, from his philosophical point of view, primarily in ethical terms. In this context, we must register at once that 'character' (*éthos*) is not intrinsically a matter of psychology or individual personality. It is the sphere of ethical dispositions and choices, as these bear on, and are manifested in, action. This fundamental issue of the relation between character and action will be raised in more detail in ch. 6.

Poetics 2 provides a simple, tripartite scheme for distinguishing between genres (or even between poets within the same genre) by reference to the broad level or tone of characterisation. But it is not at first clear just how strictly Ar. intends his ethical categories to be taken. When he refers to the portrayal of 'people better than ourselves' in tragedy, epic and Polygnotus's paintings – Polygnotus appears to have concentrated on material akin to the two poetic genres – he might naturally be assumed to be alluding to the heroic world embodied in Greek myth, a world, above all, of figures of exceptional prowess, courage, and glory (as well as a capacity for exceptional suffering). But we can learn from Ar.'s ethical philosophy that his own code of virtues did not precisely match the heroic scale of values. This presents us with the possibility of an uncertain, or even conflicting, relationship between the values held within the dramatised world of the poetry, and the values brought to bear on the poetry by the critic. Ar. nowhere openly acknowledges or faces the problem of this disparity, though I shall later argue (*à propos* of ch. 13) that it explains the need which he feels to discriminate between what he regards as ethical and non-ethical attributes, when specifying the contours of the ideal tragedy.

It is consequently not easy to relate the categories of ch. 2 with the criteria used later in antiquity, and in neo-classicism, for demarcating the characteristic subject-matter of genres. But a basic point can nonetheless be made. While later criteria have a consistent element of *social* differentiation tied to them (so that tragedy's agents become commonly defined in terms of high status or standing, comedy's low), this does not seem to be a necessary implication of Ar.'s doctrine. It is true that in ch. 13 he refers to tragic agents of 'great esteem and prosperity', where he is evidently thinking precisely of figures of *heroic* myth. Other passages, though, make it relatively clear that Ar.'s theory does not require either tragedy or comedy to be restricted to certain kinds of social character or material. Just as comedy might operate with burlesque versions of heroic myth (end of ch. 13), but might equally create its own fictional characters (ch. 9), so tragedy too could afford, Ar. thinks, to go well beyond traditional Greek practice in inventing the fabric of its plots (ch. 9). What is regarded as indispensable is a certain generic level of *ethical* characterisation. It may well be that this aspect of the treatise, though left undeveloped, offers a more flexible conception of genres than the persistent later orthodoxies which base themselves on essentially social criteria.

The following propositions can now be listed by way of summarising the major arguments and implications of the first two chapters of the *Poetics*:

(a)   poetic mimesis is an art susceptible of rational and objective analysis, which will produce a theory of its principles, standards, and aims.

(b)   poetry can be placed within a larger scheme of mimetic arts (including painting, music and dance), whose common concern is the representation of human action and life, but which differ in their media (materials), their ethical level of subject-matter, and their manner or mode of representation.

(c)   the content of mimetic works is inherently fictive, which means that they are to be sharply distinguished from discourse which makes direct claims about reality.

(d)   poetic mimesis represents, and dramatises, human life in its essential aspect of purposive, ethically qualified action.

(e)   the mimesis of action/character can reflect different levels or areas of possible reality, from the base to the outstanding; these levels are correlated with particular species or genres of poetry.

Ch. 3

Ar. now completes his framework of basic analysis by indicating the possible modes of poetry. Little needs to be said about his concentration on just two primary modes – narrative and dramatic enactment – since this is part of the restrictive conception of poetry which I have already discussed under ch. 2 and will discuss further under ch. 24. From a post-Romantic point of view, Ar.'s framework (which borrows various elements from Plato) is limited and rather rigid, lacking the suppleness to be adapted to the breakdown of traditional generic categories which has proceeded steadily in the aftermath of neo-classicism. But that is hardly surprising. Ar.'s aim is not to furnish a pliant scheme which can be modified to cater for changing poetic practices. Indeed, the scheme is not even elaborated sufficiently to encompass, for example, the extensive use in tragedy of a mode (archetypally represented by the messenger-speech) which is at the same time dramatic *and* narrative. This only serves to confirm that the purpose of the analysis is to narrow down the focus of the enquiry onto just those modes which comport with the mimesis of human action. The effect of this is to push towards the understanding of mimesis as essentially *enactive*. We shall later discover (ch. 24) that Ar. is prepared to carry this process even further.

It needs to be noticed that when Homer's dramatic technique is here described as a matter of 'impersonation' (literally, the poet 'becomes a different character'), the implication is that any poetic utterance which is not explicitly assigned to a character or persona must be attributed to the poet himself. This way of thinking was not peculiar to Ar. We find it prominently in a passage of Plato (*Republic* 3.392-6) on which *Poetics* 3 is closely modelled, and there are grounds for supposing that it was a normal Greek supposition that the 'voice' of a poem is the poet's own except where a dramatic speaker can be identified. (There was even a common tendency, not unknown in other times, to treat dramatic utterances too as though representing the authorial point of view.)

The supposition may have been partly influenced by the presence of explicit authorial statements in many poetic texts (including, prominently, works by Homer, Hesiod and Solon); but its wider application posed a difficulty for Ar.'s wish to separate fictional mimesis from affirmative or declarative uses of language. In ch. 24 this problem will induce Ar. to the extreme principle that when the epic poet speaks in his own person (which, as ch. 3 indicates, must include even the narrative mode) he is not fulfilling the proper, mimetic role of the poet. Such was Ar.'s determination to disengage poetry from modes of discourse which could be subjected to criteria of truth and falsehood.

The latter part of ch. 3 need not greatly concern the ordinary reader of the *Poetics*. The details of the dispute over the origin and names of tragedy and comedy have little bearing on the main arguments of the work, but the following points can be concisely suggested:

(a)   the section is clearly digressive or parenthetical; like some other parts of the book, it has not been smoothly integrated, but would make much more immediate sense in the context of oral teaching.

(b)   it is hard to believe that Ar. attaches much weight to the linguistic considerations cited on behalf of the Dorians. In particular, the later reference to phallic rituals in ch. 4 puts it virtually beyond doubt that he accepted the derivation of *kômôdia* from *kômazein* (revelling) not from *kômê* (village).

(c)   equally, however, the later reference to Sicily in ch. 5 shows that Ar. did regard Epicharmus as important in the history of comedy.

(d)   Ar.'s interest in the history of poetry was less in the individual data than in an overall pattern of significant evolution (cf. p.82): there is therefore no reason why he should have felt it necessary to reach a definitive solution of the Dorian claims in question.

Ch. 4

Having given in chs. 1-3 a 'static' analysis of the distinctions necessary for the study of poetry, Ar. now offers a sketch of how, from the roots of certain human instincts, and through a gradual, evolutionary process; poetry's particular cultural forms have historically developed or unfolded. The argument of the chapter is ambitious but highly compressed. It would be a mistake, though, to suppose that if only fuller detail were supplied, we would inevitably be able to see the clear historical foundations of Ar.'s position. In the latter part of his life, Ar. is known to have compiled chronological records of tragic performances at Athens; but even assuming (as we do not know) that this section of the *Poetics* owes something to these researches, the approach found in this chapter remains heavily theoretical. After all, Ar. had no evidence whatever for the origins of poetry, nor, on his own admission, for much of its early history in Greece. His premises are therefore necessarily *a priori*, and this holds true to a considerable extent even when the argument comes within the ambit of literary history for which documentary evidence was available.

Ar.'s theory of the origins of poetry is bold yet essentially simple. The two 'natural causes' of poetry are stated as a universal instinct to engage in mimetic activity (exhibited in children's imitative and fictionalising behaviour) and a propensity to take pleasure in the products of mimesis.[1] Both these premises are further reduced to a common factor: a human need for, and pleasure in, the processes of learning and understanding. The theory reflects Ar.'s general philosophy of man as a distinctively rational creature rooted in the natural world. The application of this conception to the understanding of poetry as a cultural phenomenon allows the work of poets to be given an obvious respectability and importance (both of which Plato had denied): poetry is seen as deriving from, and satisfying, the impulse to understand the world of human action by making and enjoying representations of it.

The theory is no doubt *too* bold and simple, but it does at least do some justice both to the prevalent Greek belief in poetry's and art's objective concern with reality, and to Ar.'s own view of man. It is useful to compare and contrast characteristically Romantic theories which imagine poetry to have been the

---

[1] An alternative interpretation takes the two causes to be instincts firstly for mimesis, and secondly for 'melody and rhythm'. I do not think the point is ultimately important, since Ar. regarded melody and rhythm as themselves mimetic at root: see my *Aristotle's Poetics* p. 68 n. 29.

original expression of emotion and passion.[2] Such theories naturally reflect the outlook of a cultural age which relates art much more closely to the emotional state of the artist, and it can fairly be said that they project their own outlook onto the unknown origins of poetry in a way which is precisely analogous to Ar.'s enterprise in *Poetics* 4.

It should not, however, be thought that Ar.'s argument in this passage excludes emotion and spontaneity from the origins of poetry. Indeed, a kind of spontaneity, in the form of improvisation and experiment, seems to be presupposed as a motive force at various experimental stages in the evolution of poetry. But the scope for purely natural improvisation in Ar.'s scheme diminishes as poetic activity is gradually channelled into generic types, which are regarded as embodying the regular (and so repeatable) principles of 'art', without which Ar.'s whole notion of a poetic treatise would be unthinkable. Whereas a Romantic might regard the freshness of primitive spontaneity as a kind of mythical ideal of artistic expression, for Ar. it is a necessary step, but also only a *first* step, in the cultural process which culminates in the much more sophisticated achievements of regular artistry.

As for emotion, not only will its place in poetry be later exemplified in the specific analysis of tragedy, but its necessary involvement in mimesis is also implied by the two basic streams into which Ar. imagines poetry as separating from an early stage – the serious, which was in origin encomiastic, and so entailed admiring and laudatory feelings towards its objects; and the humorous or satirical, which incorporated feelings of hostility and disapproval. But these emotions are presented not so much as the primary springs of poetry, but rather as natural consequences of the concerns of the poetry with *ethical* features of human action. It is essentially in terms of these ethical concerns that Ar. interprets the two great branches of the poetic tradition. In this way, the evolutionary scheme of poetry connects with the observations on character(isation) which we have already met in ch. 2: tragedy's and comedy's respective dealings with superior and inferior characters are traced back to

[2] On such theories see M. H. Abrams, *The Mirror and the Lamp* (Oxford 1953) pp. 78-82.

the impulses operative in the earliest (hypothetical) stages of poetry's growth.

The dichotomy between serious and humorous poetry (with the emotional and ethical implications of the two types) gives Ar.'s sketch of poetic history its shape and purpose. For each side of the framework, certain major stages of evolution are posited: in the one case, 'hymns and encomia' – epic – Homeric, 'tragic' epic – Attic tragedy; in the other, primitive invective – iambus – the (supposedly) Homeric *Margites* – dramatic comedy. There are many problems, some I believe insoluble, arising from these schemes, not least because to the series of stages just indicated Ar. adds separate suggestions for the emergence of tragedy and comedy from further forms of improvisation. But no effort is made to relate these suggestions (which may well not be original with Ar.) to the larger evolutionary picture, within which Homeric works are deemed to have been the crucial factor underlying the emergence of both tragedy and comedy.

What this means, I think, is that the factual data of literary history, in so far as we take Ar. to have had access to them, are subordinated or even sacrificed to a theoretical view of the direction of change and development within what we might term poetry's 'natural history'. Thus, for example, whatever the exact historical relations between them are supposed to be, Ar. leaves it in no doubt that the dithyrambic improvisations which produced proto-tragedy in Attica are of a lower order of importance in his scheme than the decisive discovery of tragic form by Homer in the *Iliad* and *Odyssey*.

The pivotal significance of the Homeric poems in Ar.'s perspective raises an interesting issue. Epic poetry, according to ch. 4, developed from the original impulse to portray and celebrate the actions of outstanding or noble men; but the essence of tragedy, both in its Homeric and in its later Attic form, involves such characters in great changes of fortune, or transformations, which arouse pity and fear in those who contemplate them. Thus the evolution of serious poetry moves, on this hypothesis, from a simply encomiastic origin to a stage at which a distinctively tragic viewpoint and feeling are introduced.

It is for this innovation, as well as for the bringing of new dramatic qualities to the genre, that Ar. regards Homer as responsible and important, and in both respects the judgement may well rest on fine insight.[3] But it is integral to Ar.'s argument that Homer's achievement is not considered just as the contingent work of an individual at a particular historical juncture, but rather as the *discovery* of a potential which existed 'naturally': Homer *revealed* the possibility of both tragedy and comedy, and Ar. goes on later to describe the final flowering of Attic tragedy as the attainment of the genre's 'natural fulfilment'. Where a modern literary historian, perhaps influenced by Romantic ideas of genius, might be inclined to see the Homeric poems as the unique achievements of individual poetic creativity (albeit working with partly traditional material), Ar. places Homer in the vista of a naturally unfolding pattern of mimetic possibilities. This is not to suggest that the *Poetics*' view of literary history diminishes Homeric greatness, but that it involves special presuppositions about cultural evolution which we cannot afford to ignore in reading the treatise, or in reusing its claims for our own historical purposes.

Moreover, if the whole argument of ch. 4 rests on naturalistic assumptions, then it should follow that the characteristic subject-matter of tragedy, as Ar. sees it, must in some sense be natural for a poetic genre which aims to portray 'noble actions and noble agents'. This means that Ar. accepts vulnerability and instability, which he will later identify as the crux of tragedy, to be an inescapable part of the human pursuit of excellence and goodness. It also means that tragedy exemplifies the principle that literary genres are firmly tied to the perception of certain aspects of reality, rather than being an autonomous matter of convention and institutionalisation.

Ar. had few if any predecessors in the enterprise of finding order in the whole course of Greek literary history. It is true that a sense of an important affinity between Homer and the tragedians appears on a number of occasions in Plato, but beyond this it is difficult to find germane Platonic material other than occasional and unsystematic contentions. An example of these is the idea that the history of Greek 'music' (which here includes poetry) had declined from an original state of order to a

---

[3] On the link between tragedy and Homer's dramatic technique see J.Herington, *Poetry into Drama* (Berkeley 1985) pp. 133-6. For modern reexaminations of what Homer and tragedy have in common at a deeper level, see J. Gould, 'Homeric Epic and the Tragic Moment', in T. Winnifrith et al. (edd.) *Aspects of the Epic* (London 1983), and Rutherford, 'Tragic Form and Feeling'.

modern, audience-centred decadence (*Laws* 3.700a ff.). In fact, Ar.'s scheme in *Poetics* 4 contradicts Platonic premises. While Plato objects to the Homeric poems and Attic tragedy, and wishes to go back to the simple austerity of 'hymns and encomia' (*Republic* 10.607a), Ar. treats the latter as *primitive* forms of mimesis which have been made effectively obsolete by later discoveries. For the specific history of tragedy at Athens there must have been more pre-Aristotelian ideas than we can now identify; the reference near the end of ch. 4 to changes 'which are said' to have occurred in the genre clearly implies the existence of at least a popular account of the matter. But it must remain doubtful whether anyone had put forward a historical *theory* of the kind which the *Poetics* adumbrates.

Contrary to what is still often maintained, this theory is not designed to present the culmination of tragedy as specifically Sophoclean. This is a point on which Ar.'s lack of explicitness ought to be taken at face-value. It is obvious enough that he regards tragedy's finest potential as having been first realised in the middle and second half of the fifth century, the age dominated by Sophocles and Euripides; and the frequent citation of plays by these dramatists throughout the work indicates that both could supply instances of what Ar. deemed to be the highest standards of the genre. But it should not be overlooked that neither *Oedipus Tyrannus* nor *Iphigeneia in Tauris* emerges with wholly unqualified approval. This goes to confirm that Ar. is not committed to basing his theory entirely on existing works, nor on the pragmatic assumption that the excellence possible in the genre has no meaning outside the actual achievements of dramatists. The theory is *normative*, and its principles, while partly dependent on exemplification from existing works, are not simply deduced from them. The theorist's insight claims a validity which may well contradict much of the practice of playwrights hitherto. That is why, when we come to consider comedy, we shall see that it is uncertain whether Ar. believes the natural potential of the genre yet to have been fully actualised in the theatre.

For the details of the evolution of tragedy, I restrict myself to tabulating the following brief points:

(a) Ar. mentions, but seems uninterested in, the (proximate) dithyrambic origins of tragedy. I have already suggested that this is largely due to his own theory of literary history, within which Homer is a much more vital influence on tragedy. Cf. also (e) below.

(b) the lack of interest in dithyramb is further explained by Ar.'s teleological emphasis: it is the eventual, perfectly developed form which matters, not the first stage in the growth towards it. Contrast the essentially Romantic concern with *origins* in Nietzsche's *The Birth of Tragedy*, where the heart of tragedy is located in the Dionysiac satyr chorus of dithyramb.[4]

(c) changes in the number of actors are mentioned not simply as a technical convention, but as a precondition for the dramatic portrayal of action of increasing complexity.

(d) Aeschylus' reduction of the choral role is similarly significant for Ar. as pointing the way towards the drama of action, rather than of lyric reflection.

(e) it is unclear where the light, 'satyric' stage of tragedy derives from, though a connection with dithyramb is presumably intended.[5] The whole of the subsequent account of tragedy will show how negligible Ar. must have regarded such early material to be for the true nature of the genre. This corroborates the superior importance of Homeric epic over dithyrambic antecedents in the philosopher's view of tragedy's growth, as well as the teleological emphasis noted in (b) above.

(f) the comments on the iambic metre not only illustrate the natural development of rhythm within the genre's history, but they also indicate Ar.'s belief that the language of tragedy should come close to that of ordinary speech: on this see ch. 22 and p.163 below.

Ch. 5

This short chapter indicates why Ar. is unable to supply as full a scheme for the history of comedy as for that of tragedy; but we

---

[4] Contrast *BT* §7-8 with Ar.'s ideas that tragedy developed away from the style of satyr-plays, and away from an essentially choral form ((d) above). Cf. M. S. Silk & J. P. Stern, *Nietzsche on Tragedy* (Cambridge 1981) pp. 236f.

[5] For a recent attempt to make sense of this element in *Poetics* 4 see R. Seaford, *Euripides: Cyclops* (Oxford 1984) pp. 10 ff.

can still see his assumption that the genre has gone through stages and changes which carry it gradually towards its natural perfection. Just what Ar. took such perfection to consist in, we can no longer say, since the analysis of comedy in the second book of the work has been lost. But a few hints survive to give us some idea of the Aristotelian conception of comedy and its evolution.

The first two sentences of ch. 5 touch on Ar.'s basic view of comedy. The passage gives us an instructive example of the way in which prescriptive and empirical propositions tend to coalesce within the *Poetics*. We start with a principle – the essential association of laughter with ridicule and denigration, and its use against targets regarded as 'shameful'. This would have commanded wide assent from Greeks, since it ties comedy to the observable function of derision in a culture which possessed a strongly developed sensitivity to public reproach and dishonour. But Ar. at once qualifies this principle with a condition which is at the same time ethical and aesthetic, by stipulating the exclusion from comedy's domain of subjects which are either too grave (real evil) or too painful (as with material suitable for tragedy).

It is arguable that these exclusions owe something to empirical observation: certain topics are just too serious to lend themselves to effective humour. But there is more to Ar.'s point than this. It is not difficult to find matters of the proscribed kinds both in the iambic genre practised by Archilochus, and in the style of dramatic comedy represented by Aristophanes (both these poets invite laughter, for example, towards cases of grave physical pain). Ar. wishes, in other words, to define the realm of the truly comic in such a way as to contradict some of the uses of laughter which had found a place in earlier parts of the comic tradition. It is, in fact, just such improper and excessive practices which are denoted by the phrase 'the iambic concept' in the present chapter. By 'iambic' Ar. means chiefly the targetting of denigration against identifiable individuals, which was characteristic of both the iambic genre itself and of Aristophanic Old Comedy. But he probably has in mind also the general transgression (in these same genres) of the boundaries of the truly comic or ridiculous, as he conceives it.

Ar.'s understanding of comedy consequently depends on a firm dissociation between the 'iambic' and the comic proper. This is confirmed both by ch. 4 (the *Margites* dealt 'not with invective but with the ridiculous') and later by ch. 9, where the comedy of Ar.'s own day is used to illustrate the generalised or universal significance of comic plot-structures, as opposed to the specific abuse of individuals by iambic poets. These two passages put it beyond question that the development of the comic branch of the poetic tradition is taken to have moved gradually away from coarse, personalised invective, towards a style of humour whose characters and actions represent fictional universals.[1]

But we can deduce from the importance attached in ch. 5 to Crates, whose career predated that of Aristophanes, that this process was not believed to be tidily linear. The same, in fact, would have to be said about tragedy too. In both cases, certain turning-points in literary history are identified as crucial by Ar., and these are the junctures at which progress was made towards the realisation of the intrinsic and natural potential of the genres. The passage cited above from ch. 9 implies that Ar. regarded the Athenian comedy of his own day as coming close to fulfilment of such potential, and this suggests that he had in mind plays centering on the relatively innocuous failings of somewhat standardised comic 'types'. Although it would be going too far, on existing evidence, to align Ar.'s ideal of comedy precisely with the 'comedy of manners' which was being developed during his lifetime, and which was to reach a climax with Menander in the following generation, it is only fair to say that the temptation to do just this is extremely strong. Comedy restrained within inoffensive bounds, and shirking subjects of a potentially disturbing kind, is the broad ideal which Ar. apparently sanctions. But Greek culture certainly knew more disruptive uses of laughter than this.

It is worth reiterating that Ar.'s ideal is simultaneously aesthetic and ethical – which is to say, it defines *both* the distinctive tone of comedy (its generic ethos), *and* its inherent tendency to imply an adverse evaluation of its objects. For this latter aspect Ar. employs Greek terms which denote the idea of shame or reproach, and this effectively opens up for comedy a wide scale of features, attributes and types of behaviour which

---

[1] For an attempt, utilising Ar.'s own hints, to reconstruct the nature of early Greek invective, or 'the poetry of blame', see G. Nagy, *The Best of the Achaeans* (Baltimore 1979) chs. 12-14.

might cause a person to be perceived as inferior by the shared standards of a society. If Ar.'s immediate example of an ugly mask seems to lie outside the sphere of the ethical, that should alert us to the much more heavily shame-based nature of Greek ethical attitudes in general. But it also needs to be noted that Ar. may have in mind the use of distorted masks to represent other 'faults' in those who carry them: irascibility or miserliness, for example, or perhaps positive shamelessness. The example of a mask also serves to illuminate Ar.'s contrast between comedy proper and the 'iambic' mode. The mask is almost certainly meant to imply a *fictional* identity, and so to provide a focus for laughter directed against human features whose significance is universal not particular. To mock an ugly individual, by contrast, would be regarded by Ar. as ethically offensive; and to be invited by comedy to indulge in such laughter would therefore compound an ethical with a poetic mistake.[2]

A short comment must now be appended on the last part of *Poetics* 5, which makes the transition from the introductory section of the treatise to the analysis of individual genres. Ar.'s purpose here is to explain why he will give tragedy – the historically younger genre – prior (and lengthier) treatment over epic. The basic factor behind this decision is what we have already seen to be Ar.'s evolutionary view of literary history, a perspective within which tragedy is regarded as having developed to a higher or more complex level than epic. When Ar. later offers an explicit comparison of the two genres in ch. 26, his claim that tragedy yields a more *concentrated* pleasure can be related to the remark in the present chapter on the restriction of tragedy's dramatic time (and hence its performance time, though the two are not identical) to a single day. This restriction does not amount to the Unity of Time which was eventually extracted from it in the Renaissance. It is, instead, an observation on an existing tendency in the genre, and one which partly explains why Ar. believes tragedy to be capable of tighter unity of plot-structure than epic. The limited time-span of a

---

[2] For a clear exposition of Ar.'s ethical views on laughter and amusement see his *Nicomachean Ethics* Bk.4, ch.8, where he argues for a mean between excessive jesting and boorishness. In so doing he mentions the contrast between older and newer styles of Athenian comedy, indicating his clear preference for the latter's more restrained style of humour.

dramatic work will conduce to the singleness of action which we shall find that the *Poetics* ideally looks for in poetry (chs. 7-8).

Ch. 6

Poetics 6, one of the richest sections of the treatise, can be read as comprising three closely related critical exercises: a definition of tragic drama; an analysis of the genre into its constituent parts or elements; and an evaluative ranking of these elements from the most to the least important. For convenience, the chapter can be discussed under these three headings, though this should not disguise their integration within Ar.'s method. Definition is required by this method not simply to demarcate an area of enquiry but to state the essence, the true nature, of the subject. Definition also allows the subject to be broken down into its major components, and this analytical exercise can be considered as drawing out, and expanding, the implications of the definition. Finally, since Ar. applies to poetry, as to so much else, *teleological* criteria (which concern questions of function and purpose), he has reason to discriminate between the parts of tragedy in terms of their importance for the fulfilment of tragedy's aims.

Definition – The modern reader may well have a double aversion to the Aristotelian definition of tragedy: firstly, to the very idea of attempting to state the essential nature of a literary genre, because this might seem to imply a fixity which is alien to the creativity of poetry; but also, in particular, to a definition which could be thought to fall far short of capturing the significance of the greatest tragic poetry. Such feelings arise in part from the great cultural distance between ourselves and the *Poetics*, a distance which contains types of tragic drama never conceived of by Ar. This simple fact makes one wonder why modern critics have often persisted in even considering Ar.'s definition of tragedy as a formula capable of holding together the whole history of tragic poetry.

This is a particularly strange critical practice when one registers the large disparity between Ar.'s definition and the constant tendency of modern writings on tragedy to move towards an existential or metaphysical conception of the genre (or of the world view which it is often taken to represent). Ar.'s aim, by contrast, inevitably looks much more pragmatic and less ambitious. Much of his definition places tragedy within the scheme of mimetic types and categories sketched in the first three chapters of the work, and only two indications are given of what it is difficult for us not to regard as the distinctively tragic features of the genre. Even these two indications look decidedly limited in scope: they are, first, the description of a tragic action as 'serious' (in accordance with the basic dichotomy of poetry given in ch. 4), second, the identification of the effect of tragedy as one of pity and fear, bringing with it a *katharsis* of such emotions. There seems little if any scope here for a metaphysical view of tragedy, and this will be confirmed by further consideration of each of these two points in the definitions.

Seriousness may be difficult for us to come to terms with precisely because of its fundamental simplicity, though it is hardly taken care of by Matthew Arnold's sweeping and somewhat pious reference, in 'The Study of Poetry', to 'the high and excellent seriousness which Aristotle assigns as one of the grand virtues of poetry'. 'Serious' is a word which now suggests questions primarily of tone or ethos, but Ar.'s Greek term has *both* this suggestion *and* an ethical import. It is explained in ch. 4 as a derivation from the original cultural impulse to engage in the mimesis of, and thereby to celebrate, the actions of outstanding men. The later development of tragic poetry by Homer qualifies and deepens this idea by introducing forms of plot-structure in which suffering and unhappiness are implicated, and Ar. will himself put some further critical qualification on the idea by his restrictions on the degree of goodness appropriate to the characters of tragedy (ch. 13). As this last passage intimates, the essential point is ethical. This is shown by ch. 6's later remarks about the active quest for happiness (by which Ar. means the virtuous fulfilment of our human potential). One basic component, then, in Ar.'s conception of tragedy is no more and no less than that the genre should portray agents engaged in pursuit of the ethical goals of life.

But a serious action only becomes a properly tragic action, on Ar.'s terms, when it incorporates features, and assumes a form, capable of eliciting pity and fear from its audience and of effecting a *katharsis* of such emotions. It had better be said at once that we do not really know what Ar. meant in this context by *katharsis*. We can be moderately confident only that it offers a response to the Platonic view that tragedy arouses emotions which ought, for the sake of general psychological and moral well-being, to be kept in check (*Republic* 10, 603-5). If it is true, as I believe, that we can best conjecture the nature of Ar.'s response by looking at his own philosophical psychology, then the likelihood presents itself that *katharsis* does not stand for a notion of pure outlet or emotional release, still less for a discharge of *pathological* emotions.[1] It is more probable that the idea of release is only part of a more complex concept built around Ar.'s belief that the emotions have a natural and proper role in the mind's experience of reality.

Arguing along this sort of line it is possible to move towards a very tentative interpretation of *katharsis* as a powerful emotional experience which not only gives our natural feelings of pity and fear full play, but does so in a way which conduces to their rightful functioning as part of our understanding of, and response to, events in the human world. It can probably also be said that *katharsis* is meant to be not just something we are left with *after* a tragic performance, but an intrinsic element or dimension of the total emotional experience itself. Beyond this, it is scarcely worthwhile for the ordinary reader of the *Poetics* to struggle with an idea of which Ar. gives no direct elucidation at all in the work itself.[2] The main reason in recent times for the irresistible but largely fanciful obsession with the term is undoubtedly the appeal of such speculations to a Freudian age. But those interested in the deep psychology of the tragic experience should turn to sources other than Ar. for enlightenment.[3]

[1] The pathological view of *katharsis* was established by mid-nineteenth century German scholarship, and has been prevalent ever since. But the idea that pity and fear were considered in any way morbid by Ar. is wholly without foundation. Nietzsche's criticisms of *katharsis* (e.g. *Antichrist* §7) are based on this misconception, and overlook the fact that Ar. links the emotional experience of tragedy with *pleasure*.

[2] Outside the *Poetics*, we have some help from *Politics* 8.7, where *katharsis* involves a highly excited emotional experience followed by relief. But Ar. is there discussing abnormal emotions, and the implications of the passage therefore need to be adjusted to take account of the very different nature of pity and fear.

[3] A fuller reexamination of this difficult issue can be found in my book, *Aristotle's Poetics* ch. VI. Unfortunately, *katharsis* continues to provoke various forms of fantasy: D. D. Raphael, *The Paradox of Tragedy* (London 1960) pp. 13-15, for example, produces a tasteless and erroneous travesty of Ar.'s concept, which he not surprisingly finds it easy to deride.

What has been said above about Ar.'s general understanding of the emotions is probably the most pertinent point to be made about his identification of the effect of tragedy as pity and fear (an identification which seems to have been well established before his time: see p.9). Ar. takes our emotions to operate naturally in connection with cognitive experiences of, and judgements about, the world. Pity and fear as aroused by tragedy are not, on this view, raw, elemental passions, which is what Plato implies in the passage cited above, but an integral component of a full response to the plot-structure of events designed by the poet. To anyone who argued that it is a mistake to confuse a poetic work with its emotional effects, Ar. would respond that the understanding of kinds of poetry, as of kinds of reality, cannot but involve us in judgements on their emotional power.

In Ar.'s interpretation of the response which tragedy generically invites, pity represents a strongly sympathetic sense of undeserved affliction, and fear, while resting on an analogous sympathy, entails (according to the discussion at *Rhetoric* 2.5) an implicit awareness that *we too* could be exposed to similar sufferings. This last point lies behind the statement in ch. 13 that we feel fear for those 'like ourselves', and both the tragic emotions call for a recognition of some affinity between ourselves (the audience) and the agents who act and suffer. The combination of pity and fear is meant, therefore, to comprise both a strong flow of altruistic feeling towards the tragic agents themselves, and an underlying recognition that their tragedy exposes the vulnerability of the humanity, and the conditions of existence, which we share with them. Ar.'s definition is not meant to exclude all other emotions from the experience of tragedy, only to identify pity and fear (probably in accordance, as already indicated, with a common Greek apprehension) as the dominant emotions aroused by the genre's typical forms.

It will be possible to refine the interpretation of this strand of the *Poetics* in dealing with some of its later chapters, but we can offer a provisional observation. We have seen that the notion of 'seriousness' commits tragedy to dramatising action in pursuit of ethical goals and fulfilment (the quest for 'happiness', in Ar.'s terms). But the kind of dramatic material required by pity and fear must embody a vulnerability to suffering which can touch an audience's deep sense of common humanity. This combination of ideas would seem to find the heart of tragedy in the poetic demonstration of ways in which suffering is entangled in even the finest strivings of human action. Having said this, however, it is important to emphasise Ar.'s reluctance to reduce the significance of tragedy to an unequivocal formulation in existential terms. The *Poetics* puts a valuation on tragedy which gives it the capacity to stir the emotions and deepen the understanding of its audience, but it does not share the belief of some later critics that the genre offers an all-inclusive attitude to human experience.[4]

Analysis – Ar.'s analysis of the component parts of tragic poetry can be seen from a number of angles. In technical terms, it involves the application to tragedy of the basic categories set out in the introductory chapters. The connection is made explicitly when, after listing his six components, Ar. aligns them with the media, mode and objects of mimesis. It is worth setting this alignment out diagrammatically:

style   } – [language + rhythm (metre)]   }   _ media
lyric poetry   } – [language + rhythm + melody] }   = (ch.1)

plot-structure }
character   } = objects (i.e. the characterised 'men in action'
thought   }   of ch. 2)

spectacle   } = mode (i.e. dramatic enactment, as in ch. 3)

The earlier framework of distinctions is now, in other words, converted into a concrete set of concepts for the criticism and interpretation of a particular poetic genre, and it is undoubtedly part of Ar.'s aim to provide a comprehensive terminology and a perspective which will make precise critical discriminations possible. In the process, however, he introduces some points and emphases which go beyond the earlier chapters, and these deserve to be noted.

---

[4] For a careful and subtle attempt to formulate the implications of Ar.'s view of tragedy see Nussbaum, *Fragility of Goodness* pp. 378-91.

1. the sharp distinction between the poetry of the spoken scenes (style) and that of the choral odes and related sections (lyric poetry, including music), while having a foundation in poetic practice, also prepares the way for the demotion of the latter to the category of 'garnishing' or embellishment, and for the fact that Ar. will pay scant attention to the lyric dimension of tragedy.

2. the further analysis of the objects of poetic mimesis not only brings in a new element (thought, on which see p. below) but lays the ground for the evaluative judgements which are developed in the remainder of the chapter: these judgements will clarify just what Ar. understands by his earlier phrase, 'men in action'.

3. the use of 'spectacle' to denote the *mode* of drama is paradoxical for Ar. In ch. 3 dramatic enactment was conceived purely in terms of internal poetic use of a persona (i.e. direct speech), which is why it was possible to find it employed in Homer as well as drama proper. Ar. now implicitly equates enactment with full theatrical performance, but we shall see this idea rejected at the end of the chapter, and in the course of the treatise as a whole his attitude to performance will emerge as decidedly equivocal.

Evaluation – Although Ar.'s terminology could be, and has been, made serviceable for rather different critical purposes,[5] in his own train of argument it leads naturally on to the business of evaluative ranking. The 'parts' of tragedy are not all equally important, and Ar. proceeds to build a kind of hierarchy out of them.

Of supreme importance is plot-structure – the one indispensable component of tragic drama, the 'soul' (or life-source) of tragedy, and, in graphic terms, its form rather than its colour.[6] This fundamental doctrine of Aristotelian poetics receives its

---

[5] Cf. my Introduction p.22 n.26.

[6] The Greek term which I translate as 'plot-structure', *muthos*, retains in Ar. something of its basic senses of 'story', 'legend' etc. But it is hopeless to retain the antiquated translation 'fable', as Potts, *Aristotle on the Art of Fiction*, does. We have no precise equivalent in English, but 'plot-structure' does at least emphasise what Ar. himself repeatedly emphasises in his use of the term. For an interesting but excessively analytical discussion of *muthos* in the *Poetics* see E. Downing, *Classical Antiquity* 3 (1984) 164-78.

intended justification not just from what is said in ch. 6, but from the disproportionate weight given to plot-structure in the subsequent treatment of the genre (chs. 7-14 and 16 are devoted to it). In trying to understand Ar.'s position, we must be careful not to think of plot-structure as 'form' divorced from content. Ar.'s ideas on form, and particularly on unity, will occupy chs. 7-8, but it can already be seen that his theory requires plot-structure to be both form and substance – or, better, dramatic substance (action) in its formal dimension (unity). The plot-structure is defined and treated as a designed pattern of action, and since human action is purposive and significant, no such pattern or design could intelligibly be regarded by Ar. as a matter of merely schematic form. Plot-structure, then, is not a vehicle or framework for something else, but constitutes the primary significance of poetic drama. Ar.'s comparison with painting is apt: the image without colour already has its essential visual meaning, and this meaning is not changed, only enhanced or enriched, by the addition of colour.

What is more challenging (and frequently misunderstood) is Ar.'s subordination of characterisation to action. The challenge arises from the disparity between the philosopher's rather spare and strict notion of character as a matter of ethical dispositions, and the typical modern idea of character as something more diffuse, pervasive and strongly psychological. Modern ideas of character are matched by, and in turn reflect, techniques of characterisation in modern literature, above all in the novel, whereas Ar.'s owe something to the presentation of character in Greek tragedy through explicit and even rhetorical statements of purpose. Ar. believes in a reciprocal relation between character and action – character motivating action, and action cumulatively helping to shape character. But he nonetheless sees a clear conceptual disjunction of motive and intention (character) and their realisation in action; whereas much modern thought and literature, grounded in psychological presuppositions, posits only a rich complexity of human life, which makes the analytical distinction somewhat arid.

Ar.'s views on this matter connect a conception of drama with a conception of life: both, in the philosopher's mind, fundamentally concern activity rather than static qualities. What matters in life is that people should engage in the pursuit of suitable aims and ends, not that they should rest quiescent in a fixed or achieved state; and since drama is, on Ar.'s premises, the mimesis or representation of life, it too must centre on people's actions rather than their characters as such. But this does not eliminate the need for characterisation, since the latter can help to give a fuller dramatisation of the significance of the agents' actions.

On this point there are signs of a slight equivocation, since Ar. seems at different times to suppose both that some degree of characterisation is inevitable (ch. 2), and that it can (though should not) be dispensed with altogether (ch. 6). The fundamental principle, I think, is that many actions will necessarily have a degree of characterisation built into them, since their nature will presuppose particular ethical dispositions; but some actions are not of this kind, and in these cases characterless action is a possibility. There is, then, probably a sense in which Ar. considers that character can be either implicit or explicit, but it is the latter – the positive ways in which a dramatist can illuminate the moral motivations of his agents – which he has in mind when making most of his remarks on the subject. Ar. returns to the topic of characterisation in ch. 15.

Most of the considerations on action and character given in ch. 6 would apply equally, it should be stressed, to non-tragic drama. But one in particular depends on distinctively tragic features (which the genre shares, according to the *Poetics*, with Homeric epic). It will later emerge that the emotions of pity and fear hinge around changes of fortune in the lives of the tragic agents, but Ar. requires such changes to come about in and through action, rather than consisting of wholly passive sufferings (cf. p.120). This point is implied in ch. 6's reference to the components of what will be called the 'complex' plot-type, namely reversals and recognitions. These highly charged turning-points in a tragic plot-structure presuppose a larger context of dramatic movement and progression, and this gives a decisive importance to Ar.'s understanding of the place of action in dramatic poetry. Tragic drama offers us images of the actions on which depends the difference between happiness and unhappiness, terms which for Ar. signify judgements on the success or failure of a life in the fullest ethical sense. Against such a background, 'action' is no loose or empty term for whatever may occur in a play, but a way of denoting tragedy's encompassment of the significant goals of life.

Once Ar. has asserted his priorities regarding action and character, he can deal increasingly briskly with the remaining parts of tragedy. His isolation of 'thought' as a separable poetic element needs to be seen in the light of Greek tragedy's pervasive techniques of rhetorical exposition and argument. When Ar. later (in ch. 19) comes to consider thought's place in tragedy, he says little more about it than here in ch. 6, and he relegates the study of it precisely to his 'discourses on rhetoric'. That later passage indicates that 'thought' is the sphere of the *'internal'* rhetoric of tragedy, the rhetoric used by the characters to explain, defend or justify themselves, or to state their attitudes to one another.

It is therefore not surprising that ch. 6 gives two hints of a potentially close relation between thought and character: first, in the statement that the agents are to be characterised 'in both their character and their thought'; secondly, in the reference to the 'political vein' of thought in early tragedy, where the phrase denotes morality in the public or social sphere. Again, ch. 6 more than once implies, in a way which is wholly consistent with Greek tragic practice, that characterisation will readily take the form of the set or formal speech, thus inevitably working in close connection with the rhetorical thought which represents the expository, argumentative and persuasive techniques used in such speeches.

It is necessary, therefore, to keep Ar.'s category of 'thought' wholly apart from the sense in which this word is sometimes applied by modern critics to the controlling ideas of a dramatic work. The 'thought' of the *Poetics* is not at all that of the poet himself, a concept which Ar. positively eschews. Ch. 19 draws an analogy, but also a contrast, between the rhetoric of dramatic speeches and the techniques employed by the playwright in building certain effects into his plot-structure. One implication of that later passage is that while we recognise the thought of the speeches as the intentional discourse of the individual agents, the effects of the play's design and organisation involve a response to the actions and events themselves, not to a level of 'thought' which is communicated through them: the poet-dramatist's thinking is realised in, but also effaced by, the design of the plot's structure of action. There is, then, here a pointer to the Aristotelian view of poetic impersonality which I shall say more about in connection with ch. 24.[7]

The fact that Ar. restricts his initial comments on three of the components of tragedy (style, lyric poetry, spectacle) to just the last few sentences of ch. 6 ought largely to speak for itself. We have here a symptom of some of the major shortcomings of the *Poetics*, as well as a negative reflection of Ar.'s extreme preoccupation with the 'soul' of tragedy, plot-structure. On the style of the spoken poetry of tragedy Ar. will, it is true, later have a good deal to say (ch. 22), but from a nonetheless narrow point of view. The fact is that he attaches relatively slight importance to the verbal texture and detail of tragedy (or any other poetry), and this must be in part regarded as a mark of his particular sensibility, which finds the stylistic level greatly inferior to that of poetic substance and design considered in wider terms.

This same point carries over to Ar.'s neglect of the lyric aspects of tragedy, which is even more acute: it will become apparent at the end of ch. 18 that his theory does not allow for a distinctive or independent function for lyric poetry in drama, and this can be judged to be perhaps the highest price to be paid for the singlemindedness of his poetic principles. Ar.'s poet simply is not conceived as essentially a verbal artist, a special user of language.

Finally, on the place of spectacle at the bottom of the ranking of poetic elements, I have already suggested that Ar.'s position is somewhat equivocal. In fact, the evidence of the treatise as a whole suggests that there is a tension between two impulses or points of view. On the one side, there is a strong urge to separate drama (as poetic structure) from any necessary embodiment in theatrical production. On the other, we find a recurring acknowledgement of the potentially enhancing role of the visual in the final realisation of the playwright's aims (see esp. chs. 14, 17 and 24). Ar.'s views on this matter are more complex than is often recognised.[8] Certainly he should not be condemned as simply insensitive to the theatre, but equally we cannot ignore his relative reluctance to discuss drama in close relation to

---

[7] Ar.'s concept of 'thought' should be contrasted with that found, for example, at Plato *Ion* 530c, where it is directly identified with authorial assertion.

[8] This complexity lends no credibility, however, to the extraordinary claim of Potts, *Aristotle on the Art of Fiction* p. 68, that for Ar. a dramatic poem is 'the whole performance'.

performance. By Ar.'s own day, tragic poets at Athens probably had less control over productions of their plays than ever before, and it is against this background that his dilemma between tragedy as self-sufficient poetry, and tragedy as theatre, should be interpreted.

Ch. 7

Ar. now embarks on one of the most important and exacting sections of his argument. In expounding his criteria of form, scale and unity in poetry, he allows us to see the way in which his thinking about the art rests on the foundations of a wider philosophical system.

At least three major tendencies can be identified in the history of attitudes to unity in poetry (and to art more generally). The first can be called 'formalist', and comprises many of those approaches which define properties such as proportion, balance, harmony and beauty entirely in terms of intrinsic features of the work of art. Secondly, there are those views which I would categorise as belonging to the neo-platonic tradition of thought, and which see in form some intimation of a metaphysical level of reality: the unity which the work of art exhibits is treated, on this assumption, as expressive of a sphere of being beyond the world of the senses. This tradition of ideas is now most familiar from certain Romantic notions of *organic* unity, which can be shown to stem from a philosophical view of the unity of matter and spirit.[1] Finally, there is a more diffuse range of pragmatic views which regard unity as a precondition for, but not necessarily a central part of, artistic success and effectiveness, and which employ variable criteria that are adapted to the nature of individual genres or works.

The canon of form and unity set out in the *Poetics* does not fall neatly into any of these categories. It has equally little in common with both the metaphysical and the pragmatic views of unity, and while it has often been read as advocating a formalist doctrine, that is to overlook the ways in which Ar.'s argument refers inescapably to the cognisable structure of the human action portrayed in a plot-structure. This will become clearer in

---

[1] See J. Benziger, 'Organic Unity: Leibniz to Coleridge', *Publications of the Modern Language Association of America* 66 (1951) 24-48. The neo-platonic roots of this tradition lie in such seminal passages as Plotinus *Enneads* 5.8.2.

ch. 8, where we are told that a unified mimetic work is one which represents a *unitary object*. But within ch. 7 we can observe how the dramatic logic and coherence of a tragedy are taken to be embodied in the organisation of events portrayed in the work: a unified tragedy dramatises a connected sequence of actions which lead to a single, sharply focussed conclusion. The sense of what will make a fitting 'beginning, middle and end', therefore, cannot be separated from the understanding of what is entailed in the causation and motivation of the dramatic action itself. Unity, in other words, is tied to the requirements of mimesis – the portrayal of a possible reality – and appreciation of unity (and hence of poetic beauty) is part of the perception of a work's mimetic or representational content.

The point is confirmed by Ar.'s famous reference to *natural* unity and beauty. This is not something which the philosopher supposes that we intuit or grasp by a kind of pure act of sense-perception (as some later aesthetic theories would maintain); it depends, rather, on the comprehension of the purpose or function which gives significance to a creature's form – which sees an end or *telos* in the form. So the fact that Ar.'s view of nature is teleological should enable us to interpret his analogy correctly, and thereby to see the more clearly that his theory of artistic form does not depend on abstract standards of scale and proportion. A poetic plot-structure is required to have a certain magnitude and a certain organisation of parts, in order that we can hold together and understand the chain of events which it dramatises.

But in addition to seeing Ar.'s concept of unity as an exemplification of his teleological approach to phenomena, we can also connect it with his deep interest in logic. This is, in fact, a prominent implication of the very terminology which is introduced in this chapter, and thereafter used repeatedly, to indicate the standards of coherence which he demands of a plot-structure. The phrase 'probability or necessity' invokes criteria which appear often in the philosopher's analysis of logical relations between propositions in a syllogism or other argument. 'Probability' signifies a degree of likelihood or plausibility which Ar. elsewhere connects with things that hold true 'for the most part'; while 'necessity' (which in the *Poetics*, incidentally, has nothing to do with ideas of the force of destiny) refers to complete certainty or inevitability, whether in a logical argument or in a relation between events. So the causal or explanatory significance of a dramatic sequence of action is analogous, by Ar.'s way of thinking, to the degree of cogency obtaining between the elements of a connected argument.[2]

The importance of this point, confirmed as I have said by the repeated appeal to probability and necessity in subsequent chapters, is to establish a clear association in Ar.'s theory of poetry between unity and *intelligibility*. The coherence of tragic plot-structure is presented not as a matter of clarity of framework (which is what the neo-classical Unities tended to make of it) but of clarity in the very substance of the drama – in its pattern of action. Ar. will later expand on this aspect of his theory by linking probability and necessity with the doctrine of poetic universals (ch. 9), and that link will only serve to corroborate the argument I have put for the inseparability of unity and poetic significance.

In summing up his judgement on tragic unity, Ar. ties the appropriate scale of a play to the kind of action which is distinctive of the genre. In doing so, he mentions for the first time the key idea of a tragic transformation or change of fortune (*metabasis*). This idea was not included in the definition of tragedy, though Ar. would probably consider it to be effectively implied there, or at least provided for, by the tragic emotions, pity and fear. There was, in any case, nothing either original or contentious in the association of tragedy with great changes of fortune; the association derives directly from the nature of the mythical material traditionally used by the tragedians, and it can be found in other authors than Ar.[3]

What we do, however, need to register at once is the firm connection which Ar. makes between a tragic transformation and his criteria of poetic unity. Since these criteria involve intelligibility in the causal structure of the action, Ar. is unequivocally prescribing that tragedy should dramatise pitiful

---

[2] It is curious that Ar. should repeatedly mention necessity in the *Poetics*, since he elsewhere states that few things in the human world can be seen as truly necessary. I take the essential point to be that Ar. wishes the links in a plot-structure to be as causally tight as possible, and the reference to necessity stresses this. Cf. p.107.

[3] Tragedy itself contains many reflections on the nature of transformations: for pertinent examples from the *Iphigeneia in Tauris* see lines 721f., 1120-22. Cf. also e.g. Plato *Republic* 10.603c-e, Isocrates 9.70.

and fearful swings of fortune, *and yet* make them explicable. There is here, in other words, the first clear sign of a rationalising view of tragedy which ought immediately to provoke the question of whether, or how, Ar.'s theory can cope with the darker side of the genre's characteristic material, and in particular with the interpenetration of human and divine causation which is one of the marks of traditional Greek mythology. This question will have soon to be pursued further.

Ch. 8

Ar. now explains what unity does *not* entail. Although his principal target here seems to be epic poems of the kind telling the life-story of an individual hero, it is possible that he also has the views of certain critics in mind (cf. 'as some believe'). His remarks in any case have implications for tragedy. Later, in ch. 13, he appears to assume that the ideal play will centre on an individual, though in ch. 14 he thinks more in terms of the bonds between two or more characters in a tragedy. The present chapter establishes that Ar. does not *require* a work to have a central character, though he obviously has good reason in the nature of Greek myth for his later belief that many of the finest plays do possess one. The essential point is this: whether in epic or tragedy, the action, not the individual character, is the primary consideration; and if many tragic myths lend themselves to construction around a prominent hero, that does not show that such a figure *per se* lends unity to a work.[1]

Ar.'s clarity of insight on this point, and its connection with the recognition of Homer's artistic selectivity in his treatment of myth, is all the more impressive when we compare it with the confusions sometimes apparent in the modern criticism of Greek tragedy. Two of Sophocles' plays, the *Ajax* and *Antigone*, for example, have repeatedly provoked debates about unity which

---

[1] A poem built around a character, but lacking a unifying action, would be subject to the strictures made more generally on actionless characterisation in ch. 6 (p.38). This view is explained by Ar.'s philosophy of action, on which I commented in connection with that earlier passage; but it does mean that Ar. is not open to the possibility of tragedy whose locus lies in an individual's consciousness, even though it is arguable that Greek poets (above all, Homer in *Iliad* 9 and Sophocles' *Ajax*, in the hero's great speeches (646ff., 815ff.)) sometimes do portray such tragic consciousness (albeit within a larger dramatic framework).

have far too often presupposed an equation between unity of action and the existence of a central character. Many critics have found it a problem that Ajax's suicide should occur halfway through the play named after him, leaving the rest of the play without the living presence of the 'tragic hero'; and this has sometimes been judged as an impairment of unity. Even more critics have altercated over whether Antigone or Creon should be deemed the major character in *Antigone.*

Ar. can help us to see the futility of, and the false premise behind, such arguments. Both works can unequivocally be said to possess unity of *action*, residing in the dramatisation of a coherent arc of tragic myth: in each case, Ar.'s idea of 'wholeness' (beginning-middle-end) can be applied so as to show how an integrated set of actions and events develops to its completion, to the point at which the issues have been resolved. The lack of a single, central character dominating every scene of the play surely is, as Ar.'s position implies, of no direct bearing on the question of unity. Similarly, the unity of the *Iliad* around the theme or action of the wrath of Achilles is none the weaker for the fact that Achilles' own appearances are limited to certain crucial scenes of the poem. Conversely, a work dominated by a single hero but lacking a unitary action would be regarded by Ar. as inevitably 'episodic', a term which is introduced in chs. 9 and 10.

It must be said that Ar.'s notion of unity of action suits particularly well the concentrated focus characteristic of Greek tragedy, a genre which isolates junctures of climactic significance from the larger blocks of myth to which they belong. But unity of action can hardly be satisfactorily universalised into a canon for all forms of Greek poetry, still less for the poetry of other times and places. Even epic may require a less strict and more generous sense of unity, as Ar. seems to acknowledge in ch. 24 (only to equivocate on the point in ch. 26: see p.183 below). and it is difficult to see how unity of action could be at all readily applicable to many types of lyric poetry, where coherence of effect is more likely to be a matter of emotion, thought, thematic association, or even of tone. But the fact is that Ar. seems uninterested in non-dramatic forms of poetry, as I have already emphasised (p.74), and he therefore sees no need to consider alternative poetic resources of unity.

Ch. 8 makes it clear that Ar. considers artistic unity in general to be something which the artist must incorporate in his work, not something which he finds ready-made in the world. Much of what happens in the world does not possess intrinsic unity of the kind which would conform to Ar.'s standards: that is why it is insufficient to dramatise the life of a particular individual. This point will tie up with the distinction drawn in the next chapter between history, which is a matter of contingent and often incoherent events, and the structures of universals which poetry is capable of dramatising. So it becomes gradually clear that poetic mimesis is certainly not, for Ar., a matter of direct realism. Poetry must somehow make more sense than much of the raw material of life does, and this higher intelligibility is part and parcel of what Ar. understands by unity.

But such unity is not a matter only of aesthetic or artistic organisation, since Ar. takes the unity of the work of art to depend on the unity of the object represented, and it is probably the latter which he understands to be primary in our perception of art: when we see or read a unified tragedy, it is the inner coherence, and hence the intelligibility, of the action which we recognise and respond to. Successfully unified works of art therefore, on Ar.'s premises, allow us to experience images of a fictional reality ('events which *could* occur', ch. 9) which has a more lucid or transparent significance than we can readily find in the world around us. The implications of this position must be pursued into the reading of ch. 9, which leads on explicitly from the remarks on unity in the two preceding chapters.

But some difficult aspects of the concept of unity must first be explored a little further. At the end of his discussion of linguistic units in ch. 20, Ar. explains that a proposition can be unitary either by signifying a single concept, or by connecting several elements; and he refers to the *Iliad* as an example of the latter. The term which is used for the first of these kinds of unity is the same as that found in ch. 8's principle that 'a unitary mimesis is a representation of a unitary object': in both cases, Ar. speaks of the content (of proposition/mimesis) as literally 'one thing'. This should alert us to a crucial, but little noticed, ambiguity in his attitude towards unity of poetic plot-structure. In ch. 8 a unified plot is said to portray a *single* action, but if taken literally this would make a tragedy into something like a proposition signifying one thing, rather than, as ch. 20 suggests for the *Iliad*, a cohesive structure of parts. But there is no doubt that a dramatic work must fall into this latter category; the whole of the analysis of tragedy presupposes an organisation of parts into a unified design, and ch. 7 has explicitly linked beauty and unity to the ordered arrangement of components.

If we ask, then, whether a plot-structure portrays 'one thing' or more than one, the answer must be: both, depending on how these terms are interpreted. Ar. regards true artistic unity as yielding an essentially single object (in poetry's case, a single action) for our contemplation, but at the same time residing in a complete cohesion of several parts. A plot-structure contains both several, individual actions, and one composite or total 'action' (see the opening of ch. 8). This ambiguity is reflected in Ar.'s original use of the same term, *praxis*, for the separate actions and the total action. Once the ambiguity is recognised, we can start to see why there must ultimately be an arbitrary aspect to judgements on unity of action, as, for example, in the final adjudication between tragedy and epic (ch. 26). It may be possible to agree that unity of action is desirable, without committing oneself to a fixed notion of what will satisfy this requirement.

For Ar., unity will be fully satisfied only by action which is both single and whole – that is, which forms a structure of events leading up to, and completed by, a single end (*telos*). This conception has great positive merits in appropriate application. Applied to Sophocles' *Ajax*, for example, which I mentioned earlier, it can help us to formulate a crucial fact about the play and its action: the death of Ajax, though central to the drama, cannot stand as an end to it, since it naturally leads on (in the sense of Ar.'s 'middle') to the question of how the Greeks will treat the dead hero (a fundamental question for the heroic world). Only when this question has been dramatised and answered, have we the completed action which calls for nothing further. In a case such as this, then, Ar.'s understanding of wholeness of action formulates something which is attuned to some of the finest dramatic practice.

But if this vindicates the criterion of wholeness, it does not establish the need for *singleness* of action. This point will reappear in connection with Ar.'s final verdict that the Homeric poems, though supreme within the possibilities of epic, do not achieve the purity of structure which the greatest tragedies do (see ch. 26). Ar.'s theory similarly cannot allow that a play with a double action could ever be as artistically effective as one with a single (cf. ch. 13, p.45). The reason for this clearly lies at a very deep level in the philosopher's outlook.

Ch. 9

Ar.'s observations on unity lead to the inference, at the start of ch. 9, that poetry should deal with possible and probable, not actual, events; and ch. 9 goes on to elaborate the famous claim that poetry's material approximates to the status of 'universals'. This chapter has often rightly been regarded as central to the treatise's thinking. It shows us Ar. applying his philosophical intelligence to the formulation of some of his clearest and most fundamental insights into the status of poetry. But it is also, for this same reason, a particularly abstract piece of reasoning, and it calls for patient consideration.

How, first of all, does the line of argument proceed from unity to universals? Unity, we have seen, entails a kind of cohesive 'logic' in the sequence of action dramatised by a tragedy; each link in the dramatic chain must be firmly interlocked with what precedes and follows it, and the limits of this structure (the beginning and end) must be bounded in a way which does not require us to move outside them in order to understand the internal significance of the action. We have also seen that Ar. contrasts such unity with the frequently disconnected or discrete episodes in an individual life. Ch. 9 draws this contrast again, now using history (a comprehensive category for all actual and particular events) to represent the contrary of the ideal of a unified poetic action. It is not that life or history *cannot* furnish coherent structures of action, but just that they do not regularly do so, according to Ar. (though most historical writing is based on an implicit rejection of this premise). So the poet may sometimes be able to find historical material for a tragedy or other poem (as Aeschylus had done in his *Persians*) but he will not usually be able to. This means that he will have to turn to possible or imaginary actions – things that could plausibly occur, but are not known to have done so.[1]

---

[1] When Ar. refers to poets holding 'to the actual names' (where the Greek wording reproduces the phrase already used for historical events), he seems to spoil his history/fiction dichotomy by implying that traditional myths themselves incorporate *historical* details; and the following parenthesis apparently reinforces this. My view on this controversial passage is that Ar. is

From here Ar. moves, then, to the idea that poetry's content comes close to the status of universals. These are the general categories and concepts used to understand and describe the world, but the connection between the fictional and the quasi-universal significance of poetic content remains difficult. In the Renaissance the view was sometimes held that poetry is, in the words of Francis Bacon, 'nothing else but *feigned history*',[2] and it would be possible to interpret this to mean that poetry's material consists of fictional particulars. Ar. does not deny that poetry portrays ostensible particulars: what he says in ch. 9 about 'particular names' could be extended to other details too, and it implies that the fabric of poetry offers an apparent or immediate world of particular people and events.

So every dramatic character and action *could* be treated as a (fictional or invented) particular. To modern readers, used to the conventions of the novel as well as to forms of highly realistic drama, it may seem especially important to ask why Ar. is not content with the view of poetry as 'feigned history', or an imaginative representation of the particularities which we experience in life itself. Clearly it is not enough (though it is true) to say that universals are for the philosopher more closely related to knowledge: Ar. believes that true knowledge and understanding only begin when we move beyond discrete particulars and begin to grasp universals. But that still does not tell us why he wishes or is prepared to attribute something of the power of universals to poetic art. The answer lies not just in the concept of unity, but more especially in the basic criteria of unity – namely, probability or necessity.

Probability and necessity were first mentioned in the final sentence of ch. 7, and they thereafter recur frequently in the *Poetics* to indicate the standards applied to the internal coherence of a poem. Probability represents a general criterion of regularity which falls short of invariability – Ar. is fond of explaining it in terms of things which happen or hold 'for the most part'. Necessity simply is the invariable – that which happens 'always'. (Necessity in the *Poetics*, incidentally, has

---

referring to, but without meaning to accept, the common Greek belief that traditional stories such as the Trojan War did indeed preserve historical events.

[2] *Advancement of Learning*, Bk. 2, IV.1.

nothing whatever to do with tragic *destiny* or inevitability, as is occasionally supposed.) So 'probability' stands for general human realities and conditions of existence, 'necessity' for the extreme case of such general validity, i.e. the truly universal.

It is curious in fact that Ar. should invoke necessity at all in this context, since he elsewhere admits that little or nothing in the sphere of human conduct can be referred to it. The reason must be that the phrase 'probability or necessity' (sometimes inverted) helps to emphasise his requirement of as tight and intelligible a causal sequence as possible in the plot-structure of a poem. Take, for example, the case of Sophocles' Oedipus, when confronted with someone (the Corinthian herdsman) who has the key to his identity. Despite the attempt of Jocasta to dissuade him from proceeding, the likelihood that a man of Oedipus' character in such a position will press on to full discovery of the truth, is so strong that Ar. might have considered it a virtual 'necessity' – something we would expect universally in such a context. But in practice probability is clearly of more use and relevance to the critic of literature, standing as it does for a sense of plausibility or credibility more widely applicable to human action and its springs.

Now Ar. has posited causal or explanatory lucidity as a prime requirement for an effective tragedy, so that all its constituent elements (its actions and characters) will be not only individually believable, but also comprehensible as parts of a unified totality. Such lucidity, and the unity which goes with it, requires the criteria of 'probability or necessity', and these bring with them an implicit appeal to *universals*. According to Ar., we make sense of poetic fictions by interpreting them in the light of the general or universal concepts derived from our cumulative experience and understanding of human life. Because this experience rests ultimately on actual particulars in the world, Ar. would not deny that we frequently employ universals (or, at least, probability) in our cognitive response to real events. But what he does deny, in *Poetics* 8 and 9, is that raw life can often produce whole structures of action capable of satisfying probability in an entirely unified fashion. So in contemplating poetry (or other works of mimetic art) we draw on our real experience of the world, but we do so in order to understand events which possess a special degree of coherence and, therefore, significance.

It remains open to someone, of course, to reject this Aristotelian argument, and to contend that art presents us only with a simulation of the particulars which we meet with in the world. But we can say that, for Ar., to believe that poetry offers no more than fictional particulars is to deprive it of any true meaning: once taken in this way, a work of art is open to the simple objection that its contents are, by definition, *false* (otherwise, we could treat it as history or some other form of factual discourse). We shall see later (ch. 25) that precisely this objection was brought against poetry by some Greeks, and that Ar.'s interpretation of the status of mimetic works was designed to counter it. The *Poetics* contends that it is only when we cease to regard mimesis as simply matching or reproducing some definite and individual reality, and instead respond to it as an embodiment of factors of more general validity in the human world, that we can do justice to its significance.

The formulations in ch. 9 cannot simply be taken over and applied as permanent truths about poetry; but we can at least treat them as one of the first major attempts to grapple with issues which have repeatedly concerned later critics and theorists, as well as artists. It is telling, for example, that even a movement such as nineteenth-century naturalism, which brought with it an often meticulous concern with the presentation of life-like particulars, rested in origin on certain convictions about the universal conditions and determinants of human existence: the extreme particularity of artistic fabric was believed to mediate an insight into larger, non-particular truths. It is perhaps only with the most concerted attempts (as with some modes of the Absurd) to dissolve the very possibility of reading general significance into the lives of men, that the basic sense of artistic universals comes under threat.

Ch. 9 of the *Poetics* contains, then, an important doctrine of poetic universality, which addresses itself to basic questions about both the status of artistic works and our cognitive experience of them. But it is essential to stress that Ar.'s doctrine has nothing to do with *abstraction* – or, to put the point more pragmatically, that it says nothing about the degree of realistic or particular detail which is desirable in poetry or art. Ch. 4 refers, in fact, to the keen pleasure which we take in contemplating 'the most precise images' even of intrinsically unpleasant objects; and there are various passages in the treatise (esp. ch. 17) which place explicit value on dramatic vividness. There is, consequently, nothing inhospitable in Ar.'s position towards an interest in the kinds of artistic effectiveness which derive from specificity, (though that is not to say that either the *Poetics* or the types of Greek literature with which it is primarily concerned show anything comparable to the concern of much modern literature with particularity and subjectivity).

Nor, conversely, should *Poetics* 9 be read, as it often was by neo-classicists, as containing a doctrine of the role of the typical in poetry's portrayals of reality. Such an emphasis on verisimilitude or *vraisemblance* must be carefully distinguished from Ar.'s position: verisimilitude, at least on a common interpretation of the concept, can be satisfied by a convincing simulation of particulars. Besides, any simple artistic concern with norms or typical standards of human reality can hardly be reconciled with Ar.'s view of tragedy and epic as genres portraying men 'better than us', or of comedy as a representation of men 'worse than us' (ch. 2 etc.). What Ar. requires, by probability and necessity, is not the direct reproduction of any one type of reality, but something more like an underlying correspondence to the general concepts and truths which we derive from experience of the world. *Poetics* 9 should be seen above all as a serious response to Plato's devaluation of poetic 'falsehood': Ar. restores poetry's respectability by recognising that its fictions can, through the preferably dramatic presentation of action and character, entail significance which has a kinship with the mode of understanding employed by the philosopher (who, for Ar. as for Plato, has supreme access to truth and wisdom).

It is difficult, however, for many modern readers of the *Poetics* to accept the qualification that must now be added. Ar. is not prepared to attribute to the poet himself any special insight into the nature of things, and he does not conceive of the dramatic content of a poem as in any strong sense representing the poet's own ideas or vision (see p.171 below). The poet does not treat universals in the way in which the philosopher does, as the immediate subject of a discourse whose purpose is the attainment of truth. Universals are implicit in poetic drama, but they are not there as a subject for assertion or firm belief. We need, in other words, to put ch. 9 in the larger perspective supplied by the notion of mimesis. If we do so, it becomes undesirable to reduce Ar.'s doctrine to a simple formulation. Plato (like many others) had treated poetry as directly *affirmative*; Ar. moves towards a sense of poetic discourse as non-affirmative yet still in touch with reality through the power of its mimetic nature to embody universals. So poetry is 'more philosophical' than history in that its materials are not just pseudo-occurrences ('feigned history', in Bacon's phrase) but can be interpreted as approximating to universals. At the same time, however, these universals are the stuff of fiction, and their status is intrinsically that of the possible not the actual.

Ar.'s comments on the quasi-philosophical nature of poetry should not, then, be inflated into a grand claim of gravity and deep truth for the poet's art, and the function of universals should not be translated into the terms of artistic idealism. It is a later tradition, stemming from neo-platonism, which turns art into a vehicle for transcendent ideals, and it is this tradition which leads to such Romantic documents as Shelley's *Defence of Poetry*, in which poetry is associated with 'ideal perfection' and 'eternal truth'. As I pointed out in my Introduction (p.23) some Romantics tried hard to assimilate the *Poetics* to this type of belief, but this is not seriously possible. We can note, for example, that Ar. finds in contemporary comedy a clear illustration of his point in ch. 9: this shows that his chief concern is not to claim great portentousness for poetic universals, but only to distinguish them from the individual particulars with which history has to deal. In the sort of comedy which he has in mind, the names of characters are not meant to signify a strong individuality, for the characters themselves, and their actions, demonstrate that the drama is constructed in terms of probability: the ostensible uniqueness of the stage-figures, in other words, does not disguise the fact that we understand their behaviour and experiences on the level of general or universal categories.

It is into constructing just such dramatic material that Ar.'s playwright is expected to put his energies, for it is the fictional framework of a poem, *not its verbal texture*, which marks its essential poetic nature. This bears out the priorities established in ch. 6, and confirms Ar.'s relatively low regard for the poet's use of language as such. This point will have to be pursued further in connection with chs. 20-22.

Towards the end of ch. 9 we meet a short, and possibly

misplaced, section on 'episodic' plots. It is worth pointing out here that Ar.'s attitude to episodes is significantly ambiguous. On the one hand, episodes are accepted as the basic dramatic divisions (the 'scenes') of both tragedy and epic: this is so, not only in the definition of 'episode' in ch. 12, but also in ch. 4 (the growth in tragedy's 'number of episodes') and at the end of ch. 18. On the other hand, episodes can be regarded as expansions of, or even digressions from, the central action of a poem (chs. 17 twice, 23 and 24), and it is this sense which allows the adjective 'episodic' to carry the derogatory sense that ch. 9 presents us with. This variation is perfectly understandable as a matter of general usage, but its appearance in the *Poetics* can nonetheless be related to the uncertainty which I earlier diagnosed in the criteria for unity of plot-structure (p.103). It is unclear to what extent Ar. is prepared to allow an independent and enriching function to episodes, or whether, to be justified in the terms of his theory, they must bear directly on the central action. This uncertainty reflects, I think, the tension between the idea of *singleness* of action, and the more inclusive conception of plot as an integrated structure of parts.

The final point of importance in ch. 9 is the observation that a specifically tragic drama can best arouse a sense of wonder, and also the tragic emotions of pity and fear, by paradoxical but nonetheless causally coherent events. We can get a glimpse here of one of the points at which Ar.'s understanding of unity does come under some strain. As a general doctrine of dramatic 'logic', the view of unity which chs. 7 and 8 set forth has obvious enough merits. But by equating unity of plot-structure with unity of action, Ar. presupposes that poetic drama can always afford to present an internally perspicuous and intelligible sequence of events.

Tragedy can pose a challenge for such an assumption by dealing with obscure events whose underlying causes may not be accessible to our ordinary powers of comprehension. Ar. recognises in this passage that the genre has a particular need for remarkable and disturbing dramatic materials, but he is unwilling to compromise on his standards of unity and coherence of action. The 'sense of wonder' to which he refers is an experience which startles and challenges our capacity to understand what we witness in a play, but it is not one which allows for a deep or final inscrutability: wonder must give way to a recognition of how things do after all cohere through 'probability or necessity'.[3]

Critics have sometimes been misled by the reference to 'the arbitrary or fortuitous' into supposing Ar.'s point to be simpler than it really is. If all that were excluded could be covered by these terms, then no immediate objection would be called for. But Greek tragedy still leaves us with the whole realm of divine involvement in the causation and explanation of human events, and it is Ar.'s attitude towards *this* which remains in doubt. It is true that this passage in itself might be taken to allow for religious ideas of the kind in question: events arousing wonder will fall into place, perhaps, once the divine element in them is revealed or understood. But elsewhere Ar. baulks at divine interventions in poetic drama (see p.48), and the summary of *Iphigeneia in Tauris* in ch. 17 suggests that he is prepared to reinterpret existing plays, where possible, in such a way as to minimise their religious dimension.

Ch. 10

The fact that Ar. only now introduces the distinction between simple and complex plot-structures suggests that the reference to the former towards the end of ch. 9 may have become misplaced: the two passages can at any rate be taken together here.

The way in which Ar. explains the terms 'simple' and 'complex' suggests that they were not well established in critical usage. Certainly they are so well integrated into Ar.'s theory as to make it hard to imagine their being used in quite this way within the wider culture of the Athenian theatre. They are best regarded, then, as distinctively Aristotelian ideas which clarify the possible patterns and dynamics of tragic plot-structure. Moreover, it is directly stated that simple and complex plot-types are not just a matter of dramaturgical artifice or technique; their defining characteristics are those of the actions

---

[3] 'Wonder' appears as a motif in tragedy itself, as, to take a pertinent example, at the climax of the recognition scene in Euripides' *Iphigeneia in Tauris*, 839f. ('these things are beyond wonder ...'). But the implications of such a context serve to reinforce the idea that whereas Ar.'s wonder stems from things which happen unexpectedly 'yet still on account of one another', the wonder that arises in the world of tragedy may carry us into a sphere of causation that lies beyond the human.

which they represent. So we receive further corroboration of the
basic fact that Ar.'s ideas on poetic form are grounded in the
sense of mimesis's capacity to handle certain patterns of possible
reality.

Both simple and complex dramas have in common the basic
requirements of wholeness and unity, as already set out; as
tragedies, they must also, Ar. assumes (cf. the last sentence of
ch. 7), lead up to a 'transformation' or change of fortune. This
last point is especially important, as it has so often been
confused: Addison, for example, wrongly defined a simple plot as
one lacking a change of fortune, in contrast to what he, as later
Johnson, called the 'implex' type.[1] Ar. in fact makes it clear that
every tragedy requires a change of fortune, a drastic
transformation in the life of the agent(s). But 'reversal'
(*peripeteia*) involves a specific swing in the direction of events,
and is a particular device and feature of the complex plot (see ch.
11). Where the simple and complex differ is in the precise
handling of the transformation, which can be either part of a
unilinear development (the simple plot) or the climax of a play
which hinges around nodal moments of tragic revelation and
paradox (the complex).

It is worth trying to combine the brief definitions of ch. 10 with
the opening section of ch. 18, where Ar. again mentions simple
and complex plots, but also puts them in a larger scheme of
plot-types, and offers a new pair of structural terms,
'complication' and 'dénouement', for the analysis of all
tragedies. The relation between these latter terms and the
simple-complex distinction is curious, since Ar.'s word for
'complex' and one of his words for 'complication' are indeed
etymologically cognate. I suggest that the connection is as
follows. In ch. 18 the complication is said to consist of 'events
outside the play, and often some of those within it'. This implies,
when put together with ch. 10, that the complication of a 'simple'
tragedy is likely to lie entirely in the events which precede the
starting-point of the play itself: thus the enacted drama will
represent a resolution or completion of a process whose direction
has already been fully determined; the entire play will consist of

---

[1] 'Implex' appears in *Spectator* no. 297, Feb. 9, 1712, borrowed, it seems, from
the French classicist, Dacier.

'dénouement'.[2] The complex tragedy, by contrast, contains both a section of 'complication' (though this may have its origin in events before the the opening of the play) and a dénouement which is mediated through the special characteristics of the type, namely recognition and reversal. So the relation between the structural terminology of chs. 10 and 18 can be indicated schematically by a diagram:

EARLIER EVENTS	*THE ACTION OF THE PLAY*
simple: complication	*dénouement* ....
complex: complication	*dénouement* ....
	(incorporating reversal & recognition)

If this is right, then we can see that what primarily separates the simple and complex plot-structure in Ar.'s thinking is that the complex shows us, and builds a context around, the decisive (and paradoxical) twist which forms the hinge of the tragedy, while the simple dramatises the final part of a sequence of events which have already, by the start of the play, reached the point of their tragic resolution. Certainly it is possible to draw some such broad distinction between Greek tragedies. In a work such as Euripides' *Trojan Women* the poet is concerned with the final stages of an action (the Trojan War, and more particularly the fall of Troy) whose development and direction have already been decisively determined; we are already *within* a tragic dénouement when the play opens in the camp of the prisoners-of-war, and what follows can bring only, so to speak, further working out of the tragic implications, rather than the discovery of any new tragedy: an episode such as the killing of Astyanax is part of a proceeding resolution (the crushing and humiliation of the Trojans, the moral barbarity of the Greeks) not an independent tragic action. Sophocles' *Antigone*, on the other hand, though it begins against a background of existing

---

[2] Ar.'s 'dénouement' (*lusis*) thus has a wider sense than the French word (which was originally used as a literal translation of Ar.'s term) has come to have. In this whole area, much of Ar.'s terminology has become common in dramatic criticism, but without the original framework of distinctions. The process can be seen at work, for example, in a phrase such as Dryden's 'the discovery or unravelling of the plot' (*op.cit.* (Introduction n.24) p. 31), which runs together what in Ar. are the separate ideas of recognition and dénouement.

tragedy, focusses on a new phase of tragic action at Thebes, and can be brought within Ar.'s category of complex tragedy for its use (in Creon's case) of recognition and reversal.

But it remains to ask how useful or important these distinctions, with their structural classifications, really are. About the particular features of complex tragedy more will be said *à propos* of ch. 11, but it can at least be observed at once that this concept, which formulates an idea of the potency of tragic revelation, does correspond to a major and recurring pattern of dramatic organisation to be found in epic (see ch. 23) as well as in tragedy. What seems to matter most to Ar. is that the complex type incorporates within the action of the play the moments of most intense emotional force (see ch. 6 p.38) – the moments at which the nature of the tragedy is uncovered by those most affected by it. 'Simple' plot-structures are, however, defined in largely negative terms by Ar., and it is therefore hard to see how the category could be given much critical value as a means of fixing attention on significant elements of dramatic design, though it clearly remains a fact of general importance about Greek tragedy that many plays begin after the critical determinants of the tragedy have already occurred.

A further problem is that the simple-complex distinction is not always as straightforward in practice as in theory.[3] Aeschylus' *Persians*, for example, can from one point of view be classified as 'simple', since the dramatic construction is unilinear and ostensibly lacking in recognition or reversal. Yet, in a sense, these latter elements are brought into the play in the form of components in the events which have happened before the start of the play, but which impinge on it through being reported by the messenger: Xerxes' reversal (the confident Persian attack turned to disaster), and his recognition of tragic miscalculation, are at any rate forcefully communicated to us, if not wholly realised in the dramatic present, by the messenger's description of events at Salamis, and Xerxes' reaction to them.

This point in fact reflects a larger doubt about Ar.'s understanding of a dramatic action: is the action limited to what happens within the temporal and spatial limits of the play, or can it encompass reported events too? The importance of the messenger-speech in Greek tragedy is something which Ar. never

---

[3] On this point cf. D. W. Lucas, *Aristotle: Poetics* Appendix III.

acknowledges, even though it can fulfil a function, as in *Persians*, at the very centre and heart of a work.

The two terms later introduced in ch. 18, 'complication' and 'dénouement', do perhaps give us a practical way of observing and discriminating between the various strategies used by poets to produce an individual drama out of a larger block of mythic material. It is interesting, in fact, that this passage from ch. 18 does appear to attribute a greater importance to events outside the drama proper than does the ideal of self-contained unity advanced earlier in the treatise. It is at any rate a question worth asking of virtually any Greek tragedy, how and at just what point the playwright has cut into his myth, and with what consequences for the shaping of the particular portion of it dramatised within his plot. The answers to such a question are likely to take us well beyond a bipartite model of complication and dénouement; but ch. 18's reference to the relation between events inside and outside the plot can at least provoke a critical interest in some of the playwright's procedures of structural selection and focus. I shall argue, however, in my comments on ch. 18 that it can also provoke some uncertainty about the fundamental interpretation of dramatic significance in Ar.'s theory.

Ch. 11

Having distinguished simple and complex plot-patterns, Ar. now concentrates on the latter, in preparation for his argument (in chs. 13 and 14) that the ideal tragedy should be of the complex type.

Reversal (*peripeteia*) and recognition (*anagnôrisis*, sometimes translated 'discovery') are closely linked not just in Ar.'s theory but in their essential implications for tragedy. Both are devices which focus and concentrate a tragic transformation in dramatic moments of ironic or paradoxical force. Reversal entails a complete contradiction of expectation and intention on the part of the agents (and also, to the extent that they sympathise imaginatively, on that of an audience): it therefore presupposes, just as does recognition, a significant element of ignorance at work in the dramatic situation. It is important not to confuse the particular irony of reversal with the much broader idea of a tragic change or transformation. Ar. posits the latter in every tragic plot-structure, but reversal belongs only to the complex type.

Some critics have worried needlessly about whose intentions or expectations must be confounded to produce a reversal, but it is obvious enough from Ar.'s definition that various possibilities are covered by the idea: the crucial factor is that the direction *of the action* is tragically overturned, and gives rise to the very opposite of what it seemed set to produce. Thus a subordinate character may be the instrument or catalyst of a tragic reversal, as with the messenger in the *Oedipus Tyrannus*; but the implications of the reversal must bear, as they here obviously do, on the fortunes, the lives, of the central characters. The *Oedipus Tyrannus* contains two other clear examples of *peripeteia*, in the scenes where the King sends for Teiresias (316ff.) and the Theban shepherd (1110ff.), in both cases with results diametrically opposed to his expectations.

Two earlier passages of the *Poetics* should be recalled in connection with reversal and recognition: the first in ch. 6, where these resources are called 'tragedy's greatest means of emotional power'; and the second in ch. 9, where pity and fear are said to be aroused best by events which 'occur contrary to expectation yet still on account of one another'. This latter passage links the tragic emotions with 'wonder', and the association is confirmed by a passage in Ar.'s *Rhetoric* (1.11.23-4) in which reversals are singled out as especially productive of wonder.

This all clarifies the fact that Ar.'s interest in the features of the complex plot revolves around the exceptional *emotive* power which can be concentrated into moments of recognition and reversal. It is probably only a slight exaggeration to say that Ar. thinks in terms of startling *coups de théâtre* (provided we apply the expression to twists in dramatic action, not to essentially visual effects, which would be covered by the strictures on 'the sensational' in ch. 14). We must remember, however, the qualification in ch. 9 – '... contrary to expectation *yet still* on account of one another'. Wonder elicited by a startling turn of events must, if conformity to the canon of 'probability or necessity' is to be maintained, give way to a realisation of the underlying causation of events.

So, in Ar.'s own example of the *Oedipus Tyrannus*, an immediate sense of fearful alarm at the Corinthian's knowledge of the King's true identity (1008 ff.) may resolve itself into an understanding of the distant, fateful link between these two men. The reversal (which is immediately fulfilled only for Jocasta, and not combined with recognition for Oedipus until the following scene – a fact which Ar.'s remarks telescope) achieves an instantaneously powerful effect on the emotions, but without sacrificing the essential logic of events. Indeed, it is precisely the sudden and paradoxical emergence of a *pattern* connecting the distant past with the present, which gives the movement of events so much of its force. Out of dramatic surprise emerges a further and decisive stage in the unfolding of significant action.

These points apply equally to reversal and recognition, but Ar. seems to acknowledge that the latter is a more adaptable dramatic device. Despite the trio of reversal scenes in the *Oedipus Tyrannus* (see above), multiple recognitions within a single work are perhaps more easily cited: Ar. mentions the double recognition in *Iphigeneia in Tauris*, but he might just as well have noted that in *Oedipus Tyrannus* Jocasta's discovery of the truth precedes Oedipus'; and later, in ch. 24, Ar. tells us that the *Odyssey* uses recognition 'throughout'. It is presumably because of the greater frequency of recognition that Ar. thinks it worth analysing the various types of the device in ch. 16. That analysis, as will be seen, serves to emphasise that with recognition as with reversal Ar.'s concern is that the essential sequence and logic of events should be kept intact. But since the features of the complex plot-structure represent the decisive hinge or crux of a tragic action, it is right to press at this point a question which I have already raised in general about Ar.'s insistence on the criteria of probability and necessity: are these standards of causal or explanatory coherence sufficient to cope with works whose frame of reference often extends beyond the purely human?

The question can be applied to the two plays which Ar. cites most often in support of his theory. In both cases it is certainly possible to trace a causal pattern through the purely human actions and decisions of the play, so that reversal and recognition can on this level be seen as the startling but nonetheless intelligible outcome of the agents' behaviour. This is precisely the kind of reading implied by Ar.'s references to the plays, and he seems clearly satisfied with this rationalistic level of interpretation. But in both the *Oedipus* and the *Iphigeneia* there is a prominent divine context and background to all that is shown in the plays, and we do not have to assume that Ar.'s neglect of it would have been matched by the original audiences of these works.

In ch. 16 we are told that the recognition in the *Oedipus* arises out of the plot-structure in a probable sequence of stages, but Ar. does not mention, here or elsewhere, the timing of the messenger's arrival from Corinth (after Jocasta's prayer to Apollo, the play's dominating divinity) nor the seemingly coincidental fact of this same man's original involvement in the exposure of the infant Oedipus. This last point Ar. would probably call an irrational element 'outside the plot', but such a judgement would only offer a *petitio principii*: can events which impinge on the action of the play really be deemed to be outside the plot (cf. p.150)? The critical factor is that the threads of Oedipus's life are brought together by a conjunction of circumstances that is far from being simply the plausible upshot of actions contained entirely within the play. An analogous argument could be formulated for the *Iphigeneia*, whose whole ethos, arising from the mythological background, strongly resists the peculiar rationalisation of it which Ar. tries to produce in ch. 17.

After defining the particular features of complex plots, Ar. briefly adds to them what he calls a third element of plot-structure – 'suffering' (*pathos*). This tail-piece to the chapter is intriguing not just because of its brevity, but also because its appearance here is somewhat anomalous. *Pathos* certainly cannot be regarded as having a special connection with complex plots, so Ar. must be taken to be mentioning it perfunctorily in order to complete his basic remarks on plot before proceeding (in ch. 13) to prescribe for the ideal tragedy.

Yet the way in which suffering is juxtaposed with reversal and recognition may have the effect of disguising certain problematic aspects of *pathos*. While reversal and recognition are determinate types of dramatic pattern or occurrence, with (in any particular case) an identifiable structural role, tragic 'suffering' has a more ambiguous status in Ar.'s theory. The definition of *pathos* (especially the phrase 'visible deaths') suggests that this element of a tragedy will be most clearly embodied in scenes of direct physical suffering. Later references to works which give particular prominence to *pathos* lend support to this idea: plays about Ajax and Ixion (ch. 18) are

The Poetics *of Aristotle*

presumably those centring on the former's suicide and the latter's sufferings in Hades; while the *Iliad* is placed in the same category in ch. 23 on account, one must suppose, of its pervasive emphasis on death and physical suffering.

But it will gradually emerge that *pathos* can also be regarded, unlike either recognition or reversal, as a constituent factor, actual *or potential*, in the tragic situation: as such, it is more directly comparable to, say, the ignorance uncovered through recognition than to recognition itself. Ar. himself will later, in ch. 14, argue that a particular act of tragic suffering need not be actualised for a tragic effect to be achieved. Equally, an action embodying *pathos* may have occurred prior to the starting point of a play, as Ar. himself again acknowledges (in a passing remark in *Nicomachean Ethics* 1.11.4, 1101a 33-4): this is so, for example, with Oedipus's patricide.

There are grounds here for inferring that Ar. does not attach much intrinsic significance to the (usually physical) facts of tragic suffering as such, and I cannot agree that it is 'indispensable' for his theory.[1] But he is obliged to give it a nominal place in his remarks on plot-structure, since it certainly could not be brought under any of his other categories of analysis. We can put a positive interpretation on his position by saying that he defines the essential shape of tragic action in general by reference to movement between the poles of prosperity and affliction (see the end of ch. 7 and elsewhere). It is the instability represented by changes on this scale of fortune, not the concrete manifestations or scenes of affliction (the killings and other sufferings), which he sees as truly characteristic of the genre. This does not prevent Ar. from recognising, in the passages from chs. 18 and 23 mentioned above, that there are works in which *pathos* is given a dominating role.[2]

---

[1] Vickers, *Towards Greek Tragedy* p. 60. It should be noted that the more *pathos* is located in the sphere of physical suffering, the more Ar.'s relative underplaying of it can be linked with his detachment from the whole visible dimension of tragedy.

[2] Ar.'s attitude to *pathos* can be contrasted with the view that Greek tragedy concentrates on great static scenes of suffering: see, for instance, Nietzsche's *The Case of Wagner*, footnote to §9. There are ancient parallels for this view, including Plato's adverse characterisation of tragedy at *Republic* 10.605-6.

Ch. 12

Most readers of the *Poetics*, even those interested in Greek tragedy, will not need to spend long on ch. 12. It has sometimes been thought that the chapter is spurious, but while the possibility must be seriously entertained, the case has never been clinched. Most critics are worried by the inadequacy of the formal anatomy of tragedy presented here, and the loose definitions of its individual components. There is no doubt that all this can be improved on by more careful comparison of surviving plays.[1]

But these inadequacies are perhaps just as likely to be Ar.'s as anyone else's: the philosopher's general powers of analysis are not a direct consideration, since it is perfectly conceivable that Ar. would not have thought a more detailed or scrupulous dissection of dramatic forms worth undertaking. As we know that several of the formal terms occurring here were certainly in use at an earlier date, it is in fact easiest to suppose that Ar. is simply producing plain definitions for dramatic and theatrical vocabulary which would have been familiar to at any rate most Athenians. It may be worth adding that the analysis, though notionally applicable to a dramatic text, makes best sense when referred to aspects of tragedy *in performance*: this would suggest a further reason why the exercise of analysis does not really elicit much of Ar.'s interest or acumen.

The model of dramatic construction entailed by the complete set of terms offered is simply that of a sequence of spoken scenes divided by choral odes, with the additional, free-floating possibility of occasional lyric exchanges between actors and chorus. One's reaction to this model will depend on the level of generalisation and sophistication on which one is thinking. It is difficult to deny that the model gives us only a crude approximation to what we find in many of our texts, but it is also important to remember that it is not stated explicitly or for its own sake. The purpose of the analysis is to give a serviceable application to a range of already existing formal terms, and this may be achieved even if the resulting scheme does not do justice

---

[1] For a full discussion, perhaps a little unfair to Ar. in some details, see O. Taplin, *The Stagecraft of Aeschylus* (Oxford 1977) Appendix E.

to the full range of dramaturgical practice.

But there is a further consideration to be taken into account. Ar. himself later tells us, at the end of ch. 18, that in his own day choral odes have been reduced to the status of interlude songs. Although we do not have surviving evidence of the type of play he means, it is inevitable that it would come closer to the model of alternating 'episodes' and choral odes than do many of our fifth-century tragedies. Ar. may, therefore, have been unduly influenced by the usage of theatrical terminology current in his own day when framing the definitions of ch. 12. If that possibility seems paradoxical, in view of the fact that the later reference to interlude odes *condemns* the practice in question, we shall later see that Ar.'s whole attitude to the chorus, such as it is, presents us with a paradox; so the main implications of the later passage may after all turn out to be consistent with the rather self-contained notion of choral lyrics which appears to underlie the formal categories of *Poetics* 12.

Ch. 13

It is not easy for us to sympathise with Ar.'s purpose in moving from the analysis of plot-structure to prescriptive principles for its ideal form. Why should we expect there to be an ideal which can be specified in this somewhat *a priori* and definitive fashion? In fact, Ar.'s approach has been at least implicitly prescriptive from the very start, and at every important juncture of his argument there is a blend of literary observation and legislation. The reasons for this lie in the roots of all the philosopher's thinking, but it is enough to say here that most of Ar.'s evaluative judgements about poetry have a teleological foundation: that is to say, they assume the existence of a predetermined goal or aim (for example, the tragic effect on an audience) and they then work back from this to judgements on the means which will best achieve or fulfil such a purpose. In the case of tragic plot-structure, this means that Ar. is induced to lay down the essential framework which will be most conducive, as he sees it, to accomplishing the function, and fulfilling the purpose, of the genre.

For various reasons (to do, among other things, with the nature of literary and rhetorical education) such a normative or regulative appproach to literary criticism was widespread not only in antiquity but also throughout the period of neo-classicism. It is now almost wholly alien to most critical enterprises, which typically cultivate some form of relativism in literary values. Yet it is interesting that the theory and criticism of tragedy is one area where vestiges of an older didacticism can still be traced, usually taking the form of a quest for the 'essence' of tragedy and a resolve narrowly to delimit its sphere (I. A. Richards' contention that 'the greater part of Greek Tragedy as well as almost all Elizabethan tragedy' was really 'pseudo-tragedy' is only the most notorious of many possible instances).[1] Indirectly rather than through immediate influence,this tendency evinces something of the spirit of *Poetics* 13.

The chapter certainly lies near the heart of Ar.'s understanding of tragedy, though I will shortly contend that ch. 14 deserves to be treated in closer conjunction with it than it usually is. In *Poetics* 13 Ar. deals with the ideal pattern of tragic plot in a way which raises, even if it does not satisfactorily resolve, issues of responsibility and innocence, the ethical status of tragic agents, and the extent to which a play must be built around a single figure. These and other related points call for careful scrutiny.

Ar. mentioned in passing in ch. 6 that reversal and recognition, the features of the complex plot, carry a greater emotional charge of pity and fear than anything else in the resources of the genre. Similarly, ch. 9 suggested that pity and fear could best be aroused by events which happen unexpectedly yet still on account of one another, and this again pointed to the special potency of the complex plot. So the requirement of complexity, in the defined sense, is Ar.'s first premise here in ch. 13. This in itself entails a factor of active ignorance on the part of one or more of the tragic agents, a factor which makes possible the startling and ironic climax at which reversal and/or recognition occurs. Around the concentrated charge of tragic emotion carried by these devices Ar. envisages the ideal plot-structure being built. For he accepts that if pity and fear can be aroused to a sufficient pitch by the key moments of a play, then that will satisfy the purpose of the genre.

The process of elimination which Ar. then proceeds to perform is designed to settle two essential points: what is the appropriate ethical status for the agents of tragedy? and in what direction on

[1] *Principles of Literary Criticism* (reset edn., London 1967) p. 194.

the scale of fortune should their actions and experiences carry them? Some people will find it astonishing that Ar. should need even to raise this latter question, but it is clear from the end of ch. 7, as well as from other passages, that he did not hold it to be a foregone conclusion that a tragedy should *resolve* with misfortune or unhappiness, provided that the play *contains* a stage of misfortune through which the action passes. More will have to be said on this point *à propos* of ch. 14's conclusions: in ch. 13, at least, Ar. does settle with some firmness for what the later traditions of the genre established as the characteristic tragic ending of adversity or affliction.

To the question of the ethical status of tragic agents (which is synonymous, we have to remember, with their 'character') Ar. gives a somewhat equivocal answer – firstly, that they should not be 'good'; then that they should be 'not preeminent in virtue and justice'; finally that, if necessary, they should be 'better, not worse, than indicated'. What does all this amount to? It means, I think, that Ar. has a clearer idea of what he believes does *not* belong in tragedy than of what does. Above all, he wishes to exclude characters of outstanding moral qualities. Plato had objected against both Homer and the tragedians that they showed coming to great grief men who were *supposed*, by the poets and their audiences, to be exceptionally good. He meant by this the heroes who figure in epic and tragic myth, and who often possess attributes highly valued in Greek society – prowess, honour, beauty, power, keen intelligence: attributes which simply constituted, for many, an image of the finest human excellence. Plato was not prepared to sanction such values in their traditional form, and he also rejected the idea that excellence and happiness could be tragically separated. Although Ar. does not share all of Plato's ethical ideas, he is close enough to him to be disturbed by (though not actually to deny) the idea of a person of *outstanding* qualities coming tragically to misfortune: to witness such a thing is, he says, 'repulsive' or 'shocking'.

To make sense of Ar.'s position in this respect we have to realise that he distinguishes between the ethical qualities which his own philosophy would allow him to recognise as important, and those qualities which traditional views of human excellence, as embodied in myth, saw as paramount. When, in ch. 2 or 15, Ar. calls the figures of epic and tragedy 'better than us', it is to the second of these two standards that he must be chiefly referring; and this is also what he describes as 'great esteem and prosperity' in ch. 13 itself. But also in *Poetics* 13 it is ethical character as he understands it himself which Ar. limits in the figures of the ideal tragedy by excluding preeminence in 'virtue and justice'. Some uncertainty about the precise relation between the two sets of criteria will help to explain, I believe, the equivocation which we have seen in his formulations. The upshot, then, is this: Ar. wishes tragic figures to keep their traditional trappings of renown and distinction, for it is precisely to the outer fabric of their lives – which includes the bonds of kinship and friendship that help to define their place in the world – that the damage of tragic affliction must be done; but at the same time he is concerned, for reasons which give a dramatic relevance to essentially ethical considerations, that tragedy should avoid the downfall of virtuous people.

This latter point can be put concisely in the perspective of Ar.'s larger theory, which centres around the unity and intelligibility of tragedy. Even at the crux of the complex plot, where the twist of events is most acute and unexpected, Ar. still insists, near the end of ch. 9, on the fundamental logic or coherence of the dramatic action. But we can be certain that Ar. would not have been able to conceive of great adversity occurring to a preeminently virtuous character in any way that could be made sense of by a unified structure of action: such adversity would be suspended, and would have to be dramatised, as inexplicably cruel and arbitrary, and that is in part why it could only be found, on Ar.'s premises, morally repulsive.

The positive side of this same aspect of Ar.'s theory must also be stressed. The pity and fear which a properly conceived tragedy will elicit are taken to be (and defined in ch. 13 as) emotions which rest on or incorporate a cognitive response to the circumstances and ethical facts of the situation. This brings in Ar.'s requirement for tragic figures who are 'like ourselves' – that is, within the range of our moral experience and comprehension. Pity and fear presuppose and involve, in other words, a fundamental *sympathy* for the tragic agents, and a sympathy which is not purely spontaneous or unreflective, but one which engages us imaginatively in understanding the causal nexus of the tragedy. There is a risk in explaining Ar.'s conception of pity and fear that the experience of tragedy will be made to sound more intellectual than affective, but the essential point is that he is not prepared to leave the tragic emotions simply on the level of uncontrolled or irrational impulses. His interpretation of pity and fear (as his discussion of them in Book 2 of the *Rhetoric* confirms) entails the idea that tragedy offers us, through events involving characters far removed from us in 'esteem and prosperity' but 'like us' in their ethical status, a dramatisation of instability which we can imaginatively relate to our own human conditions of existence.

In reflecting on such a proposition, it is natural for us to suppose that we are moving towards a formulation of what Ar. considered to be the essence of 'the tragic', taken as a complete vision or experience of at least one face of reality. That is because views on tragedy in the last two hundred years have strongly tended to expand from critical or theoretical concerns with certain literary works, to much larger concepts of tragic attitudes towards life as a whole. But such an expansion of the idea of tragedy has no place in the *Poetics*. Unlike Plato, who comes much closer to regarding (and rejecting) tragedy as a holistic view of reality, Ar. shows no inclination to enlarge the experience of pity and fear from tragedy into anything resembling a world-view. If we try to extract or construct such a world-view from the treatise, we can hardly get beyond a broad acknowledgement, of the kind already indicated, of the instability and vulnerability of the external fabric – the social and material standing, as well as the human bonds of kinship – of a human life. But such an acknowledgement is clearly only one partial element in the total Aristotelian picture of reality.

Something should at this point be said about the issue of the 'tragic hero', which has often been prominent in modern theories of tragedy. The translation of *Poetics* 13 indicates that Ar. varies between singular and plural phrases in discussing the agents of tragedy, but that his central formulation of the preferred type of character sticks firmly to the singular ('Such a man is one ...'). Some critics have certainly gone too far in erecting Aristotelian theories of the tragic hero on the basis of this passage, though it would be equally tendentious to regard the wording of the relevant sentences as an entirely casual matter. The fact that Ar. will go on in ch. 14 to focus on the relations between agents within a tragic action is already anticipated in the present chapter by the way in which he refers us to a 'few families' around which the finest plays are now built, though then going on to list a series of *individuals* from myth. The way in which this juxtaposition of 'families' with individuals is so easily made gives us, surely, the essential clue to Ar.'s position. He is thinking, quite simply, of major Greek myths in which tragic events occur between kinsmen, but in which a particular figure can nonetheless be identified as carrying an especially pronounced role in the story. It is the nature of the tragic myths themselves (which in this respect are easily paralleled by much later tragedy) which explains why at certain points Ar.'s argument shifts focus slightly between the individual and a tragic plurality.

In ch. 13 Ar. is thinking chiefly of the central figures whose character and actions do most to determine the movement of the events in which they are involved, and he accordingly formulates an ideal of a particular kind of individual in tragedy. This is a long way, however, from much later theorising about the tragic hero. What Ar. says is essentially negative ('... not preeminent in virtue ... not because of evil...') and it would be gratuitous to suppose that the resulting concept pictures a special kind of tragic *personality* (still less, a tragic consciousness). Many of the major Romantic and modern theories of the genre, perhaps overwhelmingly influenced by Shakespeare's greatest works, have placed their main weight on figures who in themselves represent the personal locus of tragedy – whether in conflict with forces outside themselves, or even as containing a tragic conflict within their own mind and character. Such theories may well have valid scope for application to at least parts of Greek tragedy; but that does nothing to alter the fact that Ar. himself is uninterested in any such concept of the tragic hero.[2]

Ar.'s position is in fact closer to what was, from antiquity till the earlier eighteenth century, a standard notion of tragedy as a genre demonstrating the downfall of figures of great power and prosperity (heroes, in a more basic sense, and kings).[3] Even here, however, it necessary to differentiate between the tendency towards moralism in this traditional view (turning tragedy's

[2] On Sophoclean heroes, see B. M. W. Knox, *The Heroic Temper* (1964) chs. 1-2.

[3] Much evidence for this view is assembled in A. P. McMahon, 'Seven Questions on Aristotelian Definitions of Tragedy and Comedy', *Harvard Studies in Classical Philology* 40 (1929) 97 ff.

figures into *exempla* of the precariousness of power, the wheel of fortune, or some other universal principle) and the limitation of *Poetics* 13 to a concept of individual tragic figures whose status is exceptional but whose ethical character is kept within the range of ordinary human sympathy.

Attempts to extract a deeper interpretation of the tragic hero from this passage of the work have always depended on reading great significance into the term *hamartia* which is used to describe the causal element productive of misfortune. One objection to such approaches is that *hamartia* is not strictly an attribute of the agent (though it may combine with his character) but a causal factor in the sequence of action: Ar. makes a point of stating both the ethical and the external requirements for the tragic agent, to which the factor called *hamartia* is *added* to explain the reason for the change of fortune. But my translation of *hamartia*, 'fallibility', also reflects the fact that modern scholarship has moved predominantly towards a much more limited understanding of the term than traditional ideas of a 'tragic flaw' presupposed. It is true that the reaction against the latter has perhaps swung too far towards a neutral notion of *hamartia* as 'error' or 'mistake', but such translations do at least stay close to the factor of ignorance which we have seen is a necessary component in any plot-structure of the type which Ar. designates 'complex'.

What deserves to be stressed above all about *hamartia* is that its place in a largely *negative* argument leaves it with a necessarily indeterminate status. Even if we can legitimately turn to Ar.'s own ethical treatises to illustrate the kinds of action which might be covered by the term (and the range turns out to be very wide), it remains clear enough that the function of *hamartia* in *Poetics* 13 is to demarcate a fluid area of tragic possibilities left available after the exclusion of serious ethical culpability. I would suggest that Ar. concentrates so hard on rejecting dramatic patterns of action which could be objected to on moral grounds, that he has failed to define a fully coherent alternative for tragedy.

This allows critics, of course, to claim that there is much that is left implicit in the argument; and this is particularly important for anyone who wishes to make Ar.'s theory compatible with what we know of Greek tragedy, in which the individual's involvement in a tragic chain of events is rarely divorceable from a religious background of divine forces and their complex impingement on human agency.[4] Such compatibility has often been argued for, but the strongest counterargument is that Ar.'s general understanding of dramatic logic and unity leaves little or no room for the obscurities and ambiguities which are an integral dimension of traditional belief in divine influence.

Why does Ar.'s theory need *hamartia* at all? The answer, I think, is that some conception of tragic causation is required to maintain the idea that a great change of fortune can be brought about in a way which, however startling, is still fundamentally intelligible. The crucial factor in this causation must involve the agents of the drama, unless tragedy is to be seen as wholly arbitrary and of external origin. But at the same time Ar.'s combination of ethical and emotional premises will not allow him to consider a serious level of guilt in the major figures of tragedy. *Hamartia* is intended to cope with these various theoretical requirements, yet the very brevity with which the doctrine is indicated may warrant the conclusion that Ar. is more interested in establishing the essential tenets of his view than in exploring realistically its relation to the actualities of the genre.

Such a conclusion will also help to explain why Greek tragedy itself can scarcely be used to resolve the significance of *hamartia*, and why attempts to compare the theory with the practice are necessarily inconclusive. To think that the indeterminacy of Ar.'s doctrine is borne out by the multiplicity of plot-structures found in the surviving plays, would be to suppose that Ar. wishes to cater for as wide a range of tragedy as possible. There is much to contradict that supposition: not only the various suggestions of an antipathy to religious forms of tragedy (see p.12), but also Ar.'s explicit purpose of defining the finest type of tragic configuration. The tendency to exclusiveness which comes with this latter enterprise will be conspicuously shown in the next chapter.

---

[4] It is significant that Schelling, in formulating one of the first Romantic theories of 'the tragic', automatically took fate and the gods to be linked with *hamartia*: see D. Simpson, ed., *German Aesthetic and Literary Criticism* (Cambridge 1984) p. 135. This view has also been sometimes adopted in scholarship on the *Poetics*: but it would be curious of Ar. not even to have hinted at such an important point.

There are in fact deep problems about the relation between *Poetics* 13 as a whole and the kinds of issues which often lie at the heart of Greek tragedy. This can be illustrated by reference to the case of Aeschylus' *Persians*, in which a complex interweaving of divine and human responsibility runs through the play. Even if we condense the human factor into the dominant *hubris* of the Persian King, Xerxes, there remains the difficulty of weighing this against the agency of the gods, including the deception and delusion which they are said to have planted in Xerxes' mind. And even if we believe that this issue permits of a final resolution (which is highly questionable), it will not be one for which Ar.'s *hamartia* can be an adequate description: there is, at the very least, too much religious significance shrouding the action of the play to be encompassed by any use of *hamartia* that can be sanctioned by Ar.'s moral philosophy.

But the theory is in any case arguably insufficient to deal with the tragedy even on the purely human level. The reason for this is that Ar.'s ethical outlook, as implied by the language of *Poetics* 13, presupposes tragic figures who are measurable by stable standards of individual and social behaviour. But how can a Persian King be comprehended by such standards? The question could be equally asked of figures at the extreme of the Greek heroic scale, such as Ajax, Heracles or Achilles. The action of Ajax, for example, in setting out to murder his fellow-heroes in the Greek army at Troy, could hardly be regarded by the normal ethical standards of social life as anything other than the great evil which *Poetics* 13 strongly excludes from tragedy. Yet how could such a figure satisfy the tragic instincts of Sophocles and his audience? Whatever the answer, it is nothing which we could credibly claim is contained in the Aristotelian idea of *hamartia*. Nor is it easy to feel confident that the extreme impulses of Ajax's heroic mind can be covered by the idea that he is morally 'like us'. If this notion is intended to account for the imaginative sympathy which is possible with a figure such as Ajax, it surely needs also to be counterbalanced by the perception that many of the greatest tragic heroes move far beyond the compass of our normal moral comprehension.

This line of argument is intended to throw into doubt the value of *Poetics* 13 if treated as a critical basis for the interpretation of Greek tragedy. Had Ar. been striving to make as much sense as possible of the full range of existing tragedy, he might have produced something very different. As it is, his purpose is to argue through to the essential conclusions entailed in his own theoretical premises and preconceptions, and to arrive at a sense of tragedy's potential which can be reconciled with his philosophical, and especially his ethical, point of view. Whatever the justifiability of this enterprise, it is important for readers of the *Poetics* to realise what they are dealing with, rather than to assume that Ar. must have shared the critical open-mindedness which we might expect in a modern critic of Greek tragedy.

Ch. 14

Poetics 14 has been found awkward or embarrassing by many critics, some of whom have consequently tried to regard it as a marginal or unintegrated portion of the treatise. This is convenient, but will not do. At the start of ch. 13 Ar. announced two topics for further discussion: what should be aimed at in plot-construction, and 'the source of tragedy's effect'. The wording of the text patently shows that ch. 14 addresses itself to the second of these subjects, and it will emerge that it does so, as we would expect, by giving further thought to the first of them: for Ar.'s theory cannot allow plot-structure and the tragic effect to be treated as distinct issues.

The chapter begins by raising briefly, only to put on one side, a subordinate source of pity and fear, namely theatrical spectacle. It should not be overlooked that Ar. does recognise the capacity of theatrical means to reinforce the emotional impact of a play. What he probably has in mind is chiefly the visual presentation of physical sufferings (*pathos*, ch. 11) such as Oedipus's self-blinding, or the death of Hippolytus on stage. But it is equally such scenes which could, presumably, occasion what Ar. objects to under the name of 'the sensational' – that is, the gratuitous pursuit of the *frissons* associated with visual horrors. Ar. stands by the position already established at the end of ch. 6, that the management of visual effects (whether appropriate or specious) in the theatre is not part of the poetic art proper, and I refer back to what I said on that earlier passage. It may just be worth adding that this is one of a number of passages in the *Poetics* where Ar. may be contradicting a current view, but without explicitly identifying it as such (cf. p.5). In view of the long tradition of theatrical production at Athens, and the fact that a shift towards a more exaggerated style of production had probably already begun in the mid-fourth century, it seems likely that Ar. is here deliberately contesting the idea that the true effect of a tragedy depends on its manner of performance.

After the digression on spectacle, Ar. returns to his main subject, the structure of action, and seeks to establish just what configuration of factors or events will best conduce to the tragic emotions. It certainly might be asked why Ar. should want to pursue this question further, when he has already framed a conception of the ideal plot-structure. Surely ch. 13 has already offered key propositions on the finest tragic possibilities; while ch. 14 will only complicate matters by eventually recommending a plot-structure other than the one prescribed in the previous chapter.

Clearly, then, if the two chapters are to be found congruous, they must be approaching a central and shared topic from slightly varied angles. One important shift of angle was earlier noted: Ar. now focusses not on the tragic agent or individual as such, but on the kind of situation he should be located in, and the relation between the different characters involved in this situation. There is nothing irreconcilable about these two sets of considerations. On this point at least, Ar. is trying to come to terms with the types of material commonly found in tragic myth. Even the position of the most isolated tragic individual must be defined by some sort of reference to others, and Ar. is therefore justified in complementing what he has already said about individual figures with an attempt to define the kinds of human context in which tragedy can best be dramatised. Ch. 13, after all, has hardly given a comprehensive account of the tragic ideal: it has delimited the character of the appropriate agent of the tragedy and the causal mechanism of his adversity; but this leaves many questions unasked.

Ar.'s examination of possible tragic patterns in *Poetics* 14 is sometimes criticised for being too hard-and-fast; but it is important to realise that his basic categories here depend on vital Greek assumptions which themselves tend towards the exclusive. A single term (*philoi*) embraces all those who are tied by close bonds either of kinship or of friendship. This category is of fundamental importance to the Greek mind, and would bring with it in any particular social situation certain expectations of reciprocal obligation. There is, from such a cultural point of view, no fundamental objection to Ar.'s categorisation of characters into the three groups of *philoi*, their antithesis 'enemies', and a neutral class for those who fall into neither of the others. This scheme reflects basic realities of Greek life and thought, and its use allows Ar. to touch on a wide question about the scope of tragedy in relation to certain basic aspects of men's personal and social relations.

What is, however, both disappointing and open to objection is the narrowness of both the consideration and the answer given to the question. No importance attaches to the rejection of plots involving 'neutrals'; it is difficult indeed even to *imagine* any such tragedy in a serious form, since the category by definition includes those who stand in no personal or social relation to one another. But what should cause unease is the briskness with which Ar. dismisses the plot in which 'enemy is set against enemy'. Homer's *Iliad*, which Ar. accepts as an essentially tragic work in the epic genre, not only depends on confrontations between enemies for much of its material, but actually achieves some of its most intense effects in scenes precisely of this kind – scenes such as the death of Hector in Book 22, or, above all, the meeting of Achilles and Priam in the final book. The achievement of tragic effect from the meeting of enemies in war is as significant as anything else in the great vision of the *Iliad*, and the cultural importance of this fact can hardly be exaggerated: it nurtured the capacity of all later Greek poets (as well as other artists) and their audiences to sympathise imaginatively with the afflictions of both sides in war, and thereby to penetrate to elements of tragedy lying at a deeper level even than enmity itself.

It is in part, then, because of the *Iliad* that Aeschylus could conceive of making tragedy from the Persian defeat at Salamis: the poetic debt could be traced, to cite just a detail, by comparing the treatment of Xerxes' parents with Homer's portrayal of Priam and Hecuba. But other tragedies too work into the very centre of their fabric a major factor of enmity: Sophocles' *Ajax* and *Philoctetes*, Euripides' *Hecuba* and *Trojan Women*, to name only the most obvious. *Poetics* 14 automatically relegates such works to an inferior status, but it does so without attempting to come to terms with the clear conviction of Homer and the tragedians that even the deepest pity can be aroused by actions involving enemies. The criticism could be extended to include the fact that Ar. does not consider the fluctuations that can occur in the relations of tragic agents to one another (though he mentions it in passing in the definition of recognition, ch. 11). Ajax and Odysseus, for example, are former allies, bonded by the common Greek cause at Troy, but they become deadly enemies in the antecedents to Sophocles' *Ajax*. And there are other ways in which tragedy can combine elements of both kinds of relation: the *Persians*, as indicated, depends on a confrontation of enemies at Salamis, but at the same time the immediate foreground of the play explores Xerxes' tragic standing in relation to his own parents and Persian *philoi*.

Two general observations will perhaps help to put the limitations of ch. 14 in perspective. The first is that Ar.'s theory of tragedy eschews an interest in conflict, a point which can perhaps be related to the wider nature of the philosopher's thought, in which no possibility is seen that conflict may be an ineliminable factor in certain areas of value.[1] This is, in fact, borne out later in ch. 14 itself, where plots are peremptorily rejected in which direct conflict occurs between those who are related by a bond: explicit antagonism would, on Ar.'s premises, necessarily involve deliberate evil of the kind which was ruled out in the previous chapter, and so would be morally and emotionally repulsive. It is curious that *Antigone*, the Greek tragedy which has been most commonly cited by modern proponents, from Hegel onwards, of a conflict-centred view of tragedy, is mentioned here by Ar. for a subordinate aspect of its action; but we unfortunately have no other indication of his view of the work's central clash of characters and issues.

The other factor which accounts for ch. 14's restrictive approach is, as in ch. 13, Ar.'s concern to bring his argument to a fine focus on the *ideal* design of a tragic plot-structure. So once more we encounter the wide difference between the prescriptive thrust of Ar.'s theory, which brings with it a constant narrowing of attention onto what is considered of most importance, and the more liberal kind of critical approach which might seek to do justice to the variety and variability of achievement in the genre.

---

[1] See A. MacIntyre, *After Virtue* (London 1981) pp. 147f., 153, and M. W. Gellrich, 'Aristotle's *Poetics* and the Problem of Tragic Conflict', *Ramus* 13 (1984) 155-69.

It will bear repeating (see esp. p.81) that this dimension of the *Poetics* is rooted in Aristotelian teleology, whereby the understanding of a phenomenon converges on what is taken to be its true fulfilment or perfect form.

We must turn, then, to look more closely at just what Ar. does regard in ch. 14 as tragic perfection, and examine how this is related to the earlier formulation in ch. 13. One point of contact between the chapters lies in the factor of ignorance, which is here explicitly picked out as a requirement but was earlier implicit in the nature of the complex plot, whose features – recognition and reversal (ch. 11) – are impracticable without it. What this shows, I think, is not that *hamartia* should be simply equated with a character's active ignorance, but that ignorance *can satisfy* the conditions entailed in the doctrine of *hamartia*. Ignorance of a suitable kind (especially of one's true kinship bonds) can be seen to provide the most obvious way of realising what Ar. earlier used *hamartia* to define: namely, a dramatic situation in which grave moral culpability is avoided, but in which the agents move by their own unwitting choices, and so with the tragic irony which will emerge through reversal or recognition, towards terrible misfortune or, in ch. 14's terms, the execution of an 'incurable' deed (see below).

In these respects chs. 13 and 14 rest on a consistent and common basis of reasoning. Where they conspicuously differ is in their ultimate verdicts on the conclusion of the ideal tragedy: ch. 13 finds in favour of the pattern moving through recognition to an 'ending in misfortune', while ch. 14 prefers the case in which the 'incurable' is averted *by* recognition. A detail of the treatise which suggests that these alternatives did both appeal to Ar. is the fact that the two plays which he cites most often and with most general approval, *Oedipus Tyrannus* and *Iphigeneia in Tauris*, respectively illustrate the two types of ending. Similarly, on several occasions Ar. generalises about a tragic change of fortune without committing himself to just one pattern of it (see especially the end of ch. 7 and the start of ch. 18). This should encourage us to ask whether the difference between the two chapters, and the two tragic ideals, is, from the point of view of Ar.'s theory, as great as it initially looks (it should not be overlooked that the plainness of ch. 14's conclusion gives not the slightest hint of a new line of argument).

In just what does the difference reside? In – again, from Ar.'s point of view – precisely one thing: that is, whether or not the tragic adversity is actualised in an act of *pathos* (ch. 11), a painful or destructive deed. Ar. did not altogether ignore this factor in ch. 13 (the phrase, those 'who have suffered or committed terrible deeds', refers to it) but he did not dwell on it. Now, in ch. 14, he shows that what he has had in mind all along, by specifying 'fallibility' (*hamartia*) as the causal crux of tragedy, is an active movement by the tragic agent(s) towards a particular deed or moment of the kind which can issue in *pathos*. But we can see from the *Oedipus Tyrannus* itself that this *pathos* need not occur within the play itself (cf. p.120): Oedipus's patricide at least, though not his incestuous marriage, lies far in the past (and Oedipus's self-blinding is a subordinate case of *pathos*). Clearly, then, Ar.'s theory cannot *require* a deed of tragic 'suffering' (*pathos*) to be a direct part of a play, though the *possibility* of one may be presupposed; and this negative fact helps us to understand the line of thought which we meet in ch. 14.

The type of play in which recognition precedes and averts the 'incurable' deed, and the irremediable tragic affliction which that would entail,is, in fact, compatible with almost everything Ar. has earlier said about the complex plot. It provides, in Ar.'s eyes, a suitable framework of action for a great instability to be dramatised in the lives of the agents, and it offers opportunities not only for the special elements of the complex plot, but also for *hamartia*, human fallibility. Although the ultimate *pathos* (archetypally, a killing) which the action moves towards is not carried through, the prospect of the deed can still arouse pity and fear up to the moment at which suffering is averted. We should also recognise that Ar.'s allowance for a tragic movement to either good fortune or misfortune (see above) has probably all along been intended to cover plays such as *Iphigeneia in Tauris*, which in effect incorporates *both* types of material. It is at least conceivable that Ar. felt such works capable of satisfying the earlier requirements of his theory, despite the final turn from adversity to some sort of good fortune.

To say all this is necessary in order to suggest that the discrepancy between *Poetics* 13 and 14 is not, after all, as large as has sometimes been thought. But, of course, a discrepancy does remain and calls for explanation. Paradoxically, an explanation is available which will itself tend to confirm further the closeness of ideas underlying the two chapters. If we put aside arbitrary speculations about Ar.'s changing taste (and the like), we have little choice, I believe, but to conclude that ch. 14's preference for averted *pathos* rests on psychological and ethical grounds which go back to Plato's influence.

Three times in the course of these chapters Ar. refers to the possibility of dramatic events which will prove shocking or repulsive (*miaron*); in one case it is the inexplicable downfall of a preeminently good man which is so described, while in the other two the word refers to the unacceptability of deliberately evil deeds. Although Ar. makes it clear that tragic suffering brought about by ignorance will not elicit such a reaction, these passages nonetheless show how reluctant Ar. is to abandon ethical criteria in his assessment of tragedy. In the kind of actions which ch. 14's ideal presupposes, where someone is on the point of killing a close kinsman, there is no direct risk of moral revulsion. But the actualisation of the deed would still entail a terrible contradiction of fundamental ethical expectations and convictions: Ar.'s whole system of ethics posits a high degree of human responsibility, which would be severely undermined if too much weight were given to the terrible possibilities of fallibility.

But where a tragic deed is prevented by timely recognition, the final turn of the plot-structure in the direction of good fortune must in some degree mitigate the preceding experience of prospective suffering. For some, this will amount to an ultimate negation of tragedy, a final pulling back from the brink of the 'incurable'. I have argued repeatedly, however, that we should see the emphasis of Ar.'s whole theory falling on the *intelligibility* of an action which leads, through human fallibility and without the impingement of divine or other external causation, towards a terrible impairment of the fabric of the agents' existence. If this is right, then we can conclude that, at the point at which he wrote ch. 14, Ar. realised that the plot of averted catastrophe could just as well satisfy the underlying conditions of his theory of tragedy.

I said a moment ago that ch. 14's conclusion shows traces of Plato's influence on Ar.'s view of tragedy. For Plato, tragedy's demonstration of a possible gap between goodness and happiness was to be utterly rejected as false and pernicious. Ar. certainly did not follow Plato here, but, like his teacher, he did still expect tragedy to be compatible with, rather than to contradict, certain fundamental ethical beliefs. This gives rise to his entire interpretation of the genre as something capable of dramatising even human suffering in a way which will allow rational comprehension and sympathy. And it also accounts, I suggest, for Ar.'s eventual proposition that tragedy need not show the worst that can happen: it will achieve its aim, he believes, if it demonstrates the causal nexus in which suffering can be produced; and because of this it can afford by a final twist of good fortune to defuse the pity and fear which it has already sufficiently aroused.

It is implicit in this interpretation that a final turn 'to good fortune' of the sort suggested in ch. 14, and allowed for by general formulations elsewhere in the treatise, does not obliterate the preceding 'misfortune' altogether; and when Ar. conceives of the ultimate movement of a tragic plot-structure being possible in either direction, that must be because the essential instability or vulnerability of tragic experience, as Ar. construes it, can equally well be explored in both cases. This also means that the type of plot endorsed in ch. 14 should not be confused with the kind (with 'contrasting outcomes for good and bad characters') criticised at the end of ch. 13. What Ar. has in mind *there* is a plot which progresses towards some kind of 'poetic justice' and which is therefore incapable of bringing us to the full intensity of the tragic emotions.

It should be said, in potential defence of Ar.'s conclusion in *Poetics* 14, that its implications can perhaps be extended so as to cover patterns of plot-structure other than the *Iphigeneia in Tauris* type. This claim must be offered tentatively, since ch. 14 itself says so little in justification of its final proposition. But if we can regard Ar.'s prime idea here to be the conviction that tragedy should not depend for its ultimate effect on a state of incurable suffering, but rather on the dramatic exhibition of the *conditions* from which such states can emerge, then we can at least discern a challenge to alternative theories of tragedy (such as the standard view of the genre in the Renaissance) which put their chief weight on the end-state of tragic affliction. Within Greek tragedy itself, we could refer to a work such as Sophocles' *Philoctetes* to find (in some sense) a final turn 'to good fortune' which does nothing to detract from the depth of tragic experience embodied in the rest of the drama. In so far as it represents in theoretical form the idea that tragedy cannot be judged purely by what we are left with at the end, *Poetics* 14 contains an important insight about the genre.

Ch. 15

The organisation of material in this and the following chapter contains some anomalies. At the start of ch. 15 Ar. seems to be finished with plot-structure, and he moves on to the second element of tragedy, character(isation). But some further remarks on plot soon intrude into the chapter, and ch. 16 returns wholly to the earlier topic. We cannot now confidently explain these irregularities; like certain other oddities in the treatise, they could be due to the unrevised state of the document, or they may represent damage done to the work in its later transmission. Since the few comments on plot in ch. 15 confirm points already made or later recurring (and especially Ar.'s determination to restrict dramatic causation to the intelligible sphere of purely human intention), we can here concentrate on the chapter's main topic, character.

Ar.'s principles of characterisation are, in fact, relatively straightforward, and the main challenge for the modern reader is to grasp the great divide between what the *Poetics* understands by the concept and what we now commonly mean by it. Ch. 6 has earlier firmly established the equation of character with ethical purposes and dispositions, and the point is reiterated here. Ar. is not, therefore, attending to anything like the intricacies of personality or consciousness which more recent traditions of individualism and psychology have associated with the term (though 'character' once possessed in English a meaning much closer to Ar.'s).[1] When Ar. discusses *êthos*, which we have to translate as 'character(isation)', we need to divest the latter term of almost all its strong sense of a high degree of individual differentiation. Whether as critic or as philosopher, Ar. regards the fundamental question about character to be not, in what

[1] It is interesting, for example, to learn how eighteenth-century Shakespeare criticism moves from a concern with consistency and morality in characterisation (two of Ar.'s own four requirements) to a more psychological approach to character: see B. Vickers, 'The Emergence of Character Criticism', in S. Wells (ed.) *Shakespeare Survey 34* (Cambridge 1981) 11-21.

does the distinctiveness or even uniqueness of this person consist?, but, what ethical virtues or vices are embodied in his active life?

It may be helpful to think of the comparison with painting, which Ar., not coincidentally, mentions in connection with character in both ch. 6 and ch. 15. We can perhaps more easily envisage for painting than for poetry or drama the limitation of characterisation to clear-cut indications of ethical status and intention which Ar.'s reasoning presupposes. In ch. 6 Ar. mentions both Zeuxis, whose paintings are said to lack characterisation altogether, and Polygnotus, whom he describes as a 'fine portrayer of character'. From what we can gather about the art of Polygnotus, who was a contemporary of Sophocles, it seems not only to have been predominantly mythological in subject, but also to have specialised in scenes (such as a panorama of the Underworld on the occasion of Odysseus' visit) where marks of moral status could be prominently incorporated. It is such marks, not the rich life of the mind, which Ar. believes that both the painter and the playwright must use their arts to portray.

It is clear, then, that Ar.'s view of character, both in life and in artistic mimesis, is conceived in terms of explicit, unambiguous and essentially ethical attributes – above all, indeed, in terms of the virtues and vices which he defines and explores in his two *Ethics*. This allows him to state in the present chapter his series of four principles for tragic characterisation. Of these, 'goodness' is required because Ar. has built into his general theory of tragedy the idea that it is concerned with ethically 'serious' action; and this entails that its central figures should, in large, be seen to be striving for laudable aims: it is important, for example, that Sophocles in the *Oedipus Tyrannus* shows Oedipus to be acting, and to have acted in the past, for motives which a Greek audience could recognise as noble ones.

We have, of course, to combine this broad formulation with the more detailed requirements laid down in ch. 13, where the goodness of a tragic agent was restricted so as to avoid the spectacle of morally 'repulsive' suffering. How far characterisation can be used to add plausibility to the fallibility, *hamartia*, which ch. 13 calls for, is a difficult question. Even when we have put aside the old and certainly unwarranted view that *hamartia* means precisely a flaw of character, there remains the possibility that in some cases – for example, where fallibility is connected with actions performed under the pressure of emotion – character and *hamartia* could be closely linked. But the *Poetics* itself does nothing to elucidate this point.[2]

In connection with his primary requirement of goodness, Ar. mentions the matter of a character's type or class, and this is even more pertinent to his second principle, appropriateness. For reasons rooted in the organisation of Greek society, Ar. regards character as partially circumscribed or qualified by social and related factors, and here too it helps to keep in mind the difference between ancient and modern notions of character. Where, as with Ar. and with Greek attitudes more generally, character is associated with the active pursuit of goals whose estimation, whether good or bad, rests on publicly shared ethical views, it is at least culturally comprehensible why, to use Ar.'s own example, the character of a slave or a woman is inevitably deemed to have lower possibilities of achievement.[3] A fuller idea of this aspect of Ar.'s thinking can be gained by consulting his *Rhetoric* Bk. 2 chs. 12-4, Bk. 3 ch. 7.6-7; and similar views often recur in later Greco-Roman criticism, for example in Horace's *Ars Poetica* (esp. 114-18, 156ff.).

Such attitudes, applied to literature, easily turn or degenerate into a narrow notion of fixed character-types, as found, for humorous purposes, in the *Characters* of Ar.'s pupil, Theophrastus. But *Poetics* 15 does not depend on such a limited outlook, and if we accept the social basis for Ar.'s curt references to the character of women and slaves, we should at least be able to acknowledge that the link between existing social categories and the principles of dramatic characterisation is not a peculiarity of Ar.'s theory, but an issue which recurs in different forms for much later thinking about literature (for example in theories of naturalism and social realism).

Of Ar.'s two remaining requirements for characterisation, 'likeness' and consistency, the latter can pass practically without

---

[2] On this point see esp. section III of T. C. W. Stinton, '*Hamartia* in Aristotle and Greek Tragedy', *Classical Quarterly* 25 (1975) 221-54.

[3] It is important, however, that in the case of women Ar. may underestimate the special qualities of mythical material. It is not just characters such as Clytemnestra and Medea who contradict normal Greek expectations of women; the same is true of one aspect of Antigone's behaviour (cf. Sophocles *Antigone* 484).

comment, since it rests on the criteria of probability or necessity which have already been discussed (see p.99), and it was also incorporated into ch. 9's definition of universals, where action and character were parts of an integrated conception of behaviour. But what Ar. means by likeness of character is more problematic. It must presumably be related to what was meant in ch. 13 by the need for tragic agents to be 'like us', or within the range of our moral understanding, if they are to elicit fear. So there is an apparent tension between the goodness which is entailed in tragic seriousness, and the 'likeness' which is a prerequisite for at least one of the tragic emotions. The *Poetics* seems to want the major characters of the genre to be portrayed as ethically elevated, so as to allow the full flow of pity for undeserved affliction, but not so elevated as to move outside the reach of our sympathetic comprehension.

Ar. tries to indicate an equilibrium between these points by his comparison of tragic characterisation to portrait-painting, but it must be admitted that the comparison is a little contorted. He posits an analogy between *specific* likeness (in the case of a portrait) and the *generalised* 'likeness' to humanity, which resides, as the context indicates, in character that contains some of the ordinary ethical failings which any audience can recognise. Possible confusion may arise from the fact that in the case of portraits the process is one of improving on individual limitations, while in that of tragedy one would expect the point to involve an *imposition* of ethical limitations on otherwise exceptional, heroic figures such as Achilles. In fact, however, Ar.'s formulation seems to claim a precise parallelism here, as though the poet's task were first to ensure ethical 'likeness', and then, against the background of this restriction of character, to make the agents as good as practicable.

If this is so, it points to the distinction on which I have commented elsewhere (see p.124) between the philosopher's moral standards and the dominant values of the heroic tradition of myth. Ar. is thinking, in other words, with his own normal moral categories, and in terms of these a hero such as Achilles is not necessarily regarded as preeminently 'good', as he would be by traditional criteria. So, for Ar., the dramatist must positively work to raise his figures to a level where they can satisfy tragedy's need for 'men better than ourselves', though the *Poetics* as a whole leaves us with the sense that this can only be done in part by the handling of features – material, physical and so on – which the philosopher himself would not count as properly ethical.

Ch. 16

A categorisation of types of recognition or discovery looks, at first sight, a straightforward exercise. But *Poetics* 16 contains many problems of detail, and poses some larger interpretative problems too. Most of the former are too intricate to be engaged with here, but a number of wider points can usefully be made.

In the first place, it should not pass without notice that the chapter is unusual in comparison with most parts of the treatise. There are opportunities elsewhere for Ar. to produce a typology of dramatic techniques: he could have done so with reversal, for example, or with *hamartia*. In these and other cases much more detailed consideration could have been given to the variations found in actual practice, and to the kinds of choices faced by dramatists in their use. But Ar. generally eschews this approach, since his main concern is to set out the essential principles of a theory of poetry, not to account for the full diversity of existing dramaturgy. There is, in other words, a philosophical reserve or detachment in the manner of the *Poetics* which may make one wonder why in the case of recognition Ar. chose to construct a scheme of the available kinds, and, incidentally, to make a higher density of references to particular texts (most of them now lost) than anywhere else in the treatise other than the catalogue of 'problems' in ch. 25. Since the point is to reemphasise the overriding importance of a causally tight and plausible sequence of action, that is presumably what prompted the effort of collecting examples to illustrate the range of types. But Ar. could have done precisely the same, and for the same purpose, with techniques of reversal, yet he chose not to.

Another general feature of the chapter is the confirmation which its detail gives to the argument that Ar. is interested in recognition as a device or component of a structure of events, rather than as a means of dramatising a sense of tragic awareness on the part of the agents. A particularly clear-cut demonstration of this is the reference to the scene at Alcinous's court in *Odyssey* Book 8, where Odysseus weeps at the sound of Demodocus's song on the fall of Troy: Odysseus 'wept at the memory', and by thus attracting Alcinous's notice he brought about a recognition. The scene is an important one for Homer's portrayal of the power of poetry, and a remarkable simile, comparing Odysseus to a grieving woman from a captured city, is used to suggest something about the paradoxes of war and suffering. But all this is immaterial to what Ar. understands by the strict recognition, which is a matter of Odysseus's circumstantial need to reveal his identity to the Phaeacians at Alcinous's request.

This same illustration provokes a further comment. Ar. categorises the scene under 'recognition through memory', but the point appears oblique. It is Odysseus's memory which causes him to weep, but it is his weeping which occasions the request for his identity: memory plays a contributory part, but it can hardly be said to be the direct cause of the recognition. It is also difficult to see why such an instance cannot equally well qualify as a case of recognition arising 'from the events themselves', since what is involved is essentially a combination of factors plausibly emerging in the sequence of action. Something analogous could be said of Ar.'s fourth category, recognition through reasoning: in the example cited from Aeschylus' *Choephori*, Electra's inference is neither the only nor, arguably, the decisive factor in her recognition of Orestes.

While, therefore, we can readily grasp Ar.'s general contention that recognition should come about from the integral progression of the plot, rather than by some contingent contrivance, it remains hard to be satisfied with the details of the typology. The scheme is both too concerned with categorisation, as indicated, and yet also insufficiently discriminating: no clear differentiation is drawn, for example, between cases where a character's identity is revealed to him by a twist of events, those where one character willingly discloses his identity to others, and those where one character realises or uncovers the identity of another. Similarly, Ar.'s choice of instances throws together passages where the recognition is a subordinate element in a larger structure, and those where it forms part of the climax of a work. One is left with the impression that the chapter is the merest jotting of points which have not been adequately sifted, though we should not underestimate the amount of textual corruption which it may have suffered.

Ch. 17

The opening of this chapter moves the treatise onto new ground. After the dry, awkward listing of recognition types in 16, the work unexpectedly opens out into some seemingly more far-reaching remarks on how a poet should go about transforming the material imagined in his mind into a finished piece of dramatic writing. The new line of thought is doubly surprising, in that it brings Ar.'s theorising much closer to the pragmatic position of the composing playwright than elsewhere in the *Poetics*. This fact, together with the relatively miscellaneous nature of the whole of chs. 17 and 18, has made some suspect that we have here a separate, fresh set of Aristotelian thoughts on poetry. But neither ch. 17's pragmatism nor the hints of new critical ideas found in ch. 18 really amount to a radical shift of position, as we shall see.

The first part of ch. 17 addresses itself to the imaginative dimension of dramatic composition, but it does so in a way which necessarily falls short of the expectations now usually associated with ideas of poetic imagination. For one thing, Ar. does not, either here or elsewhere, go far towards considering the poet as a man apart, with special attributes or mental faculties. It is true that he perceives *some* connection with a certain psychological type (those who can easily 'mould their emotions'), and our manuscripts of the *Poetics* actually couple, rather than contrasting, the 'manic' with the 'imaginative' at this point: my translation therefore depends on an emendation. The justification for this is that it would be wholly incongruous to attribute to Ar. the view that those who are 'carried away' will make especially good poets. This sounds like the traditional Greek notion of poetic inspiration, but that is something which Ar. does not even hint at elsewhere in the *Poetics*, and which, in fact, his whole theory of a rational poetic art seems designed to contradict and avoid. Few readers of the work will bring away from it a sense of 'Aristotle's predominant interest in the psychology of the poet'.[1]

---

[1] Potts, *Aristotle on the Art of Fiction* p. 6 (and cf. the confusion on related points on pp. 66f.).

This general consideration is reinforced by the thrust of the present context. Ar.'s fundamental point is that the composing poet must use his imagination – by which he means, his mental powers of visualising hypothetical events – in order to produce a dramatic work which will conform to canons of plausibility and appropriateness. The function of imagination here has nothing in common with Coleridge's 'secondary' imagination, which 'dissolves ... in order to recreate ... to idealise and to unify'.[2] Such a concept of original or creative imagination was the product both of German Romanticism and of an older, essentially neo-platonic tradition, which regarded the artist as capable of conceiving a reality that transcends the material world.[3] Attitudes of this kind yield, or belong to, idealist systems of aesthetics, and I have already warned against seeing the *Poetics* in this light (see p.109). Ch. 17, which represents the furthest that Ar. is prepared to go in positing the psychological conditions of poetic composition, is patently not proposing a strongly creative use of imagination, but only a sustained practice of picturing the coherence and implications of the dramatic action embodied in the play. So, on this ground also, it seems unintelligible that Ar. should wish to link his remarks with the volatile minds of the 'manic' or passionate.

This remains true even when we look more closely at Ar.'s reference to the emotional component in poetic composition. The argument is, in fact, an integrated one: the basic premise is that visualisation should be employed to ensure dramatic consistency, and we move from this to the more practical suggestion that the poet should even *act out with gestures* what he composes, working himself in the process into the emotional states which he intends to portray in his characters. Some have jibbed, quite needlessly, at the idea of a gesturing poet. Ar. is thinking in terms which bring the dramatic poet closely into relation with the actor, perhaps especially the rehearsing actor. This is all the more intelligible if we remember the tradition, albeit a declining one by Ar.'s own day, of Athenian playwrights producing their own works, and sometimes even acting in them.

Ar. recommends, then, that a composing tragedian should not

---

[2] Coleridge, *Biographia Literaria* ch. 13.
[3] I have tried to indicate the main lines of this tradition in the Introduction to my forthcoming edition of Plato *Republic* Book 10 (Warminster 1988).

only visualise his material carefully, but should enact his parts with physical gesture and with a vivid, imaginative sense of the emotions involved. It is worth noticing the closeness of these injunctions to material found in Ar.'s *Rhetoric* (and in much subsequent rhetorical theory), as a counterbalance to the temptation to find a deeper creative significance in this picture of the poet than it truly warrants.[4] Whereas neo-platonic and Romantic theories of creativity typically invoke notions of imaginative originality or transcendence, Ar.'s concern with the imagination in ch. 17 focuses on its powers of *vividness* for the dramatic realisation of possible human reality. Behind this concern lie his constant standards of reference, both in this chapter and throughout the treatise – plausibility, consistency, unity and intelligibility.

So we must guard against the temptation to assimilate what Ar. says about the poet's experience of emotion to later theories of artistic expression. It is not the poet's own emotion which is in question, but the emotion which he portrays in his characters: everything said in the present passage presupposes the fundamental concept of mimesis, which for Ar. means the fictional representation, ideally in dramatic form, of human behaviour. Whereas expressionist theories stress the source of artistic material in the artist's own psyche, Ar. is concerned only to emphasise the need for the poet to form a clear mental picture of the dramatic situation which his action requires at each point, and then to conjure up as vividly as possible the feelings of the agents which he aims to embody in their language.

One could not find clearer confirmation of this than the second half of ch. 17 itself, which follows the remarks on imaginative composition with a reiteration of the importance of general coherence of plot-structure. The pragmatic point of view of the first half of the chapter is sustained, now by a suggestion that the framework of dramatic structure should first be laid out and contemplated before the episodes are inserted and elaborated. This may seem a pedestrian and mechanical compositional technique to propose, but it arises quite straightforwardly from the theoretical premises set out earlier in the work: Ar. is, in fact,

[4] Various comments on acting and oratorical delivery in *Rhetoric* Bk. 3 chs. 1 and 12 show, I think, that what Ar. has in mind in *Poetics* 17 is a basically rhetorical concept of projecting emotion before an audience.

just translating his earlier tenets into a model of practical procedure, rather than using independent evidence or ideas to construct the latter. This connection is specifically and significantly illustrated by the fact that Ar. envisages a poet establishing a structure of action before he even names the characters. Names, as ch. 9 indicated, belong to *particulars*, whereas the basic elements of the poetic drama should have the status of universal categories; and Ar. would like to see this distinction mirrored in the poet's prior compositional concern with the essential actions and events of his plot.

Having stated the apparent simplicity of this critical doctrine, one must notice its inherently problematic nature. How are we to tell what counts as essential or general structure, and what as episodes? Ar. clearly thinks that he possesses a criterion, but it must be said that neither of his summaries (of the *Iphigeneia in Tauris* and the *Odyssey*) inspires complete confidence in it. The first of them causes real uncertainty even about what is 'inside' and 'outside' the plot (cf. p.151). Ar.'s *précis* includes details of events prior to the start of the play, yet also rules as 'outside the plot' factors which could be deemed to be integral to its dramatic significance. When Ar. says, 'it happened that the priestess's brother came to the place ...', he seems to be deliberately detaching the event from the religious background which it possesses in the myth and in Euripides' play (and without which it would arguably be left as an arbitrary coincidence, though that can clearly not be Ar.'s aim). Besides, the two examples of episodes from the play both involve events which are not shown on stage but only reported: this raises a further issue about inside/outside the plot, and one which Ar. curiously neglects in his general account of tragedy.

The distinction between essential structure and enlarging episodes has not, then, been made altogether secure, and the passage leaves us with a sense of too unrefined a notion of the central and the subordinate components of a poem's dramatic substance.

Ch. 18

We saw in connection with the previous chapter that Ar.'s summaries of plots raise questions about the distinction which he draws (with slight variations of phrase, in chs. 14, 15, 17, and

24) between 'inside' and 'outside' the plot. The first topic in ch.
18 (which contains a final miscellany of observations on
plot-structure) reemploys this distinction, but now, perhaps
surprisingly, in a more positive way. I discussed in my comments
on ch. 10 the terms 'complication' and 'dénouement' which are
now introduced for the first time, and I pointed out that they
appear to be related to Ar.'s ideas on 'complex' plot-structure.
But whereas the latter centres entirely around the internal
structure of a work, Ar. is here interested in providing a model for
the relation between events inside and outside a play. The notion
of what lies outside the play or the plot is invoked elsewhere for
the negative purpose of indicating that anomalies or 'irrational'
elements should not be allowed to enter into the plot-structure
itself. But Ar. now gestures towards the important issue of how
Greek playwrights could make individual works, as they
commonly did, from material belonging to much larger blocks of
myth.

There are some problematic points about this suggestion of a
new approach to the content of a plot-structure. Why does Ar.
now regard the events of a tragedy as always involving things
both outside and inside the play, when in ch. 7 he defined the
'beginning' of a poetic form as 'that which does not have a
necessary connection with a preceding event'? And is the new
model of complication and dénouement compatible with the
earlier scheme of a self-contained structure, complete in itself? It
is possible to argue that the dramatic framework of beginning-
middle-end can be superimposed on the particular sequence of
events which falls wholly within the play, even if these have
important antecedents. The definition of a dramatic 'beginning'
need not in fact rule out a prior set of events, but it stipulates
that the opening of a play should not compel us to look
backwards in the myth for a proper understanding of it. When
the *Oedipus Tyrannus* opens with the plague at Thebes, and the
city's response to it, Sophocles has set up an event which
necessarily leads on to a further stage of action, as *Poetics* 7
requires, but which does not (on Ar.'s terms) demand an
immediate antecedent to explain it. The opening of the play
cannot spring from nowhere; it naturally has a background in
preceding events. But this does not prevent it from satisfying
Ar.'s earlier scheme of unified plot-structure by being essentially
the initiation of a new phase or turn of events, rather than simply

the continuation of an existing sequence.

However, even if strictly compatible with ch. 7, the new complication-dénouement model still seems to disturb the simplicity of the previous notion of self-contained 'wholeness' of dramatic structure, by acknowledging that any drama may present events whose practical context is temporally larger than what is enacted in the play itself. If Ar.'s point were a purely formal one, the two sets of observations could perhaps simply be left as complementary views of the nature of plot-structure, seen from different angles. But the issue is not purely formal, for Ar.'s concept of unity, and the concept of dramatic logic which underlies it, involves the fundamental *significance* of the human actions and events dramatised by the playwright (cf. p.99). Ch. 18's recognition of some necessary relation between the enacted material of a play and its antecedents, consequently entitles us to discern an uncertainty in Ar.'s interpretation of the causality of dramatic action. Whereas ch. 7 clearly suggests a chain of causation running through a play but limited by the character of a 'beginning' and 'end', ch. 18 effectively – whether or not intentionally – reopens the question, for how can we cleanly separate a 'dénouement' (whose modern sense is narrower than Ar.'s: p.114) from the 'complication' which it completes and resolves?

This forces us back, then, to the problematic distinction between 'inside' and 'outside' the plot. Two illustrations can usefully be given of the difficulty of applying the distinction consistently. Greek tragedy's extensive use of messenger-speeches and other narrative reports necessarily brings into the sphere of the play events which have happened off stage, and such events may also belong chronologically to the antecedents of the dramatic action (e.g. the account of Salamis in Aeschylus' *Persians*, or Oedipus's description of his encounter with Laius in *Oedipus Tyrannus*): Ar. himself allows for such things in a passage of the *Nicomachean Ethics* where he mentions plays whose tragic terrors have already occurred before the start of the action (see p.120 above). Are such things inside or outside the plot? Attempts to save Ar.'s position by distinguishing his use of the phrase 'outside the play' from 'outside the plot' are not convincing. It surely makes much better sense to contend, with Kitto, that 'we cannot in fact draw a circle around the play, or its action, and say that everything inside the circle is 'within the play' and everything else is 'outside the play'. Everything that is implied by the play is in the play ...'[1]

A work such as the *Oedipus Tyrannus* dramatises the final stages of a much longer sequence of events stretching back before the start of the play. Though Sophocles' dramatic art is focussed on this final stage, the total significance of the enacted drama encompasses the past as well as the present. Oedipus' past life invades and dominates his life in the present, and any final sense of the drama's completed significance surely cannot limit itself to the relatively brief span of time acted out in the scenes of the play. But why should Ar. wish it to do so? The reason, I suggest, is one we have met before. While the *foreground* of a Greek tragedy, its directly enacted sequence of events, can often be viewed, in the terms of Ar.'s own theory, as a matter of connective plausibility, the larger background of events is often not so amenable to rational explanation or interpretation. Ar. both acknowledges and tries to cope with this fact by his principle that irrational elements should be left outside the plot (chs. 14, 15, 24). But we have seen that this is to deploy a dubious distinction, and one whose usefulness belongs to a lower level of criticism than the fullest meaning of a tragic drama.

To connect the inside/outside the plot dichotomy with Ar.'s concern to provide a secular reading of the possibilities of tragedy may appear a curious line of argument. But it is confirmed, I believe, by *Poetics* 17, where we have seen that Ar. rules Apollo's involvement in the background of *Iphigeneia in Tauris* to be 'outside the plot'. But Apollo's motive and arguably causal role in these events is a constant thematic presence throughout the work, and it is difficult to see how a traditional religious Greek mentality could regard it as anything other than integral to the understanding of the action. What else can Ar.'s judgement on its marginality amount to but a refusal to countenance a dramatic significance which carries us beyond the sphere of purely human plausibility? Despite the apparent broadening of approach which the complication-dénouement model of ch. 18 represents, we are led back once again to certain fundamental features and limitations of Ar.'s interest in poetry.

This is equally true of the remainder of ch. 18's material, about which I shall be briefer. There is certainly some interest in the

[1] H. D. F. Kitto, *Form and Meaning in Drama* (London 1956) p. 88.

scheme of four types of tragedy (which will be reapplied to epic at the start of ch. 24), and perhaps a hint here of a more liberal attitude to the possible range of dramatic strengths than was taken in earlier parts of the analysis. Ar. seems now prepared to allow that certain kinds of mythical material may bring with them, or conduce to, an emphasis on 'suffering' (in ch. 11's sense) or character, and so to acknowledge that these elements may sometimes play a more pronounced role than his earlier treatment of them suggested. But it would be a mistake to suppose that this passage is in any sense a qualification on what has gone before. By a 'tragedy of character', for example, Ar. presumably means a play which develops and exploits characterisation to the fullest extent, but only in conformity with the principles laid down in ch. 6, where it was argued that excellence in characterisation alone cannot 'achieve the stated aim of tragedy'.

So the earlier priorities still stand, as, of course, do the conclusions reached in the pursuit of the tragic ideal in chs. 13-4. This last point is directly relevant to the short paragraph in which Ar. recognises the possibility of plays dealing with the downfall of a seriously flawed character. The passage is, in fact, a vexed one among commentators, and, except for its apparent recommendation of twists of dramatic 'wonder', it has no perspicuous connection with the main discussion of tragedy earlier in the work. One possible interpretation is to see here a reference to plots in which a kind of 'poetic justice' is done, but what is rather more interesting is the admission that pity and fear can be aroused by the afflictions of agents with grave ethical weaknesses. The point may be that a character who combines strong virtues and vices can satisfy the criteria for the tragic emotions given in ch. 13: that is, he is sufficiently 'like us' to arouse our sympathy (and therefore to mediate our fear), but also has enough ethical merit to allow the flow of pity for him. If this were so, it would amount to a curious qualification on the ideal tragic agent defined in that earlier chapter; but it must be admitted that this passage of the *Poetics* remains probably too contorted and textually corrupt to interpret clearly.

The final section of ch. 18, by contrast, possesses a possibly deceptive clarity and simplicity. Ar.'s advice that the chorus should be treated as 'one of the actors' and 'a part of the whole' seems to many readers to be perfectly straightforward and admirable in intention: Ar. is urging the full integration of the chorus into the unified design of the work of dramatic art, in conscious opposition to the use of the chorus as an interlude entertainment in his own day. Posed in these terms, Ar.'s position does indeed appear laudable. But the difficulty is actually to know what he means or understands by treating the chorus as one of the actors; and here we find that different interpreters have taken the phrase in very different ways, ranging from concrete actions by the chorus to a much more diffuse sense of dramatic relevance.[2]

What can unequivocally be said is that the rest of Ar.'s discussion of tragedy gives hardly any recognition to the chorus or its lyric poetry. Apart from some general references to the latter (mostly in ch. 6) there are no indications of how the chorus is conceived of as 'a part of the whole', or how a playwright is expected to employ it integrally in designing his unified plot-structure. This negative fact is, I believe, the crucial clue to Ar.'s attitude to the chorus. For the fundamental observation must surely be that the theory of tragedy as a whole posits no particular function for a lyric or choral element in the genre. This is evidently because the theory treats tragedy (and all poetry) as a representation of action, and it concentrates on the way in which various components are to be worked into a coherent dramatic fabric. So all the essential tenets of Ar.'s view of drama apply to the non-lyric portions of tragedy, and it is therefore hardly surprising if, in default of any detailed elaboration, we are not in a position to make much sense of the superficially appealing idea of the chorus as 'one of the actors'.

The problems of interpreting this passage on the tragic chorus have easily been overlooked by most modern critics for the simple reason that we are ourselves not used to a comparable tradition of drama in which a distinctive lyric element plays a constant part.[3] The chorus of Greek tragedy has long been, and continues to be, a major stumbling-block to appreciation of the genre. There have been many attempts to fix a relatively

[2] See my book, *Aristotle's Poetics* pp. 244ff.

[3] It is always tempting to cite opera in this connexion, particularly in view of its historical origins in ideas about Greek tragedy held in sixteenth-century Italy. But it would be hopelessly optimistic to suppose that opera, with all its own distinctive cultural properties, can really tell us anything about the lyric element in Greek tragedy.

determinate function onto the chorus – including the notion of an 'ideal spectator' on the edge of the dramatic action; Nietzsche's exhilarating if heady sense of the chorus as the truly Dionysian voice of existence, set against the individuated consciousness of the agents; and a variety of beliefs in the chorus as some sort of authorial mouth-piece. The first and third of these varieties can be conclusively shown to involve much too rigid a conception of the nature of the chorus in tragedy.[4]

The range of ideas which have been held about the Greek chorus reflect the difficulties which face us in coming to terms with a lyric element within drama, and, moreover, with a lyric element which varies in its voice and persona between the particular and the general, the individual and the communal. The difficulties make it consequently natural for us to be easily satisfied by the gesture which Ar.'s neat phrases in *Poetics* 18 make towards taking account of the chorus's contribution to tragedy. But Ar.'s own theory of the genre, as I have suggested, is intrinsically a theory of drama as the action of individuals in a spoken medium of mimesis, and this leaves no obviously defined room for the chorus. If this is so, then it leads us to the paradox that Ar.'s ostensibly strong recommendation for the integration of the chorus is little more than an unassimilated attempt to cover an element of tragedy which he has otherwise neglected.

Ch. 19

It may disappoint the modern reader of the *Poetics*, but it is entirely characteristic of Ar.'s general method, that poetic 'thought' is put aside for consideration as part of rhetoric. Even when we have adjusted to the restricted sense of the term in this context (and so dissociated it from, for example, the more compendious use of 'thought' to refer to a playwright's indirect communication of ideas *through* his dramatic material, or from the kind of thought which we may associate with the lyrics of Greek tragedy) it remains frustrating that Ar. should so readily leave for a separate occasion such a large part of the fabric of poetic drama.

His reason is stated, and not in doubt; and there is certainly no

---

[4] There is a lively discussion of views of the chorus in Vickers, *Towards Greek Tragedy* pp. 9ff. For Nietzsche's views, see esp. §§7-8 of *The Birth of Tragedy.*

way of denying that the connection which he makes with rhetoric genuinely reflects the predominant practice of all the major tragedians. Ar. thinks of the individual characters of tragedy as deploying language for particular effects on those around them – to persuade or dissuade, to stir their feelings, and so on. He thinks of them, in effect, as using the resources of oratory; and, again, it must be allowed that the rhetorical is a demonstrably central mode of speech throughout the genre as we know it.[1] Ar.'s critical category of thought therefore legitimately codifies the powerful influence exerted on tragedy, from an early period, of essentially public and formal types of speech.

This public, rhetorical mode – focussing the meaning and intention of speakers on their hearers (true soliloquy being rare in Greek tragedy) – helps us to understand the association between thought and character in Ar.'s theory, as indicated in ch. 6 (p.38, and cf. the end of ch. 24). We saw earlier that the concept of character in the *Poetics* is an ethical one, and its place in drama is strictly subordinated by Ar. to action. Both character and thought can be seen to concentrate not on primarily internal or psychological states (as in much later literature and criticism) but on practically orientated intentions and attitudes: to regard Ar.'s notion of 'thought' as the 'personal part of a man's inner life' is a gross misconception.[2]

It may be worth offering brief examples of what Ar.'s category of thought is designed to cover, taken from the two tragedies which are cited most often in the *Poetics*. When, at *Oedipus Tyrannus* 583-615, the King's brother-in-law Creon defends himself against Oedipus's suspicions of subversion, he does so in a reasoned speech which is both characteristic of the quasi-forensic mode of argument so often to be found in Greek tragedy, and precisely illustrative of the rhetorical factors mentioned in ch. 19's definition of 'thought'. Moreover, it is easy to see from such a speech how Ar. can connect thought closely with character, for it is in such passages that we are given the

---

[1] Euripides has often been singled out as more rhetorical than either Aeschylus or Sophocles: this common idea underlies, for example, Nietzsche's assault on Euripidean rationalism in *The Birth of Tragedy* §§ 10-12. But, while Euripides may well press certain techniques to an extreme, the basic rhetorical style of tragic speech is common to all the major tragedians.

[2] Potts, *Aristotle on the Art of Fiction* p. 66.

clearest idea of the ethical dispositions of the dramatic agents: in the present case, it is Creon's preference for modesty over political ambition, and his honourable behaviour towards Oedipus, which are put across by his reasoning. If these characteristics, and the mode of their expression, seem somewhat insipid or abstract, that is partly a symptom of the difference between the rhetoric of Greek tragedy (to which Ar.'s concepts are in this respect aligned) and modern interest in a more inwardly psychological style of characterisation.[3]

Much the same holds for the *Iphigeneia in Tauris*, from which one might select Orestes' speech at 687-715 as a good instance of combined character and thought, in their Aristotelian senses. In explaining why his own life should be sacrificed, rather than Pylades', Orestes gives a reasoned, persuasive piece of thought which is simultaneously an exhibition of his own virtues of intelligence, courage, loyalty to a friend, and concern for the survival of his family. These are general virtues possessed by an individual, rather than distinctive traits of personality; and this helps us to understand the nature of Ar.'s concept of character(isation), as well as the reason why character and thought can be presented as related facets of drama.

These very brief examples are meant to suggest that there is something in Greek tragedy's basic dramatic technique which does correspond to the *Poetics*' category of thought. But it must also be said that this aspect of tragedy has a fundamental quality which one would not gather from Ar.'s attitude towards it. Although his postponement of the topic to the separate treatment of rhetoric is in part a symptom of the philosopher's analytic method of working, it is also a reflection of, and made easier by, the relatively low importance which thought carries in Ar.'s general view of tragedy. This low value is in turn the corollary of the treatise's dominant emphasis on action. It must be grasped that for Ar. 'thought' is a specific element which is present only in certain passages of a poetic text and not in others. The categorisation of a play into action, character, thought, and so on, is not purely methodological; it is intended to highlight separable components of the poetic work.

---

[3] I should perhaps state that I am not excluding 'psychology' altogether from the poetry of Greek tragedy, but emphasising those aspects of the genre which help to justify the critical concepts and categories of the *Poetics*.

Perhaps the clearest illustration of this conviction comes near the end of ch. 24 (which discusses epic, but the point presumably applies also to drama). Here Ar. recommends the elaboration of verbal style in 'portions of the poem which ... involve no characterisation or ... thought'. Just as Ar. can conceive of action without character (ch. 6), so he regards the other elements of tragedy as not constantly or necessarily interfused, but possessing a high degree of poetic independence which enables any one of them to be prominent at a particular time, but absent at another. This point is worth stressing because it is a measure of Ar.'s distance from much modern critical practice, which makes categories such as style, character and thought pervasive not partial attributes of a poetic text, and is prepared to discuss them separately only for the most contingent reasons of convenience. It is fair to add that what has just been said about Ar. could equally be said about most ancient criticism, as well as much later criticism in the predominantly rhetorical tradition.

The separability of the 'parts' of tragedy in Ar.'s theory is nowhere more evident than in his treatment of style or verbal expression (*lexis*), to which he turns in a preliminary and mildly polemical fashion at the end of ch. 19. The rebuke delivered to Protagoras's linguistic criteria of poetic correctness, and implicitly to all similar contentions, speaks for itself. As well as giving us a glimpse of sophistic pedantry, the passage establishes Ar.'s impatience with the idea that poets should be expected to be linguistic purists: the defence of poets against linguistic criticisms in ch. 25 should be compared (p. 62).

Ch. 20

Having rejected sophistic criticisms of linguistic faults in poetry, Ar. proceeds to prepare for his theory of verbal style with a thoroughly technical linguistic introduction. But the anomaly is only superficial. Ar. uses this opportunity to set out the groundwork for a general approach to linguistics, but he does not claim that every detail bears directly on poetry. There are reasons for supposing that some of the material in this section was composed at an early date, and was perhaps originally separate. Some have wanted even to deny Aristotelian authorship to *Poetics* 20; but that would appear unnecessary.

The chapter is primarily of importance for the student of ancient grammar and linguistics, but it would be a pity for other readers of the work to ignore it altogether, and I accordingly include a few very brief comments on its character, though inevitably leaving difficult details (including some problems of translation) entirely on one side.[1]

The linguistic categories presented in *Poetics* 20 straddle phonetics and grammar – that is, they mix definitions of speech-sounds with definitions of functional units of language. Moreover, Ar. describes not only types of words but even an entire proposition (or 'sentence') as a particular kind of utterance or sound, though the rest of his definition is naturally functional or logical. This is one of a number of features of the chapter which could be faulted from a later and more sophisticated linguistic point of view; but such criticisms need to be tempered by a proper sense of the relative historical achievement represented by this attempt to produce the outline of a comprehensive framework for linguistic description. It is impossible now, for lack of sufficient evidence, to know just how much progress over earlier or other current linguistic thinking such a framework actually incorporated, but it seems at any rate possible that Ar. had achieved greater refinement and economy of definition in this area than anyone before him. If the overlap of phonetics and grammar may irritate some modern linguisticians, the fact remains that Ar. has striven with considerable intellectual finesse (unfortunately now marred by some textual corruption) both for a concise yet comprehensive set of descriptive classifications, and for a kind of hierarchical ordering of language from foundations in its basic phonetic elements up to the highest level of compound semantic units, whether single propositions or larger combinations of them.

It must be said that Ar.'s scheme suffers from an excessive economy or simplicity, though this is in part because it is only a sketch; some major Aristotelian ideas about language are not even alluded to in this section. Nevertheless, we can detect one fundamental notion in this passage which carries great

---

[1] For the wider context of Greek views on language, see ch. 1 of R. H. Robins, *Ancient & Mediaeval Grammatical Theory in Europe* (London 1951), ch. 2 of the same author's *A Short History of Linguistics* (London 1967), and ch.5 by M. S. Schofield, in *The Cambridge History of Literary Criticism*, vol. 1, ed. G. Kennedy (Cambridge, forthcoming).

significance for Ar.'s general treatment of poetry: that is, the essentially denotative model of meaning, according to which the function of sentences is to frame logically determinate propositions (whether positive or negative). This notion is of course closely related to Ar.'s own predominant interest in philosophy, but it is not one which seems hospitable to uses of language which cannot be readily analysed into affirmative or negative predications. We shall see that Ar. does not in fact qualify this view of language to take account of the special character of poetry; the distinctive status which he grants to poetry is entirely a matter of variation in lexical or stylistic choices of words. We have here surely a further reason why the lyric sections of tragedy, which diverge furthest from Ar.'s basic categories of linguistic meaning, are the most neglected in his theory of poetry.

Chs. 21 & 22

Having set out his basic linguistic terminology in ch. 20, Ar. now proceeds to produce a new series of categories which will, once defined, enable him to expound a doctrine of style. But we notice two things at once: first, that these chapters, though ostensibly part of the analysis of tragedy, say very little about this genre as such (perhaps an indication of the separate origin of this section?); second, that the categories in ch. 21 do not even encompass all the aspects of language touched on in the preceding chapter. What Ar. now offers, in fact, is essentially a set of lexical groups (a classification of words as items of vocabulary) which will allow him to generalise about poetic style.

It is curious that the definitions in ch. 21 refer explicitly only to nouns, though some of the examples of metaphor involve verbs. In view of its appearance in the narrower sense in ch. 20, it is doubtful whether Ar. can intend the Greek term *onoma* to mean just 'word' (as it sometimes does) rather than 'noun', even though it is equally clear that ch. 21's classification could be applied to other parts of speech. The point appears to be that Ar. is deliberately narrowing his focus so as to concentrate on the types of diction or lexical choice which face a poet, and he finds it convenient to do this by thinking primarily of nouns.

The partial exception to this statement is Ar.'s treatment of metaphor, to which I shall later return. But the thrust of chs. 21-2 as a whole is undoubtedly such as to present poetic style in terms of levels or registers of vocabulary. This seems especially odd in view of Book 3, chs. 1-12, of Ar.'s own *Rhetoric*, which also addresses the subject of style (chiefly in connection with rhetoric, but with many references to poetry) and which should be read by anyone who is concerned with this section of the *Poetics*. Although the two passages have much in common, including details of illustration, the *Rhetoric* provides a much fuller and richer consideration of various aspects of style: not only the lexical aspect covered in the *Poetics*, but further questions of tone, euphony, rhythm, word-order, sentence-construction, and the linguistic expression of emotion and character.

Why should such a series of topics be dealt with for rhetoric, whose stylistic range is mostly narrower than that of Greek poetry, but not for the latter? No ready explanation presents itself; but it is perhaps impossible altogether to suppress the suspicion that many questions of poetic style simply do not interest Ar. or strike him as important. The treatise, after all, locates the core of the poet's art in the design of large-scale structure (plot) not in the fineness of verbal texture or detail: 'the poet should be a maker of plot-structures rather than of verses' (ch. 9).

Ar.'s conception of style, which can be confirmed from the cited passage of the *Rhetoric*, rests on a set of categories, defined in *Poetics* 21 and applied evaluatively in ch. 22, which imply a clear model of speech-registers. At the centre or mid-point of this model lies the vocabulary of 'standard' speech (whose relativity to cultural groups Ar. acknowledges). All other registers are conceived, explicitly or implicitly, as divergences from standard speech, particularly through the choice of individual words which depart from normal usage. In the case of both poetry and rhetoric, though to different degrees, Ar. regards stylistic distinction as chiefly a matter of ornamentation: 'standard terms produce clarity, while all the other types catalogued in the *Poetics* produce elevation and embellishment' (*Rhetoric* 3.2.2).

In this connection it is worth recalling the definition of tragedy in ch. 6, which refers to 'language garnished in various forms ...': the metaphor used here occurs also, for example, at *Rhetoric* 3.3.3, where a writer is faulted for using epithets 'as the food instead of the garnishing'. Equally revealing is the passage at the end of *Poetics* 24, where intensive use of verbal style is recommended 'in portions of the poem which are static and involve no characterisation or statement of thought': the clear implication is that style is an embellishment, a decorative enrichment of the verbal texture, and that it can be cleanly separated from questions of meaning.

This notion of style can be connected with a comment I made on ch. 20, where I referred to Ar.'s 'essentially denotative model of meaning'. The supreme virtue of language-use, viewed in general terms, is taken to be clarity, and this reflects not just a sense of the functional character of ordinary speech, but also, and perhaps even more so, the bias of Ar.'s own interests towards philosophical lucidity and precision.[1] Whatever may be the larger merits or strengths of such a position, it is the essentially negative implications of it for the appreciation of poetry which must concern us here.

These implications can be most immediately glimpsed from a number of passages in *Rhetoric* Bk. 3 where 'speaking poetically' and similar phrases are used *derogatorily* (see esp. 3.3.3): although the reference in these cases is to the standards of rhetoric, the underlying suggestion is that poetry exemplifies a linguistic medium in which sense is sometimes sacrificed to empty verbal effect. Indeed, at 3.1.9 Ar. actually has occasion to mention 'poets who speak fatuities but who seemed to acquire reputation for their style', though it is difficult to know what exactly he has in mind. Even when, as in *Poetics* 21-2, Ar. is attempting to formulate a positive doctrine of poetic style, it is clear that he is concerned primarily with stylistic ornament in the choice of vocabulary, and not with any deeper features of poetic writing. Ar. assumes, in other words, that the poet, at any rate if he is a good poet, will always be striving for an essential standard of clarity, and this means that the question of style can be reduced to a matter of the degree and kind of verbal embellishment which will secure a distinctive poetic flavour without detracting unduly from lucidity.

There is only one respect in which the *Poetics*' discussion of style hints at something other than this notion of verbal

---

[1] It is not surprising that analogous thoughts on language can be found, for example, in John Locke's *Essay Concerning Human Understanding*, Bk. 3, ch. 10, esp. §§ 23 ff.

embellishment, and that is in the treatment of metaphor. Metaphor is included in Ar.'s initial list of word-types in a way which seems to imply that it is simply on a level with, say, 'lengthening' of words; and this impression might be gathered again from the early part of ch. 22. Nor, for all its precision, does the analysis of categories of metaphor in ch. 21 do much to counter this impression, although it does entail a sense that metaphor cannot be viewed purely as a matter of ornament, independently of sense. But it is only in his concluding emphasis on the importance of metaphor that Ar. makes the point explicitly and tellingly: 'metaphor entails the perception of similarities'.

What this deceptively simple formulation contains is an acknowledgement that metaphor is simultaneously a stylistic and a cognitive feature of language, capable of communicating thoughts which may not be readily translatable into 'standard' language. If Ar.'s remarks lack the Romantic enthusiasm of Shelley's claim that the 'vitally metaphorical' language of poetry 'marks the before unapprehended relations of things and perpetuates their apprehension',[2] they nonetheless share with this some awareness of the special potency of metaphor. Unfortunately, this attitude towards metaphor remains in the *Poetics* an intruigingly suggestive one, rather than a view which Ar. cares to elaborate. Metaphor is left with something like the status of the exception which proves the rule (it is the only thing 'one can never learn from another'), namely that stylistic choices are essentially a matter of register and verbal decoration.

It must be admitted that the firm dichotomy of style and meaning on which Ar.'s position depends is not peculiar to him; in fact, it was to become standard in ancient criticism, particularly under the influence of rhetorical habits of thought, and it has only been effectively challenged in relatively modern critical movements and views of language.[3] It will always, moreover, be a tempting dichotomy to apply, since at certain levels and in certain contexts of language it can be shown to have practical force in the form of alternative means of expression with functional equivalence. But it becomes questionable if

[2] *A Defence of Poetry* (1821).
[3] For a well-judged survey of ancient views on style see ch. IX of D. A. Russell, *Criticism in Antiquity* (London 1981).

treated as a uniformly valid principle for all uses of language, and Ar.'s reliance on it in the *Poetics* goes far towards explaining why he fails to produce a satisfying account of the stylistic issues raised by Greek poetry.

A final question, which follows on from what has just been said, is worth asking about the doctrine of poetic style put forward in the *Poetics* (and confirmed by the *Rhetoric*): is Ar. to be regarded as a proponent or advocate of a 'strong' theory of poetic diction? Does he, that is, commit himself to attaching a positive value to the distinctiveness of poetic uses of language? It must be concluded, I think, with only slight qualification, that he does not. *Poetics* 22 makes it clear that Ar. disapproves of a degree of stylistic elaboration which endangers what he sees as the fundamental requirement, in any significant use of words, of clarity; and there are many similar passages in *Rhetoric* 3, including the one cited earlier where he refers to poets who 'speak fatuities' but are noted for their style. This same passage goes further by claiming that tragic poets have now abandoned the adornments of this 'poetic style' and restrict themselves to the language of ordinary speech (3.1.8-10). This viewpoint is corroborated by *Poetics* 22 itself, where 'the close reproduction of ordinary speech' is attributed to iambics (the metre of tragic and comic dialogue).

When we put these passages together with *Poetics* 4, in which tragedy's evolution involves the choice of iambic metre for its closeness to ordinary speech (see p.35), we clearly have the elements of an Aristotelian theory that tragedy has improved poetically or stylistically by evolving closer to the norms of 'standard' speech. This is interesting in a number of ways, partly as a contrast to later neo-classical ideas on the need for stylistic elevation in tragedy (and cf. Aristophanes *Frogs* 1058-60 for a similar notion in fifth-century Athens). Purely on the level of stylistic doctrine, the importance of Ar.'s position can hardly be exaggerated, given that tragedy represents the highest poetic achievement which he is prepared to recognise. Regardless of the factual accuracy of what is said about tragic style (which the loss of fourth-century tragedy makes it impossible for us to evaluate), we can see that Ar. approves of what he regards as tragedy's stylistic movement towards relatively unadorned clarity of language. This shows that the twin principles of clarity and elevation stipulated at the start of ch. 22 are, as we might well have suspected, hardly of equal weight. While Ar. recognises the genuine appeal of distinctive stylistic registers above that of standard language, as well as their integral place in established genres of Greek poetry, his paramount linguistic value, rooted in his own philosophical convictions and experience, is perspicuity of meaning.

We should perhaps hesitate to equate Ar.'s doctrine of style with superficially similar later ideas on the subject, but the topic is one which would merit extensive comparative treatment. I simply mention two examples. In the case of Horace *Ars Poetica* 46-72, with its principles of the known word enlivened by new connections, and of restrained linguistic innovation, what links there are with Ar. derive from Horace's use of sources in the Peripatetic tradition which preserved elements of Ar.'s own thinking; but the whole issue has in any case been transferred into the context of current Roman arguments about the development of the language. Of later instances, Wordsworth's famous *Preface* also offers scope for both comparison and contrast with the *Poetics*. Wordsworth's advocacy of 'language really used by men' and his rejection of conventional poetic diction, clearly has a cultural context in Romantic naturalism which is very remote from Ar.'s. There remains, though, at least an interesting parallel to the philosopher's position in Wordsworth's contention that there is 'no essential difference between the language of prose and metrical composition'.

Ch. 23

Ar. starts his treatment of epic by reverting to the priorities which he earlier established for tragedy. He does so with what is virtually a paradox: epic, a *narrative* genre, should use *dramatic* plot construction. This echoes the reference in ch. 4 to Homer's uniquely dramatic work as an epic poet (these are the only passages in the treatise where the adjective *dramatikos* occurs), and it signals Ar.'s determination to apply to the earlier and larger genre the same basic principles of unity and coherence which he has carefully worked out for tragedy. Ch. 23 consequently contains a great many echoes of previous chapters of the work, especially of chs. 7-8 in which the principles of poetic unity were set out. Those early chapters themselves indicate clearly enough, despite their place in the analysis of tragedy, their general import for serious poetic standards: ch. 8, in fact, takes its illustrations entirely from *epic*.

This last point helps to explain why Ar. comes straight to the central issue of unity of plot-structure in ch. 23. It is not just the case that plot-structure – the sequence and design of action – is the major attribute of anything that Ar. is prepared to regard as poetry, and unity the primary value associated with it. The epic genre raises the issue of unity in a particularly acute form, both because of its typically substantial length and also because of its tendency to handle extensive areas of mythical material. The eleven books of the *Cypria*, for example, which Ar. refers to here, ranged over a whole series of antecedents to the Trojan War, from the time of the marriage of Peleus and Thetis (Achilles' parents) to the arrival of the Greeks at Troy – events spanning some twenty years of legendary time.

But to this and other similar poems in the Epic Cycle, Ar. was able to contrast the very special character of the two great works which (like all Greeks of his time) he attributes to a single Homer. Ar.'s fundamental observation on the *Iliad* and *Odyssey* is a shrewd one: Homer has combined the resources of epic length with a deliberate narrowing of dramatic focus onto, in each case, a limited action of real unity. So whereas other Cyclic poets are like historians in their diffuse handling of an entire (mythical) period of time, Homer is a true tragic poet (cf. ch. 4) who has grasped the greatest requirement of poetic art.

Ch. 23's comments on unity confirm that Ar.'s understanding of poetic form is not purely technical, but rests on the idea of intelligible unity of action portrayed in the poem. The difference between Homer and other epic poets is not presented as a matter of technique, as though Homer could have made a unity out of the material of, say, the *Cypria*. Homer's insight was to see that the very choice of material was itself crucial; the poet can attain unity only if he selects a story whose action is capable of being '*perceived* as a unity': that is, of being apprehended as a structure which is both 'whole', or complete in itself, and internally coherent in its dramatic sequence. Without such unity, an epic might yield all sorts of other pleasures, but it could not, on Ar.'s premises, give that concentrated pleasure which arises from the experience of a complex interrelation of parts connected by, and contributing to, a 'particular end'.

This theory of artistic or aesthetic pleasure (for ch. 8 generalised the canon of unity for *all* mimetic art) can be taken to reflect the outlook of a philosopher who seeks to find intelligible order in the human and natural worlds, and whose system of thought puts a premium on synthesising interpretations of phenomena in terms of their ends or purposes. It would be mistaken to treat Aristotelian unity of action as merely a call for literary order and design, or a protest against disorganised composition. Unity of action is a principle of order of a strict and special kind, and that is why it cannot automatically be endorsed. More will have to be said in connection with epic unity on the next chapter, but something of what is at stake can be suggested at once.

Because unity of action, as elaborated by Ar., stresses *singleness* of action, even double plots will fall below the highest standards argued for in the *Poetics* (ch. 13 contains two references to double plots of one particular kind). If two strands of action contributed to a common end, they would by definition be parts of a single action for Ar.; if they were dramatically combined in some other way (say for purposes of contrast or counterpoint), their separate 'logic' would, like the contingently related events of history or an individual life, detract from the coherence of the work. From this case we can extrapolate to the steadily diminishing unity of works which involve even more independent elements than a double plot. Ar.'s theory is ultimately based, as ch. 26 will later clarify, on deep convictions about the superior pleasure yielded by the experience of artistic structures whose unity stems from the portrayal of wholly integrated action. Conversely, it implicitly rejects the possibility of validly alternative sources of unity (unity, say, of theme, thought or emotion), and it offers no sense at all of the conceivable value of works which deliberately eschew strict unity in favour of some other aim.

This central tenet of the *Poetics* raises some problems even for the understanding of the Greek poetry which was known to Ar. (see esp. p.102), but it became an increasing difficulty about the work from the sixteenth century onwards when Ar.'s ideas were juxtaposed with, and assessed in relation to, forms of literature not contemplated by him. The earliest of these was the Romance, whose characteristically cumulative rather than integral structure, often revolving round the life of a single individual, can perhaps be compared to the type of Cyclic epic about which the *Poetics* is dismissive. Renaissance critics in Italy argued over the validity of the Romance's greater diffuseness (as well as other features of it), under the conflicting pressures of upholding the classical authority of Ar. (and others) but also responding to the achievements of modern literature. Similar problems were to arise, at least to critics open to them, from the singularly unclassical nature of much Elizabethan-Jacobean drama in England, especially Shakespeare's.

Ar.'s canon of artistic unity can only be sustained as a universal principle, I would suggest, if it is emptied of all its most significant implications. Interpreted as if it were simply an insistence on coherent organisation by whatever means, as it has often been, it can of course be made to look like an unobjectionable, practically self-evident tenet. But once it is grasped that Aristotelian unity demands a lucid dramatic logic in the causal or explanatory sequence of a structure of events, we should recognise that as a critical principle it presupposes a particular and sharply defined way of approaching works of literary (or other) art. For some Greek tragedies, with their intense concentration on a short sequence of interlocking actions, this notion of unity has relevance and critical value, though even here I have tried to show that Ar. may be pressing for a rationality of dramatic logic which the genre's religious ethos cannot easily accommodate (see p. 118). But for other genres, and particularly those of later cultural traditions, Ar.'s understanding of poetic unity deserves to be invoked only if a critic is prepared to argue independently for its acceptability as a way of apprehending the significance of poetic representations of human life.

Ch. 24

While ch. 23 emphasises one essential priority in Ar.'s view of epic, ch. 24 contains a wide range of observations on the genre. I shall comment in turn on the following topics: plot-types; epic scale and variety; metre and ethos; the poet's status in relation to mimesis; 'the marvellous' and the issue of epic plausibility.

Ar. reproduces for epic the four plot-types which he gave for tragedy in ch. 18 (cf. n. on p.67). That earlier passage intimated that these categories need not be mutually exclusive ('ideally one should strive for all these elements ...') except, of course, in the case of the simple and complex (ch. 10). So what Ar. means by character-poems and poems of suffering are works in which characterisation or acts of suffering play a particularly prominent part. Ch. 6 had in fact already indicated the very different degrees of characterisation possible in a poem, and there have been various hints of an analogous point concerning *pathos* or suffering (see p.120). The categorisation of four plot-types, therefore, does not really introduce anything new, but essentially summarises implications of the earlier discussion of plot-structure.

The present passage confirms the nature of this categorisation by its judgement that both the *Iliad* and *Odyssey* can be classed under two of the types each. It is impossible to be sure, but it looks as though Ar. is applying the same classification to epic and tragedy purely because of Homer: from the various strictures in chs. 8 and 23 on other epics' lack of unity, it is improbable that Ar. could have exemplified all of his categories from these alone (though presumably some would at least qualify for 'the poem of suffering'). The present passage ties in, then, with what is said more generally in ch. 4 about Homer's individual discovery of the possibility of poetic tragedy.

As for the actual judgements made here on the *Iliad* and *Odyssey*, it is hard to know how categorical they are meant to be. In so far as they stress pervasive or recurring elements in the poems (pain and destruction in the *Iliad*, twists of plot and recognition in the *Odyssey*) they have some obvious validity. But the clear-cut nature of such judgements involves, it would seem, a commitment to particular readings of the poems, and also runs the risk of simplification. Is pain and destruction (*pathos*) really less important in the *Odyssey* than the *Iliad*? Does character (in Ar.'s ethical sense) have a less significant role in the *Iliad* than the *Odyssey*?

These are large questions to which Ar. appears to have neat answers from which other readers of Homer could well dissent. And there are more precise points involved too. In regarding the *Iliad* as a simple rather than complex plot-construction, Ar. does not exclude the presence of recognition or reversal altogether, but he cannot hold them to be central to the work. Does this mean, as I would strongly suggest, that he would not attach the same importance as some modern critics do to the death of

Patroclus and its tragic implications for Achilles?[1] For if this juncture, with its involvement of Achilles in reversal, recognition and *hamartia* (the sending of Patroclus into battle), is the climax of the *Iliad*, then how could the poem not be complex on Ar.'s terms? Is it possible that Ar. would instead locate the work's main 'dénouement' in the death of Hector and the treatment of his corpse? While we can hardly answer this question on the evidence available, we can at least ponder the implications of categorising whole works in the sort of terms which Ar. offers us in this passage; and to do so may bring a better understanding of the difficulties inherent in all general judgements on large-scale poems.

This leads us on, in fact, to Ar.'s next topic: epic length. Here again – but this time, significantly, without explicit admission – Homer is the focus of the argument, for both the *Iliad* and *Odyssey* were composed on a much larger scale, so far as we can tell, than other epics (they were probably at least twice as long as the largest of the Epic Cycle). When Ar. states that epics could be written to a length equivalent to a set of (three) tragedies, he is hypothesising works of no more than a third of the *Odyssey*'s size, or a quarter of the *Iliad*'s. The contrast with 'the old epics' is, therefore, largely if not entirely a reference to the two great Homeric poems, and the paradox emerges that the supremely fine plot-constructions of these works – the only ones in the genre, according to Ar., to attain true unity – exhibit a scale which carries them well beyond the requirements of epic. It is not immediately apparent that this is problematic for Ar.'s theory, since he acknowledges that epic can afford to incorporate a larger range of episodes than tragedy, and that it gains thereby in variety and grandeur. But when we reach the final comparison of tragedy and epic in ch. 26, we shall see that Ar. does find epic length an impediment in the way of achieving strict poetic unity.

One hint as to why this should be so can be gleaned from the reference to 'tragedies given *at a single performance*' (or 'hearing'). The *Iliad* and *Odyssey*, as well as some other epics, could not be performed at a single hearing, and this clearly poses a difficulty for the cognitive experience of poetic unity as interpreted in the *Poetics*. When expounding his general principle of unity in ch. 7, Ar. referred to structures which are too

---

[1] See Rutherford, 'Tragic Form and Feeling in the *Iliad*'.

large to be taken in by a single process of contemplation. Although he does not regard great epic length, such as Homer's, to be incomprehensibly over-size in quite this way, ch. 7's comments, together with the reference to performance in ch. 24, indicate that epic length does threaten to jeopardise the coherent conditions of perception or cognition which Ar. takes to provide a basis for a sense of artistic unity.[2] A final verdict on this point needs to be suspended till we consider the final chapter of the work.

Ar.'s observations on the appropriateness of the hexameter to epic narrative remind us of a similar passage on tragedy's metre in ch. 4 (p. 35), and are also connected to the discussion of rhythm in *Rhetoric* 3.8. All these passages show a belief in the *natural* potential of verse-rhythms to embody or enhance a certain tone and style of poetry. While 'it is not always easy to determine in such judgements which was primary, the inherent appropriateness of the metre to the style or the long *de facto* association of style and metre',[3] and while modern literary historians would be more likely to favour the second of these criteria (the associationist), there is no doubt about Ar.'s own naturalistic conception of what was involved: *Politics* 8.5.6 and 9 should be consulted for general statements of the emotional potential of rhythms and melodies. In fact, as Plato *Republic* 3.399e ff. shows, there was certainly an earlier tradition of ideas which assigned intrinsically expressive attributes or ethos to particular rhythms. Ar. can best be understood to be adapting such thinking to his own particular convictions about the natural foundation of cultural development (see pp. 79ff.): as genres evolved, it was necessary for their poets to discover the natural rhythms which suited their subjects and purposes. It should be noted, however, that while Ar. recognises the close relation between metre and style, he virtually ignores questions of rhythm in ch. 22 (though not in the related chapters of *Rhetoric* Bk. 3).

*

[2] Ch. 7's own remarks on the irrelevance of performance conditions to poetic scale (p.39) make a separate point.

[3] A.M. Dale, *The Lyric Metres of Greek Drama* 2nd edn. (Cambridge 1968) p. 69.

'The poet himself should speak as little as possible': Ar. uses Homer to exemplify this important negative aspect of mimesis. But just what does Ar. mean by it? It is necessary, for a start, to compare some of the phraseology of ch. 3: where my translation reads 'dramatic impersonation', Ar.'s Greek literally says (in reference to the poet) 'becoming another person'; and what I translate as 'the voice of narrative' means, again in reference to the poet, 'as himself' or 'in his own person'. Moreover, the phrase 'the poet himself' had been used as a description of *narrative* in a section of Plato's *Republic* (see esp. 3.393a and 394c) to which *Poetics* 3 shows a clear terminological debt. The strict implication of this would seem to be that 'the poet himself' in ch. 24 means all narrative, as opposed to passages of 'impersonation' or direct speech. But if such an interpretation were pressed rigorously, it would commit Ar. to an intolerable contradiction of the basic narrative status of epic poetry, which he openly accepts in several passages.

On the other hand, Ar. offers no further criterion for distinguishing only certain utterances of, say, Homer as coming from 'the poet himself', and it is not easy to see how he could have supplied one. We are bound, I think, to see in ch. 24's pronouncement a qualification on the understanding of mimesis or poetic representation, but one which is not wholly integrated with the broader exposition of Ar.'s theory. Since, as I have had more than one occasion to note, Ar.'s interest in epic is essentially an interest in Homer, it is the Homeric poems which provide the key to his thinking on this point. Even in ch. 3 Homer was specially mentioned for combining narrative with direct speech, and we can now see that this also tallies with the references, in chs. 4 and 23, to the uniquely *dramatic* quality of the Homeric epics. Homer shows, on this view, that epic can and should approach to a predominantly dramatic mode of mimesis; and in making this observation in the present passage, Ar. is induced to formulate a principle which, strictly interpreted, denies mimetic – and so poetic – status to narrative.

Though this passage in ch. 24 ultimately, therefore, remains unassimilated into the overall argument of the treatise, it does, I believe, give us a very significant clue to Ar.'s view of poetry. If we go back briefly to Plato's earlier use of the phrase 'the poet himself', we can infer that it depended on a traditional Greek sense of poetic authorship: the poet is responsible for what is said in his poem, and, unless he specifically attributes an utterance to a character (though this would not, for Plato, excuse him ethically: cf. p.178 below), his words must be taken to be his own. Such a notion had traditionally associated or matched poetic *authorship* with poetic *authority*; the voice of the poem is assumed to be essentially that of the poet. Whereas Plato had accepted the premise behind this idea, in order to challenge what he believed he heard the voice of the poets telling their audiences, *Poetics* 24 indicates that Ar. was prepared to circumvent the problems which troubled Plato by treating the poet as only truly a poet when fulfilling a *dramatic* (or dramatising) function.

This Aristotelian reinterpretation of mimesis as essentially dramatic harmonises with the larger tendency of the *Poetics* to establish the *fictional* nature of poetry (see p.72). So long as poetic utterances could be treated as those of the poet himself, they could be questioned, as Plato had questioned them, on grounds of truth or morality. For such objections to be largely put aside, Ar. needed to clear a distinctive 'space' for poetry outside the sphere of directly affirmative and truth-seeking discourses such as history, philosophy and science. He does this in a number of ways – by his positive doctrine of poetic universals (ch. 9), by his negative rebuttal of existing criticisms of poetry (ch. 25), and, here in ch. 24, by his attempt to exclude the voice of 'the poet himself' from poetic mimesis. Indirectly, and paradoxically, ch. 24 remains a testimony to the tenacious traditional idea of first-person poetic utterance as equivalent to the poet's own voice: it is just because of this assumption that Ar. wishes to minimise such utterance, rather than attempting, through some conception of a poetic persona, to fictionalise even the 'I' of poetic texts.

It hardly needs to be said that Ar.'s desire to exclude the voice of the poet from his poetry, and to turn the poetry into a 'stage' onto which the poet brings his characters, is closely interrelated with the *Poetics'* concentration on tragedy and Homeric epic (as well as comedy in the lost book). If even the narrative portions of an epic can be treated as the utterances of 'the poet himself', it has to be asked how Ar. would respond to the much more prominent 'ego' of much Greek lyric poetry (such as the odes of Sappho and Alcaeus), or to the ostensibly moralising and even didactic voice of the elegiac poet. But as soon as one puts such a question, one realises that the *Poetics* contains no positive evidence with which to answer it: the genres in question are effectively left quite out of account, allowing us to infer reasonably that Ar. has no proper place for them in his theory of the poetic art.

The inference is consolidated by consideration of the theory as a whole. Poetry as the mimesis of men in action; the primary importance of plot-structure; and the supreme value of unity of action – these central tenets are all made for dramatic or quasi-dramatic genres, and they offer no framework for an approach to lyric and other neglected types of Greek poetry. Ar.'s theory is, after all, not a historically inclusive one, but a strongly evaluative attempt to state the essential values of poetry in relation to those genres which the theorist holds to be the highest achievements of the cultural tradition. The notion of poetic 'impersonality' briefly but firmly suggested in ch. 24 is entirely harmonious with the main thrust of the theory as a whole, both in its positive stress on the mimesis of action and character, and in its negative implications for poetry which gives too prominent a role to 'the poet himself'.

Poetics 24 stands, then, as perhaps the first committed, if somewhat arbitrary, confrontation with critical problems – the poet's relation to his work, and his presence within it – which, in various guises and contexts, have often reappeared in later literary criticism. Ar.'s position can be seen as the polar opposite to the prevalent Romantic view of the poet as a person who gives full expression to his own inner being and personality. It is consequently not surprising that there should be at least superficial similarities between Ar. and certain modern views which represent a reaction against Romantic criticism – whether individual theories such as that of T. S. Eliot ('the progress of an artist is ... a continual extinction of personality')[4] or larger systems such as Structuralism, with its devaluation of the author in favour of the conventions and 'codes' of literature. In the case of Structuralism, which tends strongly towards the rejection of traditional mimeticist interpretations of literature, the resemblance may well be too distant to be helpful. The case of Eliot is more complex, and his views bear much more closely on

---

[4] *The Sacred Wood* 7th edn. (London 1950) p. 53. On Eliot and the *Poetics* see my Introduction, p.26.

non-dramatic poetry than do Ar.'s; but Eliot's position does at least have a kinship with Ar.'s conviction that the poet, though entirely responsible for the design of his work, should not be personally discernible or identifiable within it.

The last major topic of ch. 24 is the place of 'the marvellous' and 'the irrational' in epic, though Ar., as often, broadens out his observations into general poetic principles (note the illustrations from tragedy, and compare the use of examples from epic in ch. 8). Ar. earlier raised the question of the marvellous (or 'wonder') in ch. 9, and in a way which intimated why he needs carefully to define its position in his view of poetry. The sphere of the marvellous is essentially that of things out of the ordinary – things which strike and compel our attention because they diverge from, or even contradict, our normal expectations and experiences. Ar. is aware that poetry in general makes considerable use of material which can be classed as 'marvellous' in this sense. At *Rhetoric* 3.2.3, in justifying the remark that poetry can afford to employ more unusual and 'marvellous' linguistic features than prose, he says that poetry's 'subjects and people are more out of the ordinary'. *Poetics* 9 recognises that tragedy has a need for exceptional events of the particular kind which will arouse the powerful tragic emotions in its audience. And the special features of the ideally 'complex' tragedy by their very nature call for events which involve a dramatic and exceptional transformation in the lives of the agents: tragic reversal is defined, in ch. 11, in terms which make evident its precisely unexpected and startling character.

Now, Ar.'s own principles of plot-structure repeatedly emphasise causal or explanatory unity; the actions of a play should not just follow one another but should arise with full probability out of their antecedents, and lead on with equal plausibility to their consequences: 'for it makes a great difference whether things happen because of one another, or only *after* one another' (ch. 10). The insistence with which probability or necessity are repeatedly invoked as the indispensable criteria of successful plot-structure allows us to see why Ar.'s attitude to the marvellous is a delicate issue for his theory. In ch. 9 he tried to make room for the marvellous in tragedy by positing events which 'occur contrary to expectation yet still on account of one another'. In commenting on that passage I suggested that this formulation may disguise the problematic character of exceptional tragic events for Ar. I identified the problem as residing in a discrepancy between the intrinsically rational and secular standards of probability or plausibility on which Ar.'s theory as a whole depends, and the fundamentally religious outlook embodied in the traditional myths of tragedy. When Ar. now returns to the question of the marvellous in relation to epic, we discover that the problem has not been definitively solved.

But ch. 24 shows at once that the marvellous involves difficulties for Ar. that are not restricted to matters of divine causation. It is not of immediate relevance that the example of the pursuit of Hector from *Iliad* 22, mentioned later again in ch. 25, seems to strike Ar. as more 'absurd' than it need do; what matters is his sense that certain major events in Homeric epic offend against rational expectations. 'The irrational', which means the realm of events that are not intelligible by normal causal explanation, is the very antithesis of the probability or necessity to which the *Poetics* constantly reverts. Ar. is now attempting to suggest how a theory grounded on the latter can still accommodate the former.

At first sight, ch. 24 appears simply to yield the place of the marvellous in epic, even if the justification given – that epic is not performed by actors – is curious for a critic who elsewhere strains to separate even dramatic poetry from the conditions of theatrical production. But after adding an observation on how a poet can lend a semblance of plausibility even to certain irrationalities in his material, Ar. develops a new formulation regarding the whole question. He now produces the apophthegm which he will reuse in the next chapter: plausible (or probable) impossibilities are preferable to implausible possibilities. This commits Ar., it would seem, to an acceptance of superficial or ostensible credibility as sufficient for the purposes of poetry. We must note , however, what is often overlooked, that Ar.'s maxim offers a principle for 'hard cases', not a recommendation which applies to all poetic plots; after all, the poet who can produce plausible possibilities must still be expected to prefer them to plausible impossibilities.

Ar.'s concession to the strange, exotic and exceptional world of epic wonder is counterbalanced by his warning that the irrational should be kept outside the plot-structure. But this tenet reminds us of the difficulties which attach to the meaning of this criterion (see p.150). Ar.'s example – Oedipus's ignorance of Laius's death – certainly serves to make a point, but not as fully as the case requires. Oedipus's ignorance is a negligible irrationality, not, however, because it belongs to the past, but because its unintelligibility (by normal suppositions) does not bear on, or interfere with, the central significance of the play: it is the latter sense, rather than the former, in which this detail can be deemed 'outside the plot'.

But the important corollary of this is that *some* events already enacted before the start of the play may not be so easily put aside, even though they would ostensibly be outside the plot-structure. Can we, for example, ignore what, by normal criteria, would be the implausible coincidence of the meeting of Oedipus and Laius on the route between Thebes and Delphi? This too is, in one sense, outside the plot or the play, but, in a much more vital sense, it lies at the heart of the drama, and is placed there not just by the total pattern of the Oedipus myth but also by Sophocles' incorporation of it into his work through Oedipus's recollection of the event (*OT* 794ff.).

The insufficiency of the criterion of 'outside the plot', as Ar. states it, brings us back to the underlying tension which can be detected in the *Poetics*: between, on the one side, the essentially rationalising criteria of probability (and hence of intelligibility and unity) called for by the theory; and, on the other, the irreducibility of the worlds portrayed in both tragedy and epic to such a consistent and limited level of explanation. Ar. is aware in various ways of this tension, but his attempt to deal with it in the present passage is, despite some interesting remarks on poetic manipulation of credibility, more of an unresolved concession to poetry than a full adjustment of his theory to the special, and particularly religious, presuppositions of epic and tragedy. The following chapter will give us perhaps the most promising of Ar.'s attempts to cope with the problems of belief and credibility raised by poetic fictions.

Ch. 25

This is perhaps the most highly condensed (or congested) passage of argument in the *Poetics*. For this there is a specific reason. Ar. is known to have compiled a large work (several times the length of the surviving *Poetics*) known as *Homeric Problems*, in which he dealt with a great mass of criticisms ('problems') directed against the *Iliad* and *Odyssey*, and offered defences or solutions to most of them. The present chapter is almost certainly a summary of the reasoning and standards of criticism elaborated with much fuller illustration in that larger work. As such, it has a rather indigestible compactness about it. But that should not be allowed to conceal its real importance as a passage which contains, albeit in annotatory form, some of Ar.'s most important ideas on the nature of poetry (and of mimetic art more generally).

To understand Ar.'s enterprise, we need in the first place to recall the position of great educational, cultural and ethical authority traditionally held by poetry in Greek society. Poetry had for long been regarded as a repository of wisdom, knowledge and moral insight, capable of exhibiting the finest values and ideals of human life (particularly through heroic myth) and of conveying both explicit and implicit injunctions to human conduct. But for about a century and a half before Ar.'s time, this traditional poetic authority had come increasingly under attack from various quarters – from philosophers, from technical or scientific thinkers, from moralists, from independent and sceptical teachers (sophists). The culmination of this critique of poetry's credentials was to be found in Plato; but Ar. knew of a large range of earlier writers too who had tried to find fault with the standards of poetry, and particularly of the oldest and greatest poetic texts, the *Iliad* and *Odyssey*.

Ar. marks a new and important phase in the approach to Greek poetry, for he wishes neither to return to the traditional estimation of poets as wise and knowledgeable guides to life (see e.g. Plato *Republic* 10.606e) nor to assent to an outright rejection of poetry of the kind Plato had moved towards. Well used as we now are to various forms of aestheticism, which grant to poetry and the other arts a strong degree of autonomy, it is difficult for us to appreciate the nature of the evaluative problem facing Ar. in his theory of poetry, or the originality with which he tackled it. The problem was effectively to define the status of poetry in such a way as to free it from the moral and other objections which its critics had brought against it, yet without slipping back into a conventional account of the privileged nature of poetic knowledge.

The attempt rests on an interpretation of the concept of mimesis, which embraces both poetry and the visual arts. It may at first seem curious that Ar. should stress the notion of mimetic 'image-making' in the present context, since the language of 'images' appears to imply a stronger correspondence-theory of representation than he wishes to argue for. But Ar. is probably counting on his audience's automatic recognition of the ways in which Greek painters and sculptors departed from the norms of the ordinary world of visual experience. Even in the mid-fourth century, when Greek art was in certain respects growing in realism, the idea of a visual image did not necessarily import a direct or faithful conformity to the visible. The reference to the visual arts does therefore reinforce Ar.'s contention that mimesis can vary in the kind of things which it sets out to portray. In particular, it lends support to the view that artistic mimesis can go beyond the actual or the recognisable, in order to represent either a reality in which people believe or a type of existence which conforms to conceptions of how things 'should be', rather than how they actually are.

Although this categorisation of objects of mimesis may strike us as needlessly analytical, it does successfully communicate Ar.'s response to all those Greek critics of poetry who assumed a fixed and unquestionable standard of accuracy or truth by which works could be tested and, perhaps, found wanting. The argument purports to show that it is a basic critical prerequisite to consider the aim of a work of art, and to judge it by criteria which at least to some extent the work itself (or its genre, as Ar. would say) determines, rather than imposing an inflexible and wholly independent set of norms. The dictum, 'correct standards in poetry are not identical with those in politics or in any other particular art', is a bold and challenging assertion not of *complete* independence of poetic values (which would contradict the idea of mimesis altogether), but of the need to relate judgements on art to the internal nature and canons of the art.

There can be no doubt that the central impetus of Ar.'s case is directed partly against Plato, who was prepared to apply rigorous ethical and epistemological principles to all Greek art, regardless of historical or other considerations relating to the purpose of the individual works. This is not to imply that Ar. in any sense refutes Plato's position; what he does effectively do (which would not have troubled Plato himself) is to show that Platonic and similar objections to art cannot claim to be doing justice to the standards and principles which the practitioners or appreciative audiences of the arts would acknowledge. It remains open to a Platonist, however, to contend that art cannot be allowed to stand outside the realm of the supreme values of truth and morality. We have here an interesting illustration of the contrasting tendencies of the two philosophers: of Ar.'s teleological interest in the internal aims and practices of a particular activity, and of Plato's conviction that all things can be judged from an absolute vantage (an Archimedean point) of philosophical truth.

The central purport of ch. 25, then, is to offer a series of arguments for a style of criticism which works *with*, rather than from outside, the intrinsic aims and techniques of the individual art or genre. Once this is grasped, we can afford not to be deflected by the difficult details encountered in the accumulation of individual points and illustrations. The reader ought, though, to bear in mind that when Ar. uses what may seem to us a banal example – such as the question of a horse's front legs in a painting – he is probably in part reflecting the kinds of technical quibble which had actually been raised in particular instances by earlier writers. This tends to be confirmed by the fragments of the larger work, *Homeric Problems*, where we can see Ar. sometimes having to rebut points of pedantic fatuity raised against Homer.[1]

We need also, however, to realise that Ar. himself has a certain fondness for elementary instances of a phenomenon which can take much more complex forms. Thus in *Poetics* 4 he uses a simple case of recognising the subject of a portrait in order to argue for the cognitive dimension of the experience of mimetic art (see p.34). Similarly, an example such as that of the horse's legs is intended to demonstrate a point whose application is much wider – in this particular case, the difference in art between technical precision in specific areas of knowledge, and the achievement of proper artistic ends.

Behind even the driest passages of ch. 25 there remains the significant purpose of an attempt to demarcate the kind of standards which are appropriate to art. It can just be noted that Ar. here at least touches on a whole range of factors which had clearly been often neglected or misunderstood in earlier

[1] For a selection of fragments in translation see J. Barnes (ed.) *The Complete Works of Aristotle* (Princeton 1984) vol. 2, pp. 2431-3.

criticism, and whose pertinence has often had to be rediscovered and reestablished in many later periods – the difference between essential and inessential failures in art; the importance of apprehending the type or level of reality which a work sets out to represent; the impingement of historical background on a work; the character and implications of particular stylistic conventions; the importance of the individual context within the work of art. Anyone who doubts the insight which Ar. is exercising in this chapter would do well to consider the relative neglect which this section of the treatise was shown during the period of neo-classicism. While Ar.'s 'authority' was abused during the sixteenth and seventeenth centuries to erect a system of absolutist critical principles and rules, the flexible and subtle framework represented by ch. 25 was often left discreetly out of account.

Indeed, it must finally be asked whether the *Poetics* itself as a whole takes sufficient account of the considerations adduced in ch. 25. Although the treatise certainly eschews the more naive kinds of moralism or technical criticism which are rebutted in this chapter, it might be tentatively suggested that the 'liberal' and accommodating quality of ch. 25 sits a little uncomfortably alongside the more prescriptive approach to poetry which is followed elsewhere. It must be remembered that ch. 25 offers a defensive strategy against hostile critics of poetry, while the work as a whole contends for what Ar. sees as the finest standards inherent in the genres which he examines. This need not be construed as a radical inconsistency, but it can stand as an instructive example of a tension which could no doubt be found in certain later critics too: between, on the one hand, an impulse to establish general critical values, and, on the other, a desire to allow individual artists and their works a generous independence from preconceived norms.

Ch. 26

Although chs. 23-4 provided only a brief outline of a critical approach to epic, and ch. 25 dealt with problems that might be raised about more than one kind of poetry, Ar. now regards epic as adequately covered, and turns to a final judgement on the relative merits of tragedy and epic. Why should such a judgement be necessary? The primary reason is Ar.'s general philosophical conviction that to understand a phenomenon thoroughly one needs to consider its finest possibilities: so, if we want to grasp the nature of poetic art, we must look at the genres which represent its best potential; and if these, as the *Poetics* assumes, are tragedy and epic, we must press for an ultimate recognition of which of them is capable of reaching the higher level.

In fact, we can refer back to ch. 4 of the treatise to see the roots of the attitude to poetry which gives rise to the exercise conducted in this final (surviving) chapter. Ch. 4 presented an evolutionary view of poetic development, whereby a process of experiment engendered the gradual attainment of the potential *naturally* inherent in generic forms of mimesis. But not only does this process involve the improvement of genres to the point of their 'natural fulfilment' (p.35); it is also believed that one genre may reveal poetic possibilities which require an effectively new genre for their further realisation. This is precisely the relation earlier suggested between Homeric epic and Attic tragedy, and the end of ch. 5 has already expressed the notion that tragedy somehow incorporates all the best features of epic (by which Ar. understands, above all, a dramatic mode of mimesis, and unified plot-structure).

Although this view of literary history is difficult for us to share, and while Ar.'s actual comparison of epic and tragedy in ch. 26 will be seen to be unsatisfactory in more than one respect, it is still worth stressing that the basic desire to judge genres in relation to one another is one which has often been conceived by later critics. The practice was widespread in the ancient world, and in later neo-classicism (when Ar.'s judgement on epic and tragedy was commonly reversed). In both of these periods there was a tendency to operate with an evaluative hierarchy of genres, analogous to hierarchies discerned in nature and the social world. Romanticism cracked the solid foundations of such literary order, especially by its elevation of lyric genres to a much higher status than they had previously held; and the relativism present in much modern criticism has worked against explicit adjudications of one genre's superiority to another. But it remains interesting to note the underlying continuation of some degree of comparative evaluation to be found in even much ordinary critical activity. Where questions of value are admitted into the critical sphere, it is difficult to see how all genres can be

intrinsically regarded as equally important, even if (as classical
critics too admitted) each one may have some unique qualities.

In turning now to the basis of Ar.'s final comparison of tragedy
and epic, we see at once that he has an existing estimation in
view ('so people say ...'), which adds a further, though
contingent, reason for the exercise. It is a straightforward matter
for Ar. to dismiss the idea that the conditions of performance
(and in particular the audience) could settle the question, for he
has made it clear, both in ch. 6 and in ch. 14, that he regards
performance as a strictly *extrinsic* factor, of which poetry proper
is independent. Whatever may be thought of Ar.'s wider attitude
to the theatre (cf. p.97), it is clear that his present argument is
unassailable: since there is only a contingent link between a
genre and the type of audience which at any particular time
happens to go with it, a true judgement on the former cannot rest
on considerations about the latter. Ar. is able to go further, and
to point out that criticisms against tragic actors concern a
separate art from that of the poet: this again harks back to the
end of ch. 6, but it also puts into practice a principle enunciated
in ch. 25 ('one must also ask ...', p.62).

But beyond this point Ar.'s case becomes less secure. For a
start, it reverts to the argument (from ch. 5) that tragedy
possesses all epic's attributes. We are entitled to ask whether
this is actually fair: after all, even Ar. himself, in ch. 24, allowed
some special qualities to epic, including particular scope for
extension and grandeur (see below). Moreover, when Ar. then
adds music and spectacle as tragic attributes lacked by epic, he
is arguably committing the very fallacy which he has just
observed in rejecting existing arguments for epic superiority.
Music and spectacle belong to tragedy *only in performance*, and
should therefore, on the *Poetics'* own premises, not be allowed to
weigh in the judgement on the genres proper. One might add
that these two elements of tragedy are precisely the ones which
Ar.'s own earlier analysis almost entirely neglected: spectacle
was put aside precisely for the reason just indicated, because of
its inessential relation to the poetic work of art proper; while
music is part of 'lyric poetry' (*melopoeia*), which receives even
less attention than spectacle (see p.97).

This leaves us with Ar.'s main ground for the verdict of
tragedy's superiority over epic, and it is hardly surprising that it
carries us back once again to the central concern of the treatise,

poetic unity. If, however, Ar. were to rely only on his earlier observations on tragic and epic unity, it is hard to see how he could choose between the genres. The Homeric poems have established, according to ch. 23, that epic can satisfy the same requirements of unity as tragedy, and Ar.'s standards, as noted above, are those of the genre's finest possibilities, not its common practice. Besides, when epic scale was discussed in ch. 24, its greater length was regarded positively as bringing scope for grandeur and variety.

Nonetheless, in ch. 26 Ar. not only disregards this observation on epic grandeur, but finds tragedy superior to epic precisely because of its shorter scope; and to do so, he needs to invoke a new principle connected to poetic form and unity. Not only is the principle ('relative compression gives greater pleasure') a new one for the *Poetics*, but it remains obscure how it is to be related to the passage in ch. 7 where we are told: 'beauty of size favours as large a structure as possible, provided that coherence is maintained' (p. 39). At the very least, this latter point would seem to call for a recognition that epic and tragedy require their different scales of composition, and that no single criterion can be applied to both. But to make matters worse in ch. 26, Ar. now attempts to reinforce his case with a wholly specious illustration: the hypothesis of an *Iliad*-length *Oedipus* no more demonstrates the superiority of tragedy's typical scale than would the reverse, an *Oedipus*-length *Iliad* (whose inappropriateness for epic is recognised in ch.23, p.58: '... too intricately detailed').

The artificiality of Ar.'s position is shown by the way in which, seemingly with some awkwardness, he qualifies what he had earlier said about the possibility of epic unity. In ch. 23 the *Iliad* and *Odyssey* were said to deal each with a unitary action which would provide material for only one or two tragedies, while other epics have actions 'of many parts' (cf. the phrase 'multiple plot-structure' in ch. 18, p.52). Now, by contrast, epic length is taken unavoidably to entail 'a construction of several actions', even in Homer. The rewording is significant and seems designed to allow a verdict in favour of tragedy. Ar. is now prepared to press the idea of unity to a strict and narrow extreme, even seemingly at the price of withdrawing some of what he had earlier granted to Homeric epic and the special qualities associated with its scale.

If this in part reflects the exigencies of the evaluative

comparison, it is also arguably symptomatic of Ar.'s theoretical commitment to the assimilation of epic to tragedy. For all his admiration of Homer, Ar. ultimately places the highest attainments of the epic genre within the perspective of poetic development sketched in ch. 4. This means that, in the final resort, Ar.'s theory draws him into judging Homer by standards of unity which are taken from a historically later genre. On this level, ch. 26 is entirely consonant with the earlier parts of the work, and it can therefore fittingly stand, at the point where the *Poetics* breaks off in our manuscripts, as a last illustration of the theoretical character of the treatise's view of poetry.

Further reading

The most important modern English translation of the *Poetics* is that by M. E. Hubbard, in D. A. Russell & M. Winterbottom (edd.) *Ancient Literary Criticism* (Oxford 1972).

Also interesting, and with extensive annotation, is the version by James Hutton (New York 1982).

Both the translation and the exegesis in L. J. Potts, *Aristotle on the Art of Fiction* 2nd edn. (Cambridge 1968), too readily assimilate the *Poetics* to later critical and aesthetic ideas.

L. Golden & O. B. Hardison, *Aristotle's Poetics* 2nd edn. (Florida 1981) offer an extensive running commentary which is sometimes out of step with the translation, but which should be compared for views rather different from mine.

D. W. Lucas, *Aristotle: Poetics* (Oxford 1968) provides a full commentary on the Greek text; parts of it, especially the interesting appendices, can be used even by the Greekless reader.

The following works offer discussion of the *Poetics* or of the Greek literature relevant to it:

G. Else, *Plato and Aristotle on Poetry* (North Carolina 1987)
S. Halliwell, *Aristotle's Poetics* (London 1986)
H. House, *Aristotle's Poetics* (London 1956)
J. Jones, *On Aristotle and Greek Tragedy* (London 1971)
B. Knox, *Word and Action* (Baltimore 1979)
F. L. Lucas, *Tragedy: Serious Drama in Relation to Aristotle's Poetics* 2nd edn. (London 1957)
M. C. Nussbaum, *The Fragility of Goodness* (Cambridge 1986)
R. B. Rutherford, 'Tragic Form and Feeling in the *Iliad*', *Journal of Hellenic Studies* 102 (1982) 145-60.
E. Schaper, *Prelude to Aesthetics* (London 1968)
B. Vickers, *Towards Greek Tragedy* (London 1973)

Glossary

The Glossary contains brief explanations of names, technical terms etc. which occur in the translation, except for a few which are immediately clarified in their context. The Glossary's sole purpose is to facilitate reading of the *Poetics*; fuller details, where appropriate, should be sought in reference works such as *The Oxford Classical Dictionary*, 2nd edn. (Oxford 1970), or P. Grimal, *Dictionary of Classical Mythology* (Engl. transl., Oxford 1986). All dates are B.C.

Achilles: son of Peleus (q.v.), and central Greek hero of the *Iliad* (q.v.): ch. 15 refers to his mixture of characteristics in the latter.

Aegeus: King of Athens, who arrives opportunely to offer the heroine refuge in Euripides' *Medea* (q.v.) in a scene which Ar. faults for illogicality (ch. 25).

Aegisthus: adulterous lover of Clytemnestra (q.v.), whom he helped to plan the murder of her husband Agamemnon. Aegisthus was killed in revenge by Orestes (q.v.) – though not, it seems, in the kind of burlesque comedy on the theme which Ar. cites at the end of ch. 13.

Aeschylus (c. 525-456): the first of the great Athenian trio of tragedians, but probably the least admired by Ar. He is given credit in ch. 4 for a major step towards the fulfilment of tragedy's potential, and ch. 18 alludes to his grasp of the need to select material suitable for a unitary plot-structure. But Ar.'s comparative paucity of refs. to Aeschylus (*Choephori* is mentioned in ch. 16), and the fact that he ignores the question of tragic trilogies (an Aeschylean speciality), suggests a slighter interest than in Euripides or Sophocles.

Agathon: Athenian tragic playwright (active during the last two decades of the fifth century), mentioned in chs. 9 and 18 (three times). Evidently innovative. Ar. approves of his willingness to invent his own dramatic material (ch. 9), but not of his unintegrated lyrics (ch. 18).

Ajax: a major Greek hero in the Trojan War. The plays about him referred to in ch. 18 were presumably, like Sophocles' *Ajax*, centred on his fit of madness and eventual suicide, after his failure to win the arms of Achilles. They would thus be likely to contain many scenes of *pathos*, 'suffering' (q.v.), which is Ar.'s reason for referring to them.

Alcibiades: Athenian aristocrat and politician (c.450-404). Ar. uses his name arbitrarily in ch. 9 to indicate historical particulars, but he may wrily have in mind the exceptionally volatile (and therefore disjointed) nature of Alcibiades' public career.

Alcinous: King of Phaeacia, visited by Odysseus (q.v.) on his journey home (*Odyssey* bks. 6-13).

Alcmaeon: mythological hero who avenged his father Amphiaraus by killing his mother Eriphyle (q.v.); his story has parallels with that of Orestes (q.v.). He is mentioned in chs. 13 and 14 (twice) as a prominent subject for tragedies. In one of these, by Astydamas (q.v.), the killing seems strangely to have rested on ignorance of his mother's identity (ch. 14).

Amphiaraus: father of Alcmaeon (q.v.); ch. 17's ref. is apparently to a scene in which the playwright Carcinus gave him an illogical sequence of movements in the play, but the point is not entirely clear.

Anagnôrisis: see s.v. recognition.

Anapaest: a Greek rhythm and metre of a rather four-square kind, associated with marching; often used for a choral entry (*parodos*), which is why Ar. excepts it from his definition of a choral ode (*stasimon*) in ch. 12 (though the statement anyway causes technical difficulties).

Antheus: title of a play by Agathon (q.v.) which used no traditional material (ch. 9). We have no other evidence at all about it.

Archon: magistrate responsible for 'granting a chorus' (i.e. permission to perform a play) at the state-organised dramatic festivals of Athens. Ch. 5's ref. to this arrangement indicates the first inclusion of comedy in the most important of these festivals, the Great Dionysia (in the year 487/6).

Ares: Greek god of war.

Ariphrades: probably a comic poet of the late fifth century; hence the satire of tragedians (ch. 22) would belong to his plays, as with Aristophanes' parodies of tragic style.

Aristophanes (c.450-385): Athenian comic playwright, author of fantastic and scurrilously satirical works. Hence the ref. in ch. 3 hardly signifies a judgement on his status, which for Ar. was probably not altogether high (cf. p. 85).

Astydamas: a successful Athenian tragic playwright, active from 370s to 340s (i.e. a close contemporary of Ar.'s). In his *Alcmaeon* (q.v.) the hero apparently killed his mother in ignorance (though in the traditional myth he was executing his father's wish for revenge), and that is why Ar. cites it approvingly (ch. 14).

Callippides: a leading tragic actor in Athens in the later fifth century, evidently associated with a new histrionic style (ch. 26 twice).

Carcinus: prolific Athenian tragic playwright, active from 370s onwards. Cited by name for particular (and unfavourable) points in chs. 16 and 17.

Carthaginians: their attack on Sicily (480), at the same time as the battle of Salamis, illustrates historical coincidence in ch. 23.

Centaur: see s.v. Chairemon.

Cephallenians: inhabitants of Greek island (modern Kefallinía) to west of Corinthian gulf. Ch. 25 refers to a local legend about Odysseus's marriage.

Chairemon: obscure author of *Centaur*, a work in a mixture of metres (chs. 1 and 24) and called a 'rhapsody' (q.v.) by Ar. Also known to have written tragedies. Active in first half of fourth century.

Chionides: one of the earliest of Athenian comic dramatists (ch. 4), perhaps the first winner of an official prize in the genre in 487/6 (see s.v. Archon).

Cleophon: mentioned in chs. 2 and 22 as the author of poetry about ordinary characters and in a plain style. It is usually assumed that he is identical with a known tragic poet of the same name, but the ch. 2 ref. implies work by him in another genre.

Clytemnestra: wife of Agamemnon, mother of Orestes (q.v.); involved with her lover Aegisthus (q.v.) in the murder of her husband, and in turn killed by her son. Ar. regards the latter matricide as a fixed mythological datum (ch. 14). For its treatment see esp. Aeschylus' *Choephori* and the *Electra* plays of Sophocles and Euripides.

Complex: Ar.'s term for a plot-structure which contains a central use of recognition and/or reversal (qq.v.). The main points are made in chs. 10-11, and the ideal tragic patterns of chs. 13 and 14 both presuppose a complex structure. Cf. p. 112.

Complication: defined in ch. 18 as the portion of a play's material which stretches from the start of the story up to the beginning of the transformation (q.v.). Part of the complication may be 'outside' the play proper. A complication is therefore not directly related to a complex plot, though there may be an underlying link between the concepts (see p. 113).

Crates: Athenian comic poet, active from around 450. Crates appears (ch. 5) to have moved away from the iambic style of personal and scurrilous satire (which we associate with Aristophanes, q.v.) towards a more generalised and universal style of comedy, which Ar. took to be closer to the true essence of the genre (cf. ch. 9 for the distinction).

Cresphontes: a lost tragedy by Euripides, approvingly cited near the end of ch. 14 for its recognition scene, in which Cresphontes was identified by his mother Merope as she was on the point of killing him.

Cyclopes: a group of one-eyed giants, first portrayed in *Odyssey* bk. 9. In ch. 2 (the passage is corrupt) Ar. has in mind the very different light in which various poets had portrayed the best known Cyclops, Polyphemus.

Cypria: a (lost) epic poem which dealt with the antecedents to the Trojan War, starting with the wedding of Peleus (q.v.) and Thetis.

Some Greeks ascribed it to Homer, but Ar. evidently did not (ch. 23).

Cyprians: see s.v. Dicaeogenes.

Danaus: father of Hypermestra, who secretly defied his instruction to kill her husband, Lynceus (q.v.). In the tragedy by Theodectes (q.v.) mentioned in ch. 11, Danaus attempted, on discovering the truth, to have Lynceus put to death, but a dramatic turn of events (reversal, q.v.) led to Danaus's own death. It is likely that this version was due to Theodectes' own invention, rather than traditional saga.

Deiliad: the title (ch. 2) of a burlesque epic by Nicochares (q.v.); the form of the title recalls *Iliad*, but means *Saga of a Coward.*

Dénouement: defined in ch. 18 as the portion of a play which incorporates the transformation (q.v.). The term is also used in ch. 15, in a possibly misplaced passage.

Dicaeogenes: author of the *Cyprians* (about which nothing else is known), cited in ch. 16 for a dramatic recognition-scene. He is usually identified with an early fourth-century writer of tragedies and dithyrambs.

Dionysius: a painter of ordinary figures, according to ch. 2. He is probably to be identified with Dionysius of Colophon, a contemporary of Polygnotus (q.v.).

Dionysus: Greek god of nature and fertility, associated among much else with wine (ch. 21).

Discovery: see s.v. recognition (and cf. p. 116).

Dithyramb: a genre of lyric poetry, performed by choruses of fifty dancer-singers. Ar. mentions it twice in ch. 1, cites its range of ethical styles in ch. 2, and alludes to its stylistic extravagance in ch. 22. That he otherwise neglects it is due to his belief (ch. 5) that tragic drama grew out of dithyrambic origins and thus superseded the older genre.

Dorians: one of the chief ethnic and dialectal groups of the Greek world, particularly centred in leading states of the Peloponnese. Ch. 3 contains a digression on Dorian claims to primacy in the invention of dramatic comedy and tragedy.

Elegy (adj. elegiac): a poetic genre practised particularly in the archaic period, by poets such as Theognis and Solon. Its strong element of hortatory moralising explains why Ar. shows little interest in it (cf. p. 74), giving it only the most perfunctory of mentions in ch. 1.

Empedocles: Sicilian philosopher-poet, whose life spanned the first three quarters of the fifth century. Ar. uses his verses to exemplify works which should be classified as technical writings, not poetry (ch. 1), but he nonetheless uses quotations from them as linguistic-stylistic illustrations in chs. 21 and 25.

Encomia: poems in praise of great men and their achievements; one of the original forms which the poetic instinct took, according to ch. 4. One developed form of encomium is the kind of victory-ode (epinikian) familiar to us from the work of Pindar.

Epicharmus: Sicilian comic playwright, probably active in the early fifth century, though the ref. to him in ch. 3 implies an earlier start to his career. He is alluded to in the mention of Sicilian comedy in ch. 5.

Episode: (a) any scene or spoken section of a play (e.g. chs. 4, 12); (b) a digressive or expansive dramatic section (chs. 17, 23), which, if not integral, leads to the 'episodic' fault (ch. 9). Cf. p. 111.

Eriphyle: mythological wife of the Argive hero, Amphiaraus (q.v.), whom she helped to lead to his death. She was consequently killed by her son, Alcmaeon (q.v.), and ch. 14 cites the matricide as an unalterable 'fact' of myth.

Eucleides: an unknown poet, apparently the composer of some form of iambus (q.v.), cited in ch. 22 for his parodies of Homeric diction.

Euripides (c.485-406): the youngest of the great trio of fifth-century Athenian tragedians; his works were the most commonly restaged in the fourth century, during Ar.'s lifetime. He receives frequent mention, mixing praise and censure, in the *Poetics*. Particularly notable is the approval first of his unhappy endings (ch. 13), then for plays such as *Iphigeneia in Tauris* and *Cresphontes* in which an 'incurable' tragic action is prevented by timely recognition (ch. 14).

Glaucon: an otherwise unidentifiable critic, cited for a shrewd observation in ch. 25.

Hamartia: the human 'fallibility' which causes the transformation of fortune in the ideal tragic pattern of ch. 13; it is probably also assumed in the cases of tragic ignorance cited and recommended in ch. 14. For discussion see pp. 128-30.

Hegemon: writer of 'parodies' (ch. 2), i.e. burlesque epic verses (and perhaps mock-imitations of other genres too). Probably active in the fifth century.

Helle: title of an unknown tragedy cited in ch. 14 for its recognition scene. Helle became, by her drowning, the mythological eponym of the Hellespont. Nothing is known of her son.

Heracleid: more than one lost Greek epic with this title is known to have existed. Ar. uses it in ch. 8 to signify any work dealing with the whole life-story of the hero Heracles (which contained an archetypal series of labours and exploits), rather than with one unified action.

Herodotus (c.485-425): the first great Greek historian; his *Histories* tell (among much else) the story of the two Persian invasions of Greece in 490 and 480-479. In citing his work (ch. 9) Ar. may partly have in mind the very wide range of actual but disconnected events which it embraces, as opposed to the single action of a poem.

Hexameter: the metre of epic poetry (chs. 4 and 6).

Hippias: an otherwise unknown critic cited on a linguistic point in ch. 25.

Homer: the standard Greek name for the author of the *Iliad* and *Odyssey*, and sometimes of other epics too; Ar. ascribes the *Margites* (q.v.) to him. His superiority to all other epic poets, and his discovery of the essential features of what were to become tragedy and comedy, are the salient points in Ar.'s attitude towards his work (esp. chs. 4, 8, 23-6).

Hymns: poems in honour of the gods; assumed by Ar. to have been one of the chief serious forms of early poetry (ch. 4).

Iambic trimeter: the usual metre of both iambus (q.v.), after which it was named (ch. 4), and the dialogue-scenes of tragedy and comedy. Ar. regards its flexible rhythms as being particularly close to ordinary speech (chs. 4 and 22) and correspondingly suited to poetic portrayal of action (ch. 24).

Iambus: a poetic genre associated especially with scurrilous personal humour (chs. 4 and 9) and best exemplified by the remains of Archilochus's work. Ar. regards the style of iambus ('the iambic mode' ch. 4) as having historically given way gradually to the more decent and refined ethos of comedy proper.

Icadius: an alternative form of Icarius (q.v.).

Icarius: father of Penelope, hence father-in-law of Odysseus and grandfather of Telemachus. He is mentioned (ch. 25) in connection with an artificial critical 'problem' concerning Telemachus's visit to Sparta in *Odyssey* bk. 4.

Iliad: one of the two great epics universally attributed to Homer (q.v.) by the Greeks in the classical period. Ar. regards it, with the *Odyssey* (q.v.), as the prototype of tragedy (chs. 4 and 24) – among other reasons, for its concentrated unity of action (chs. 8 and 20, but cf. ch. 26 with p. 183).

Illyrians: an Indo-European people (ch. 25) whose territory included parts of modern Albania and Jugoslavia.

Invective: a (hypothetical) form or mode of early humorous poetry (ch. 4), which shaded into iambus (q.v.) and which concentrated on attacking individual targets.

Iphigeneia: daughter of Agamemnon and Clytemnestra (q.v.), sister of Orestes (q.v.). The events leading up to her sacrificial death and miraculous transportation to the Black Sea are dramatised in Euripides' *Iphigeneia in Aulis* (ch. 15). Her later reunion with her brother forms the climax of Euripides' *Iphigeneia in Tauris*, which Ar. cites frequently (esp. chs. 11, 14, 16 and 17), particularly for its recognition-scene.

Ixion: mythical Thessalian King, guilty of various crimes, including an attempted rape of the goddess Hera, for which he was punished on a revolving wheel in the Underworld. He was the subject of a number of tragedies, which Ar. takes (ch. 18) to be generally characterised by scenes of *pathos*, 'suffering' (q.v.).

Katharsis: part of the psychological impact of tragedy, resulting from the experience of pity and fear (ch. 6). Its literal sense is purification/purgation, but its one occurrence in the *Poetics* remains obscure: Ar. may mean by it a powerful release of emotion which has a salutary effect on our emotional (and hence our ethical) disposition. See p. 90.

Laius: see s.v. Oedipus.

Little Iliad: a (lost) epic poem covering the final stages of the Trojan

War and the departure of the Greeks for home. Cited in ch. 23 for the multiplicity of actions which it encompassed.

Lynceus: a tragedy by Theodectes (q.v.) which included (ch. 18) the seizure of the child of Lynceus and his wife, Hypermestra, by the latter's father, Danaus (q.v.), and the eventual death of Danaus (ch. 11).

Lyre (kithara): a large instrument used both for accompaniment to certain kinds of poetry, and for solo-instrumental performance (chs. 1 and 2).

Magnes: an early Athenian comic playwright, active in the second quarter of the fifth century (ch. 3).

Margites: a (lost) comic epic, named after its simpleton 'hero', in a mixture of hexameters and iambic trimeters (qq.v.); ascribed by Ar. to Homer (q.v.) and regarded by him as the prototype of true comedy (ch. 4).

Medea: tragedy by Euripides, in which Medea murders her children for revenge against her husband Jason. Cited in ch. 14 for its deliberate tragic action, and in ch. 25 for the 'illogical' entry of Aegeus (q.v.).

Megarians: inhabitants of Megara on the Corinthian isthmus, and of this city's colonies in Sicily. They represented a branch of the Dorians (q.v.), and laid claim to an early tradition of comic drama (ch. 3).

Melanippe: human amour of the god Poseidon (q.v.), to whom she secretly bore twins. In Euripides' play, *Melanippe the Wise*, her attempt to defend herself and the twins from her father's anger involved a sophisticated speech which Ar. judged to be inappropriate for a woman (ch. 15).

Meleager: mythical hero who killed his mother's brother(s) (accidentally, in some versions) and was killed in revenge when his mother burnt the brand on which his life depended. Ar. cites him as a figure caught in the tragic events of a family (ch. 13).

Menelaus: husband of Helen. His vicious behaviour in Euripides' *Orestes* is judged by Ar. to be a poetic fault through its excessiveness (chs. 15 and 25).

Merope: mother of Cresphontes (q.v.).

Metabasis: see s.v. transformation.

Mime: see s.v. Sophron.

Mimesis: Ar.'s basic concept of the (fictional) relation between works of art (poems, pictures, dances, etc.) and the world. It is best translated 'representation'; in poetry, Ar. shows a strong inclination to associate it with direct speech or enactment. Cf. esp. pp. 70ff. and 171ff.

Mitys: nothing else is known for certain about this person. The incident involving his statue in ch. 9 is possibly historical.

Mnasitheos: a professional singer whose antics are alluded to in ch. 26 but who is otherwise unknown.

Mynniscus: a tragic actor who is said to have worked for Aeschylus (died 456) and was certainly active as late as 422. Ar. mentions his criticisms of a younger actor's style (ch. 26).

Mysians: title of tragedies by Aeschylus and Sophocles, centring on Telephus (q.v.), who is the silent figure in the (unknown) episode criticised in ch. 24 for some improbability.

Nicochares: author of the burlesque *Deiliad* (q.v.); probably identical with the comic poet of the same name active at Athens in the early fourth century.

Niobe: mythical mother of six (or seven) daughters. Her boasting offended the goddess Leto, whose children, Apollo and Artemis, killed Niobe's daughters. Subject of tragedies by Aeschylus and others (ch. 18).

Nome: originally the name of a particular kind of melody, the word came to be applied to lyric compositions for a solo performer (chs. 1 and 2).

Odysseus: father of Telemachus (q.v.) and a leading Greek hero in the Trojan War, whose subsequent wanderings and delayed homecoming are the subject of the Homeric *Odyssey* (q.v.). One version of this homecoming was evidently presented in the unknown tragedy, *Odysseus the False Messenger*, referred to in ch. 16. Odysseus's heroic endurance made the lament given to him in Timotheus's *Scylla* (q.v.) seem to Ar. entirely inappropriate (ch. 15).

Odysseus Wounded: probably one title (another is known) of a tragedy by Sophocles in which Odysseus was fatally wounded by his illegitimate son, Telegonus (ch. 14).

Odyssey: Homeric epic dealing with the wanderings and homecoming of Odysseus (q.v.); the barest outline of its story is given in ch. 17. Ar. considers it, with the *Iliad* (q.v.), to be the prototype of tragedy (esp. chs. 4, 16, 24), esp. for its use of recognition (q.v.), though in one passage he indirectly likens its morally satisfying ending to that of a comedy (ch. 13).

Oedipus: mythological King of Thebes who had unwittingly killed his own father, Laius, and married his own mother. Ar.'s refs. to Oedipus, apart from two general ones in ch. 13, are always in connection with Sophocles' *Oedipus Tyrannus*, which is frequently cited for exemplary points of dramatic construction (esp. chs. 11, 14 (first ref.), 16), though other passages suggest possible criticisms (chs. 14 (second ref.), 15, 24).

Orestes: son of Clytemnestra (q.v.), whom he killed to avenge his father, and brother of Iphigeneia (q.v.). Euripides' *Orestes* (chs. 15, 25) deals with events subsequent to his matricide, and the same author's *Iphigeneia in Tauris* is frequently cited by Ar. for its recognition-scene (esp. chs. 14 and 16).

Parnassus: Greek mountain-range where the young Odysseus was wounded hunting, in the episode recollected at *Odyssey* 19.392-466 but left out of the main plot-structure of the poem (see ch. 8).

Pathos: see s.v. suffering.

Pauson: a painter of 'inferior', perhaps comic, figures (ch. 2). His works may have included a pornographic element, judging by Ar.'s suggestion that they could be injurious to young minds (*Politics* 8.5.7).

Peleus: title of tragedies by Sophocles and Euripides; we do not know which of them Ar. means in ch. 18. Peleus was father of Achilles (q.v.); the plays named after him probably concerned the exile and other miseries of his old age.

Peripeteia: see s.v. reversal.

Phallic songs: ribald and scurrilous entertainments, associated with fertility cults: for an example see Aristophanes *Acharnians* 263-79. Ar. takes their festive character to have contributed to the origins of comic drama (ch. 5).

Philoctetes: title of lost tragedies by Aeschylus and Euripides (as well as a surviving play by Sophocles) from which Ar. quotes in ch. 22. Philoctetes was a hero abandoned on a desert island by the Greek expedition to Troy, but later brought back for the sake of his bow (inherited from Heracles), which was needed for success in the war.

Philoxenus: a poet of dithyramb (q.v.), active in the later fifth and early fourth centuries, and associated, like Timotheus (q.v.), with a new musical and poetic style in the genre. Ch. 2 alludes to his maudlin treatment of Polyphemus the Cyclops (q.v.).

Phineidai: title of an unknown tragedy (ch. 16), *Sons of Phineus*. The sons were blinded by their father after a false allegation against them; both Aeschylus and Sophocles wrote tragedies on the subject. But it is unclear how the episode mentioned by Ar. would fit into either one of these or any other play about Phineus.

Phorcides: an unknown play, *Daughters of Phorcys*; we have no reason to identify it with the satyr-play (q.v.) of the same name by Aeschylus. Phorcys was a sea-god who sired the petrifying Gorgons and other formidable monstrosities.

Phthiotides: a play of this name, *Women of Phthia* (Phthia being the Thessalian territory of Peleus and Achilles), was written by Sophocles, but nothing is known of its subject-matter.

Pindarus: an unknown actor (ch. 26), criticised in the same terms as Callippides (q.v.).

Pipe (aulos): reeded, oboe-like musical instrument, normally used for accompaniment to sung poetry (e.g. in tragic lyrics), but sometimes for solo performance (chs. 1 and 2). An *aulos*-player in tragedy or dithyramb might, it seems (ch. 26), engage in excessively mimetic antics.

Polygnotus: major Greek painter, active in Athens and elsewhere in the middle two quarters of the fifth century, and notable especially for large panel-paintings of mythological and heroic subjects (chs. 2 and 6).

Polyidus: Ar. calls him a 'sophist' (a professional teacher-cum-lecturer) and refers twice (chs. 16, 17) to his treatment of the reunion of Iphigeneia and Orestes (qq.v.). It is unclear whether this treatment was contained in a show-piece oration, of the kind which some sophists wrote, or in a poem.

Poseidon: god of the sea, and enemy of Odysseus (q.v.) on his long journey home from Troy (ch. 17).

Prometheus: the *Prometheus Bound*, traditionally ascribed to Aeschylus (q.v.), dealing with Zeus's brutal punishment of the Titan Prometheus for his gift of fire to mankind.

Protagoras: a major fifth-century sophist (see s.v. Polyidus) who interested himself, among much else, in grammatical analysis and normative linguistic theory (ch. 19).

Recognition (*anagnôrisis*): one of the main elements of the complex plot (q.v.). Sometimes translated 'discovery', it constitutes a major change from ignorance to knowledge in the tragic agent(s), with a determinant impact on the outcome of a tragedy. Various types are analysed in ch. 16. Ar. also identifies recognition in the *Odyssey* (q.v.), esp. in ch. 24.

Reversal (*peripeteia*): a complete and startling twist in the direction of a dramatic action (ch. 11); one of the components of the complex plot (q.v.). It should not be confused with the basic tragic transformation (q.v.) from prosperity to adversity.

Rhapsody: this term, which normally signifies the performance of epic poetry by professional reciter-actors, rhapsodes (cf. ch. 26), is applied in ch. 1 to an individual and highly peculiar poem (perhaps of a quasi-epic character) by Chairemon (q.v.).

Salamis, battle of (480): sea-battle in which the Athenians inflicted a major defeat on the invading Persians (ch. 23); recounted in bk. 8 of Herodotus (q.v.).

Satyr-play: a short dramatic work with a chorus of satyrs (companions of Dionysus, q.v.), usually performed as a tail-piece to a series of tragedies. Ar. associates satyr-play with a light, semi-comic style of plot and diction which he also believed to have been found in early tragedy (ch. 4).

Scene-painting (*skênographia*): the term probably refers in ch. 4 to the decoration of the stage-building (*skênê*) in the Athenian theatre so as to give visual embodiment to the spacial setting of a play; but its detailed implications are controversial.

Scylla: title (ch. 15) of a dithyramb (q.v.) by Timotheus (q.v.), in which Odysseus (q.v.) lamented the fate of his companions, swallowed by the sea-monster, Scylla. The same work is probably meant in the ref. to an energetic *aulos*-player in ch. 26.

Simple plot-structure: a tragic plot whose transformation (q.v.) occurs without the dramatic twists of the complex type (q.v.), which Ar. prefers to it. See chs. 9, 10 and 13. The *Iliad* (q.v.) is also classed as 'simple' (ch. 24, but cf. p. 168).

Sisyphus: mythological figure noted for his cunning and for his punishment in Hades, which involved the eternally unsuccessful attempt to push a stone up a hill. The ref. in ch. 18 is extremely obscure.

Socratic dialogues: prose works dramatising philosophical conversations between Socrates and others (ch. 1). The best known are those of Plato, which Ar. may have in mind.

Sophocles (c.496-406): major Athenian tragic playwright, responsible for certain technical innovations (ch. 4) and commended for his handling of the chorus (ch. 18). But Ar.'s main refs. to him mostly concern just one of his plays, the *Oedipus Tyrannus* (see s.v. Oedipus).

Sophron: Sicilian writer of mimes, i.e. short, racy comic dramas, in rhythmically heightened prose, on a range of mundane and vulgar subjects (ch. 1). Active in the fifth century.

Sosistratus: a professional performer of epic poetry (cf. s.v. rhapsody), noted in ch. 26 for the extravagant use of gesture. Otherwise unknown.

Sthenelus: minor Athenian tragic poet of the later fifth century, noted in ch. 22 for his common style.

Suffering (*pathos*): a tragic action productive of great pain or death, or a dramatic scene in which such suffering is dominant (ch. 11). The prominence of this element in certain works makes Ar. classify them as 'tragedies/poems of suffering' (chs. 18 and 24). But a tragic action need not always contain actualised *pathos* (see ch. 14 with p. 136).

Tegea: town in the Peloponnese, where Telephus (q.v.) was born, before being taken by his mother to Mysia.

Telegonus: see s.v. *Odysseus Wounded*.

Telemachus: see s.v. Icarius.

Telephus: a son of Heracles and king of Mysia in N.W. Asia Minor; the subject of a large number of tragedies. In ch. 13 Ar. probably has in mind plays dealing with his loss of identity and his unwitting killing of his uncles.

Tereus: a tragedy by Sophocles, in which Philomela, after being raped and having her tongue torn out by Tereus, revealed the facts to her sister Procne through a tapestry (i.e. 'the voice of the shuttle' in ch. 16).

Tetrameter: see s.v. trochaic.

Theodectes: rhetorician, tragic playwright, and friend of Ar.'s, active at Athens in the mid-fourth century. Ar. cites both his *Lynceus* (q.v.) and his *Tydeus* (q.v.).

Theseid: the title of any epic poem dealing with the exploits of Theseus, the national hero of Athens. The wide range of these exploits, which include the killing of the Cretan minotaur, would make such poems less than unified, which is Ar.'s reason for citing the type (ch. 8).

Thyestes: mythological figure notable for (a) crimes against his brother Atreus, for which the latter tricked him into eating his own children, (b) unwitting incest with his own daughter. Cited in ch. 13 for his tragic potential.

Timotheus (c.450-360): poet of dithyramb (q.v.) and other lyric poetry, associated with radical innovations of a musical and stylistic kind. In addition to the named ref. in ch. 2, Ar. cites what seem to have been the emotional excesses of his *Scylla* (q.v.).

Transformation (*metabasis*): the passage of the tragic agent(s) from prosperity to adversity (good fortune to misfortune), or *vice versa* (end of ch. 7, etc.); it thus represents what Ar. regards as an essentially tragic instability in human affairs. On the variable direction of the transformation see p. 135.

Trimeter: see s.v. iambic.

Trochaic (*tetrameter*): a lively metre which Ar. associates with early tragedy (ch. 4) and whose rhythms he regards as apt for dancing (chs. 4 and 24). Its replacement by the iambic trimeter (q.v.) represents, for Ar., the movement of tragedy away from its early chorus-dominated form towards a greater concentration on action.

Tydeus: a tragedy by Theodectes (q.v.). Tydeus was a mythical hero and father of Diomedes. In the usual accounts his death occurs on the famous expedition of the Seven against Thebes and is not connected with his son; the ref. in ch. 16 is therefore obscure, but it is possible that we are dealing with another invention of Theodectes' (cf. s.v. *Lynceus*).

Tyro: tragedy by Sophocles, in which Tyro escaped from a life of suffering when she recognised her sons through the boat (or cradle) in which she had exposed them as infants. The play was a Sophoclean instance of a transformation (q.v.) from adversity to prosperity.

Xenarchus: Sicilian mime-writer, mentioned with his father, Sophron (q.v.), in ch. 1.

Xenophanes: polemical philosopher, poet and sage, active in the later sixth and early fifth century. Ch. 25 alludes to his contention that the traditional anthropomorphic gods of Greek religion were simply a projection of human features (including immorality) onto the supernatural.

Zeuxis: Greek painter of the later fifth and early fourth century, famous for his technical realism. Ar. thinks his works lacking in ethical character (ch. 6), and a corrupt passage in ch. 25 seems to have referred to his unidealising treatment of figures.